TROPICAL RENDITIONS

REFIGURING AMERICAN MUSIC

A series edited by Ronald Radano and Josh Kun

Charles McGovern, contributing editor

TROPICAL RENDITIONS

MAKING MUSICAL SCENES IN FILIPINO AMERICA

Christine Bacareza Balance

Duke University Press *Durham and London* 2016

Typeset in Chaparral Pro and Knockout by
Graphic Composition, Inc., Bogart, Georgia

Library of Congress Cataloging-in-Publication
Names: Balance, Christine Bacareza, [date]– author.
Title: Tropical renditions : making musical scenes in
    Filipino America / Christine Bacareza Balance.
Other titles: Refiguring American music.
Description: Durham : Duke University Press, 2016.
    | Series: Refiguring American music | Includes
    bibliographical references and index
Identifiers: LCCN 2015038470
ISBN 9780822359586 (hardcover : alk. paper)
ISBN 9780822360018 (pbk. : alk. paper)
ISBN 9780822375142 (e-book)
Subjects: LCSH: Filipino Americans—Music. |
    Filipino Americans—Ethnic identity. | Filipino
    Americans in the performing arts. | Music—
    Philippines.
Classification: LCC ML3560.P4 B353 2016 |
    DDC 780.89/9921073—dc23
LC record available at http://lccn.loc.gov/2015038470

Cover art: Louie Cordero, "My We," 2011.
Courtesy of the artist. Collection of the
Singapore Art Museum.

Duke University Press gratefully acknowledges
the support of the University of California,
Irvine, Humanities Commons, which provided
funds toward the publication of this book.

For Gary

CONTENTS

....

ACKNOWLEDGMENTS

....

I belatedly give thanks to the thinkers and teachers whom I was so fortunate to meet more than fifteen years ago in a site of fugitivity and theory, an undercommons where performance was/is a serious matter and object of study, a way of not only tracing the past but rehearsing some futures. It is one thing for those, so brilliantly sharp yet softhearted, to notice you. But it is a life-changing thing for them to believe in you, sometimes more than you even believe in yourself. José Esteban Muñoz's trust and love set me on this unexpected path. In his life and writing, he has shown and continues to show me other ways of being and worlds beyond. Fred Moten's voice and presence have been lifesaving navigational devices, both in the world and writing. My deepest thanks to him for teaching me how to listen. The steadfast character and razor-sharp intelligence of Karen Shimakawa and the precisely thoughtful insights of Kandice Chuh have taught me so much. Since my pre-graduate school days, Lucy San Pablo Burns has proven to be a friend and collaborator extraordinaire. Her relentless pursuit of learning, her disciplined yet loving ways of being are what I aspire to every day. In her no-nonsense manner, Laura Kang has modeled how to bring both rigor and curiosity to study and life itself. Allan Punzalan Isaac's grounded optimism and crafty command of language bring fabulousness to every room he enters. Daphne Brooks's refined style on the page and crackling humor onstage continue to model, for me, ways of paving one's own path. I cherish and look up to the level of commitment Gayle Wald brings to ideas, to writing, and to the politics they engender. In her writing and mentorship, Deborah Wong has sounded calls to writing and action at the most crucial moments. At critical moments in its making, this book greatly benefited from the close editorial eyes and care of Ann Cvetkovich, Laura Kang, and Alexandra Vazquez. I owe the world to Sonjia Hyon for taking the time to read parts of this work, even at the latest stages of its writing. Back in 2009, Josh Kun believed in this project, even in its most amorphous state. Since that time he has impressed on me the importance of listening broadly and writing in a forthright manner. Martin Manalansan's unwavering support and scholarly example over the years have emboldened me to think more deeply and shine more brightly. Feedback from all of the aforementioned folks has proven to be so vital because it helped push this book to all of the places it still needed to go. Any mistakes or omissions in the final text are completely my own doing.

My deepest thanks to my colleagues in the Department of Asian American Studies at UC Irvine—Jim Lee, Linda Vô, Claire Kim, Dorothy Fujita-Rony, Julia Lee, and Judy Wu—for working on behalf of and alongside what might have seemed like a never-ending book project. Your collegiality and faith has meant the world to me. To three colleagues who have taught me so much about commitment and a love for the work: my fellow Angeleno, Bridget Cooks, for helping me see the music; my survivor sister, Vicky Johnson, for reminding me that it's not just the destination but the journey; and my fellow traveler, Bliss Cua Lim, for sharing her Manila and Pinay pop sensibilities with me. To Arlene Keizer, Jeanne Scheper, Jennifer Terry, and Tiffany Willoughby-Herard for your constant reminders of the political potency of form. To Nahum Chandler, for his steady intellectual presence. To Michael Montoya, for his infectious excitement in the transformative possibilities of scholarship and teaching. To June Kurata, Cathy Nguyen Yates, Francine Jeffrey, Roberta Geier, Caroline McGuire, Kasey Ning, Jasmine Robledo, and Lien Nguyen, whose administrative know-how keeps the whole enterprise afloat.

I grew up an only child, but along the way, I have always benefited from the pleasures of living, learning, and growing up within various kinship networks of fellow writers, thinkers, misfits, and artists. Alexandra Vazquez is my scholarly sister, through and through, a pathfinder whose fearless commitment to listening and work I aspire to daily. Ricardo Montez is my forever-radiant kin, an aesthete whose critical eye and generous heart are unmatched. Nothing shines as bright as Shane Vogel's clean, crisp prose, right-on politics, and effortless smile. Hypatia Vourloumis is the archipelagic sister who has always brought me back to the feeling of acoustic guitar melodies riding on Pacific tradewinds. Joshua Chambers-Letson, just like a younger brother, has believed in me so much that he has pushed my work beyond what I could have ever imagined. Jeanne Vacarro is a crustacean sister and bold fashionista with whom I have shared so many sentiments, both closely and remotely. Patty Ahn is the Piscean sister and Angeleno fly girl sensation with whom I've shared so much of this work. I look forward to reading more of their work in print and in the near future. To all of my students, from NYU to Vassar to UC Irvine to Cornell, with special shout outs to: Elaine Andres, Erica Cheung, Marko Cristal, Emily Hue, Kimarlee Nguyen, Mark Pangilinan, Ray San Diego, Mark Villegas, and the students of my "U.S. Pop Music and Racial Commonsense" seminar at Cornell University. Thank you for patience with me, at various points of this book writing process, and for always reminding me that the learning, growing, joy, and music need never end.

This project is the result of many years of archival and ethnographic research supported by various funding sources and institutions. Many thanks to the Consortium for Faculty Diversity (CFD) predoctoral program and Vassar College's American Cultures program, most especially Eileen Leonard and Linta Varghese, for the time and support necessary to complete the dissertation, from which this book only retained one chapter. The UC President's Postdoctoral Fellowship program has provided a wonderful network of scholars that helped with the transitions from graduate school to tenure-track faculty life, from East Coast to West Coast living. I extend so much gratitude to Sheila O'Rourke and Kimberly Adkinson for their leadership and administrative efforts and, of course, to my faculty mentor Deborah Wong. Her support helped push my research into new and important terrain, most especially her sponsorship of the "Tropical Renditions: Popular Music and Performance" concert and symposium, an event that prompted much of this book's thinking. My thanks as well go to the performers and participants of that event: DJ Kuttin Kandi, Ron "Kulintronica" Quesada, Liz Katindig Dykes, Oliver Wang, Theo Gonzalves, Mary Talusan, and Lakan de Leon.

My deepest gratitude to the Ford Foundation Postdoctoral Fellowship program, most especially, to my mentor Fred Moten, Laura Harris, Lynne Feeley, and all of my other interlocutors during my visit through the New Americanist Series at Duke University. Extra special thanks go to Lorenzo and Julian Moten for their levity and hospitality. Cornell University's Society for the Humanities is where the important final steps of the book were completed. My deepest thanks go to our faculty host, and most especially to the all-star administrative staff—Mary Ahl, Paula Epps-Ceppero, and Emily Parson—who provided me with the warmest support. And to my writing buddies, fellow sister-fellows, and Ithaca pals—Ann Cvetkovich, Dana Luciano, Munia Bhaumik, Saida Hodzic, Arnika I. Fuhrmann, Gretchen Philips, and Karen Jaime—for making life on the hill that much warmer, even in those intense winter months.

Since I began my time in the UC system, various system- and campus-wide programs have proven critical in my efforts to conduct research not only across the United States but also in the Philippines. Under the auspices of the UC Pacific Rim Mini-grant (2009–10), UCI Humanities Committee on Research and Travel (2011), and the UCI Council on Research, Computing, and Libraries (CORCL) (2011–12), I was able to conduct ethnographic research, in both countries, as well as archival research at the University of Michigan's Bentley Library and UC Berkeley's Bancroft Library. This latter work was aided greatly by the wonderful archivists and staff at both institutions. My deepest thanks go to Karen L. Jania at the Bentley Library and to David Kessler, Crystal Miles, and Susan Snyder at the Bancroft Library for their assistance with accessing and reserving materials, photocopies, and permissions requests. I also send my appreciation to Rei Magosaki, for sharing the magic of diving into the Hagedorn collection at UC Berkeley, and to Patty Ahn, for her assistance with additional historical and bibliographic research.

Various events have served as rehearsal spaces, many groups of thinkers as jamming buddies, for the crafting of this book's research and writing. Thanks to the UC Humanities Research Institute (UCHRI) for funding the first "California Dreaming" faculty working group (June 2011), to my coorganizer Lucy San Pablo Burns and to our distinguished collaborator-colleagues—Kevin Fellezs, Nayan Shah, Allan Isaac, Alexandra Vazquez, SanSan Kwan, Lan Duong, Mariam Lam, and Eric Reyes. Much gratitude to NYU's A/P/A Studies, most especially Jack Tchen, Laura Chen-Schultz, and Amita Manghani, for the opportunity and support to organize "Renaissance Renegade: A Jessica Hagedorn Retrospective" (2013) and the event's illustrious participants—Mark Bennett, Lucy San Pablo Burns, Thulani Davis, Jojo Gonzalez, Allan Isaac, Robbie McCauley, Nicky Paraiso, Ching Valdes-Aran—for sharing in the celebration of our favorite gangster. Much of this book also received direct critical feedback, on both sides of the United States and the Pacific, through talks given at Princeton University's "Too Cute: American Style and the New Asian Cool" (2010), organized by the fabulous Anne Cheng, and its "In the Mix: Asian Popular Music" conference (2011), organized by Noriko Manabe; UC Berkeley's Center for Southeast Asian Studies speaker series (2011), thanks to the work of Joi Barrios-Leblanc, Catherine Ceniza Choy, and Sarah Maxim; the University of the Philippines College of Music's inaugural Ph.D. conference, "The Impact of Music in Shaping Southeast Asian Societies" (2011), daghang salamat kay José Buenconsejo; an organized panel titled "Popular Music and Asian America" at the 2013 International Association for the Study of Popular Music, U.S. chapter (IASPM-US) conference, with additional thanks to our respondent, Deborah Wong; Cornell University's Musicology Colloquium series and Southeast Asian Studies Program's Gatty Lecture series, thanks to the generous invitations of Alejandro Madrid and Arnika Fuhrmann, respectively.

Every year, the EMP Pop Music Conference has provided a place for and reminder of the sheer pleasures and joy of listening, thinking alongside, and writing about popular music. Through it, I have found the smarts and talent of writers such as Daphne Brooks, Jon Caramanica, Jeff Chang, Hua Hsu, Loren Kajikawa, Josh Kun, Summer Kim Lee, Emily Lordi, Shana Redmond, Gustavus Stadler, Ned Raggett, Barry Shank, Karen Tongson, and Gayle Wald. All of this, of course, would not have been possible without the tireless efforts of Eric Weisbard and Ann Powers. In other places, I have also found the important work of Patty Ahn, Wendy Hsu, Hyunjoon Shin, Grace Wang, and Oliver Wang, colleagues dedicated to the careful study of Asian and Asian American popular music. I look forward to seeing how our field grows.

In the field of Filipino and Filipino American studies, the work and dedication of Lucy San Pablo Burns, Oscar Campomanes, Theo Gonzalves, Dawn Bohulano Mabalon, and Allyson Tintiangco-Cubales served as my impetus for embarking upon graduate school and study. Since that time, their writing and camaraderie, along with that of Allan

Isaac, Martin Manalansan, Neferti Tadiar, José Buenconsejo, Victor Bascara, Francisco "Kikoy" Benitez, Rick Bonus, Christi-Anne Castro, Denise Cruz, Robert Diaz, Vernadette Vicuña Gonzalez, Bliss Cua Lim, Victor Roman Mendoza, Raul Navarro, Martin Joseph Ponce, Rhacel Parreñas, Robyn Rodriguez, Sarita See, Roland Tolentino, Celine Parreñas Shimizu, and Benito Vergara, have functioned as vital signposts and welcome respites on this intellectual journey.

For the past six years or more, it has been an honor to meet, get to know, develop friendships, collaborate with, and think alongside musicians and artists living in and traveling to all the cities that I now feel I can call home—New York, Manila, and San Francisco.

The original gangster, Jessica Hagedorn, is an artist I have admired ever since I first read *Dogeaters* in Oscar Campomanes's "Filipino/American Literature" class in 1995. Words cannot express how much I continue to cherish her mentorship, friendship, care, and generosity. Diego Castillo is the most *lambing* rock star you will ever meet. Daghang salamat 'dong for the hospitality and deep cultural history lessons that help me feel at home, no matter what city we find ourselves in. To Quark Henares, the most *kilig* and humble indie director: your joy for life, art, and music is infectious. I am so glad to have gotten to know that much better "that director from the Philippines who uses so many exclamation points in his e-mails." To Marie Jamora, thank you for your continued support of this book, ever taking time to read it in its draft form. I look forward to our continued collaborations. Interviews and informal conversations with Marie Jamora, Myrene Academia, Mikey Amistoso, Jason Caballa, Toti Dalmacion, Diego Mapa, and Raimund Marasigan were filled with stories and deep insights on Filipinos, culture, and music that helped to guide and challenge, in important ways, my own ideas. Thank you so much for the many nights of good music and laughter, beer and spirits, as well as days filled with record diggin', movie watching, food trips, and musical excursions. To the members and management of Sandwich, Taken by Cars, Pedicab, and Ciudad—thank you for the opportunities to share the same stage and to help bring your music and positive vibes to fans and audiences in the United States. To RA Rivera and the "Word of the Lourd" crew (Lourd de Veyra, Jun Sabayton, Ramon Bautista, Tado, Erning)—your astute political satire and cultural commentary inspire me every day. I am so glad that you are in the world. Here's to many more chances for writers and scholars to prove to the world that OPM [and punk] is not dead! I hope this book spurs others onto the necessary work of listening and writing closely to the Philippines' pop musical pasts.

Interviews, conversations, and meals shared with Jesse and Ogie Gonzales were important reminders of how music and musicians travel, of how we can make home in many places. I am so grateful for their friendships and all the work they have done for the San Francisco/Bay Area and Asian American indie rock scenes. To Alleluia Panis, Ann Borja, Anthem Salgado, and the artists of Bindlestiff Studio and Tongue in a Mood (Allan and Joyce Juan Manalo, Patty Cachapero, Kevin Camia, Rene Acosta, Michell Arellano, Chrystene Ells, Ogie Gonzales, Theo Gonzalves, Mark Marking, L. A. Renigen, Gayle Romasanta, Lorna Chui Velasco, and so many more)—for the mayhem and kritikal kalokohan and creative support that helped shape me and a generation of artists, scholars, and community members. My utmost thanks and respect to the many artists of New York and Los Angeles who have taught and fed me, in so many ways: Angel Velasco Shaw, Ching Valdes-Aran, Amy Besa and Romy Dorotan [from Cendrillon to Purple Yam], AJ Calomay, John Castro, Wendy Hsu, DJ Icy Ice, Robert Farid Karimi, Mia Katigbak, Jorge Ortoll, Ralph Peña, Suzette Porte, Joel Quizon, Mark Redito [Spazzkid], Rona Rapadas, DJ Rhettmatic. To the many folks of the Asian Cinevision film festival crew and the various bands and musicians of Riding Mower Records (RMR), most especially—Risa Morimoto, Eric Lin, John Wong, P.I.C. crew and my band sister-wives (Steve Mallorca, Cindy Mallorca, Jason Grey, Eric Gonzales, Jeff Gray, Christine Bachas, Rick Bartow, Sam Rosser, Mark Desierto, Marie Capasullo, Mas Yamagata, Annie Kim), Jason Gonzales, Johnny Ariz, Steve Cannarelli, Sarah Kricheff, and, of course, my own beloved band of merrymakers, The Jack Lords Orchestra (Micah Valdes, Riley Sumala, Joel Bernardo, Wady Sarmiento, Adam Charity, Bernard San Juan)—your love and music and levity have kept me going through it all.

To my SF/Bay Area and New York chosen family members and band of free thinkers, outsiders, dreamers, and doers. Olivia Malabuyo Tablante is my BFF and soul sister #1, my spiritual adviser, and the best cheerleader/PR manager a girl could ask for. Mark Tristan Ng is my wonder twin, a fellow world traveler and a fellow deviant overachiever who makes many, if not all, things possible. Sonjia Hyon has taught me so much about the ethics of friendship and has been the best writing buddy through the years. Philip Huang has always been a forthright and inspiring friend, a poet and writer whose sense of style and openness to the improvisatory I can only aspire toward. From the laundromats of Berkeley to the *inihaw* of Waipahu to the multiple levels of Manila's inferno to the perfectly timed poetry-filled e-mails, my sisterhood with R. Zamora Linmark crosses borders and time zones. Jorge Ignacio Cortiñas's logic of emotions is unmatched. I aspire to his passionate discipline and composed cariño. Randy Bunnao is the best writing buddy a girl could ask for. Thanks for the laughs and accountability. To each of the life-sustaining folks whom I have had the privilege of sharing "home" with: Chris Bucoy Brown, Allyn Nobles, Christopher Punongbayan, Angie Carrillo, Aimy Ko, Elisa Paik, Jef Castro. Thank you for teaching me daily how to be a better person.

In their making, musical scenes are always already a collaborative process: In the way that no artist, no listener, no reader is ever really out there on their own. In the way that even solo performances require a production crew and audience. In the way that single authors and writers require an editorial and life support team. Over these past few years, Ken Wissoker has been so much more than just an editor. He has been a writing coach and therapist, a champion, a cheerleader, and, most of all, a friend. His belief in this book (and its writer) has carried me through. My biggest thanks go to him as well as Elizabeth Ault, an invaluable woman, who knows how to get things done. As project editor, Susan Albury has kept me on task and on time. I have much appreciation for her steadfast and forthright nature. My gratitude goes out, as well, to Chad Royal and the rest of the Duke marketing team for helping my book make its proper ways out into the world. From the bottom of my heart, I need to thank this book's designer, Amy Buchanan, as well as Louie Cordero, for their patience and generosity in my relentless pursuit of the perfect cover for this book. It is here and I am so very happy. Many thanks to Marilyn Bliss, indexer extraordinaire, and Ray San Diego for the final proofreads. Finally, my deepest gratitude goes to this book's developmental editor (and one of its main architects), Allison Brown. Thank you for the vision and structure that carried me through!

To the many friends and family members across Filipino America who, through their love and support, have helped spur on this book: in New York and New Jersey, the Bernardo, Canton, Fromm, Gabisan, Gonzales, and Marquez families; in the San Francisco/Bay Area, the Mala-buyo families; in the Los Angeles/Southern California area, the Jabines, Gacula, Gage, Louischaroen, and Sumalpong families; in Hawaii, the Dumaran clan; in Virginia Beach, Ronsolo and Joy Lomibao; in Balti-more, the Caragays; in Davao, Philippines, the Ng clan; in Maribojoc, Bohol, the Bacareza family; in Talisay, Cebu, the Gabisan clan. Extra spe-cial thanks to Glenn and Leizle Gabisan, Eric Gonzales, Christian Alivio Marquez, Olivia and Marlone Malabuyo-Tablante, Peter, Phalin, and Steve Louischaroen, Auntie Dixie Dumaran, Neil and Nikki Dumaran, Al, Polly, and Jay Caragay, Ronsolo and Joy Lomibao, Mark Tristan Ng, Keith Gabisan Cuizon, Uncle Cardet and Auntie Pamee Echavez, Willie and Candace Impoc, and Marcel Mabala for their hospitality during the research trips and fellowship years that this book required.

I am a child of Filipino immigrant parents. I grew up in 1980s sub-urban Los Angeles. Even with the large number of Filipinos and Fili-pino Americans around me, my school textbooks, TV, film, and radio told nothing about Filipino and/or Filipino American history, let alone about Filipino music. But, my parents owned a number of records fea-turing Filipino traditional songstresses—Pilita Corrales, Susan Fuen-tes—albums that sat comfortably next to The Platters, Frank Sinatra, and Nat King Cole discs housed in their coffin-sized turntable player. On weekend mornings, this music blasted throughout our home—Latin rhythms caressed by disco beats, melodies filled with words from lan-guages that my parents only spoke to each other and at family parties sweetly gliding on top. *Daghang at maraming salamat* to my parents, Rosenda Bacareza Balance and Romeo Gonzales Balance, for building a foundation for my learning and for teaching me that there are so many ways to sing and listen; and to my second set of parents, Uncle Val and Manay Luz Gabisan, for showing me their unconditional love.

For those who did not live to see this book in its physical form—Romeo Gonzales Balance, Nancy Chang, Eric "E" Fructuoso, Luz Gabi-san, and José Esteban Muñoz—your presence in my life fills every one of these pages, your love will always stay alive.

Gary Gacula Gabisan's open and loving ears, critical and important insights, and commitment to the work and to the world, make this book as much his as it is mine. Whether physically or in spirit, he was there at every gig and rehearsal; every interview and archive visit; every conference panel, film screening, and organized event; on every flight, bus, train, and car ride; each morning when I woke up to write and every evening I went to bed with the words and songs still in my head. For all that, I am eternally grateful. *Ang gugma ko kanimo, Gars* . . . the words will never be enough. But never mind *Naman*. We have the music.

Flip the Beat

An Introduction

Black and white shot: the corner of a sparse, brick-floored room. A Victrola sits center, its mouth agape toward the right side of the screen. A man dressed in black enters screen right and positions himself, seated, in front of the phonograph's horn. He cranks the instrument's arm and then slowly places the needle on the record. The horn emits the prefatory crackle of a recording and, then, percussive rhythms beaten against multiple drums. Scene fades out and repeats again: the corner of a sparse, brick-floored room. Victrola, center. Man enters, cranks the arm and places the needle. Crackle of a recording and, then, percussive rhythms. Scene fades out and repeats a third and final time: Sparse room. Victrola. Man. Arm. Needle. Crackle and, this time, a voice from the machine, words spoken in a foreign and faraway tongue. Close-up on the phonograph's needle riding the vinyl's uneven grooves, awakening sounds from beyond.

Director Marlon Fuentes's film *Bontoc Eulogy* opens with these repetitive scenes of methodical listening. It follows the fictionalized tale of the Narrator's search for his grandfather Markod, a long-lost Bontoc chief and warrior. The trail leads the Narrator to the historical event of the 1904 World's Fair and its Philippine Reservation, an eight-month in situ exhibition of more than one thousand lowland Christian, mountain tribal, and Muslim individuals to introduce fairgoers to the newly acquired territory of the United States. Presenting itself as an autoethnographic documentary, *Bontoc Eulogy* depends on, as much as it upends, the generic qualities of ethnographic film and photography.[1] It features archival footage and photographs that depict tribal and lowland members of Philippine society in either of two registers: the ethnological or the pedagogical.[2] Staged stills focus on the traditional dress and customs (rituals, dance, music-making) of the Reservation's inhabitants. Live action shots capture scenes of primitive Filipinos being taught in the ways of modern dance, language, and technology by fairgoers and organizers alike. Anthropometric front- and side-view photos recall criminology's mug shots, visual means of characterizing distinct facial features, hairstyles, dress, and body parts for later classification. In these turn-of-the-twentieth-century U.S. imperialist visions, the Philippine Islands and its people figure as innately primitive yet potentially assimilable. Rather than an exceptional relationship to the Filipino body, the Fair's images are indicative of a longer history of Filipino compulsory visibility within a U.S. colonial imaginary. For U.S. government officials and scientists, these photographs were modes of surveillance and documentation of cultural and biological difference that undergirded the moral and civilizing need for U.S. presence in the Philippines.

Produced by the Center for Public Broadcasting (CPB) in 1995, the film's content and reception brought together two particular eras of Filipino American cultural history. *Bontoc Eulogy* not only marked the 1904 World's Fair but also the late 1990s centennial celebrations of the end of the Spanish-American War, the declaration of Philippine independence, and the beginning of the Philippine-American War. Screened at events and venues in both the United States and the Philippines, *Bontoc Eulogy* underscored the politics and limits of memory, history, ethnographic representation, and diasporic imagination. Released during a time of heightened exploration of Filipino American identity, and in the wake of forgotten wars and colonial or neocolonial relations, the film's reception delineated the burden of representation for artists such as Fuentes. In corners of the ethnographic film community, the demand to operate as a native filmmaker—that is, one with "an unique insider perspective on the culture under study"—often arose.[3] Eager for visibility and recognition, Filipino American audiences also latched onto the premise and promise of *Bontoc Eulogy* as Fuentes's personal tale, unaware of or perhaps choosing to dismiss its metadiegetic interventions and politics of form. In both instances, many viewers never let go of the idea that the film was autobiographical.

Bontoc Eulogy exploits what Barbara Kirshenblatt-Gimblett defines as the "art of mimesis," the means by which ethnographic objects are "displayed" and "re-presented."[4] A mode of display guided by "representational conventions," in situ installations such as the 1904 Philippine Reservation can never be regarded as politically "not neutral." Yet, Fuentes's film is guided by the representational techniques of not only the (auto)ethnographic but also the experimental. The film draws viewers in by moving effortlessly between archival visual and audio sources and re-creations. But it is through sonic representational techniques—the sound of birds chirping and insects buzzing, the crackle of a spinning record, sounds that connote the pastoral and the past—that Fuentes listens against the desires for holistic narrative structure and smooth transitions. Ever aware that "film has the power to impose a sense of order, purpose, and interconnectedness upon [this] vortex of events," Fuentes invites viewers to take note of the authenticating force of images and sound in concert. An anti-illusionistic piece, it works against the classic Hollywood model techniques of "invisible editing and a musical score that "is not heard . . . while simultaneously obliterating the presence of the narrator/filmmaker."[5]

The case of *Bontoc Eulogy* illustrates the strategies of and desires for autoethnographic filmmaking in the aftermath of an oft-forgotten U.S. imperialist project. These tropes of forgetting and memory organize the "everywhere and nowhere" condition of belonging for Filipinos in the United States and the incomplete project of Filipino nationhood as much as it does a narrative of U.S. exceptionalism. By making the familiar strange, *Bontoc Eulogy* requires its viewers to actively study their assumptions, both in form and content, regarding the authenticity of these narratives. Importantly, *Bontoc Eulogy* emphasizes film as a medium where the visual and sonic meet. It draws viewers' attention to the incommensurable yet productive relationships between the sonic and visual, between the personal and historical. In emphasizing the fissures between sound and sight, Fuentes makes his viewers aware of the fictive and constructed nature of memory, history, and narrative. Returning to the film's opening sequence, the experimental filmmaker is a listener who continually returns to the documents and events of history, his artistic vision greatly depending on his listening practices.

Through his interplays between historical documents and a personal narrative, between the visual and the sonic, Fuentes-as-"native"-filmmaker retells a "straight historical story," while presenting "strategies of ethnographic representation" and "issues related to the documentary form" that "make familiar" the exotic and other by foregrounding the interplay between the visual and the sonic.[6] He oscillates between the real-life historical events of the 1904 World's Fair and Philippine Reservation and a fictionalized ancestral character and story. Fuentes listens against the familiar and compelling tropes of ethnography and multiculturalism—the autobiographical, the native informant, and the teleological. By highlighting the sonic as a formal expression, his film's interpretation of these tropes exposes their authenticating force and uncovers the various burdens of representing that accompany them. Using these same objects and methods, but toward different artistic and political ends, *Bontoc Eulogy* employs techniques and acts of disobedient listening, in order to defamiliarize the viewer's assumptions of what is real and natural and instead render something anew.

Tropical renditions designate this "something new," musical performances, such as *Bontoc Eulogy*, which bring together the sonic, visual, and bodily. These musical renderings occur in various mediums, such as popular music, film, video/installation art, poetry, theater, and music videos. Tropical renditions tune us into the work that popular music does, into the burdens of representation under which racialized performers operate, and into the translocal scenes produced by and productive of U.S.-Philippine relations. Through disobedient listening practices, tropical renditions emerge.

With a method of disobedient listening, we are able to move through and beyond preoccupations with authenticity by listening against and beyond the dominant discourses that continuously constrain and narrow our understanding of the sonic and musical in Filipino America. These scholarly and popular holdings take the shape of visibility politics, naturalized notions of the voice, and cultural imperialism's nation-based models. These containment discourses, mobilized by both ruling and oppositional forces, produce a set of cultural givens that take the form of tropes, the common figures and narratives for describing Filipino listening, voice, and music: the native and/or authentic Other; the alien; the machine; the primitive/child; the hybrid/multicultural; the derivative. Disobedient practices listen against such discourses. They draw our attention to listeners' and critics' attitudes and manners toward a performer and performance—not just in the moments of audition/listening but, also, in their subsequent acts of retelling. They require us to renew our interest in listening as an ethical, social, political practice. They force us to question the hows and whys of established ways of thinking and to identify their impact, their *doing* in the world. Through these lines of questioning, other forms and ways of being— other performances—materialize.

Disobedient listening—or listening against—defies the smooth yet violent framings of colonialism and imperialism's visual regime. Disobedient listening refuses to play the roles of an authentic other, native informant, or indebted giver. Disobedient listening disavows a belief in the promises of assimilation by keeping one's ears open to hidden and distant places often not of this world. Practices of disobedient listening rehearse other types of poiltics and affiliations than those merely based on the promises and demands of visibility. Instead, it is a method that turns to the sonic and musical not just as replacements for a cultural logic of racial visibility but instead as a way to amplify this discourse's limits and demands.

In his "imaginary interview" with fictionalized critic Maria Blumentritt, Fuentes articulated: "The authorial voice of the Narrator clues the viewer into the potential fissures of the tale. This idea is introduced in the first sequence of the film, with the three successive shots of him listening to an ancient Victrola, reminiscent of 'his master's voice.'" This opening sequence invokes a genealogy of images associated with "his master's voice," a trope whose history and meaning frame "what is to come" in the film. A familiar figure loaded with cultural meaning, "His Master's Voice" was most famously captured in Gramophone Company (1900) and RCA-Victor (1921) images. Originally painted by Francis Barraud in 1899 and originally titled "His Late Master's Voice," it is a portrait of Nipper, the painter's late brother's fox terrier, quizzically staring at the phonograph's horn, hearing but not seeing his deceased master speaking. "His Master's Voice" speaks to the early history of the phonographic machine as it "displac(ed) the visual from the site of performance" and troubled the thin line between sound as reality and sound as representation.[7] A magical "ghost machine," it crossed the line between the living and the dead, as voices from the great beyond lived in perpetuity on vinyl.[8] The trademark image's widespread success as a phonographic mise-en-scène of obedient listening, according to cultural anthropologist Michael Taussig, also corroborated a U.S. popular imaginary shaped by scientific and colonial photographs capturing scenes of primitive listening.[9] Thus, the film's prologue calls our attention to the political and ethical stakes of listening.

As Fuentes continues in his imaginary interview, "This prologue suggests the possibility that the whole film, the whole story about to follow, is really a concoction of the character's imagination—a fleshing out of the sound artifacts he has heard."[10] While the prologue sets up Fuentes as the film's author, the Narrator-cum-filmmaker's continuous returns to the record—to hear something new each time—and his film's subsequent narrative interruptions warn us not to regard this "author" as omniscient or all-knowing. Instead, we are asked to remain open to the imaginative possibilities of his faulty memories by regarding his "fleshing out of the sound artifacts he has heard."[11] He fleshes out the sound artifact by adding details, stories, personal background, and physical bodies to these two-dimensional recordings. He fleshes out the sound artifact, as fragment, into the film's narrative order. For Fuentes, "fleshing out" is an artistic practice: along with Doug Quin, his musical collaborator, he composed the film's visual and sonic tracks from archival sound recordings and historic popular music recordings, as well as brand-new sound and musical tracks reconstructed and reimagined from previous audio and written texts. Keeping in mind this artistic practice of "fleshing out," these repetitive shots of Fuentes, methodically placing himself in front of a Victrola to listen, require us as viewers to reimagine him as something more like a turntablist-DJ—digging through, listening to, and drawing from archival materials to stage encounters between texts from disparate sources, in order to flesh out a new composition.

As a tropical rendition, Fuentes's film both indexes and is produced by a long-standing history of U.S.-Philippine "special relations." It is a history of war, empire, and neocolonialism that has produced two paradoxical situations. The first is a racialized one in which Filipinos are hypervisible and invisible, "everywhere and nowhere," perceptually absent and racially ambiguous within a U.S. popular imaginary.[12] The second is a cultural one in which Filipinos are figured as innately musical people who possess no unique musical traditions. Rather than argue for either side of this paradox, in this book, I aim to think deeply about what this paradox has produced and continues to produce, the ways this paradox points us to how musicality [listening, voice, genre] is naturalized; how musical tradition or culture is politicized; and how the place of the Philippines is imagined through music. These cultural paradoxes, produced by and productive of U.S.-Philippine relations, are what persistently set the stage for tropical renditions to take place.

In a political sense, renditions signal the transfers, or handings over, of something or someone to be detained and questioned. Often associated with acts of violence, especially during times of war, renditions contain and retain traces of previous acts—their performers and performances—that emerge despite their covert intentions. In this book, "renditions" invokes the long history of U.S.-Philippine special relations and its enduring political, economic, and cultural aftermath. These scenes of surrender and transfer between two nations are what resonate throughout: the sale and transfer of the Philippines (from Spanish to U.S. hands) in 1898; the transfer of U.S. government and public systems (health, education, culture) throughout the American period (1899–1945); the handing over of governing power from American colonial to Philippine elites (1945); Marcos's declaration of martial law (1972); and the closing of U.S. military bases (1992). This long history of renditions engenders the double-edged meaning of "belonging"—both within their nation-state and diasporic homes—for Filipinos in today's global economy. Quoting noted Philippine theorist E. San Juan Jr., Martin Manalansan writes, "Belonging to the world characterizes the Filipino overseas contract worker's (OCW) ability to find, feel at, and make home in almost any nation as much as it describes her condition, upon migration, of 'becom[ing] assets . . . human capital . . . (and) exchangeable commodities' as part of the global labor market (1998, 7)."[13] The history of special U.S.-Philippine relations has also produced "popular imageries" and "imaginary topographies" that continue to further establish narratives of political friendship and affiliation between these two countries, ones that undergird the socioeconomic realities of Philippine labor and its exploitation.

Tropical renditions are performances that direct us to the tropics of the Philippines—its archipelagic landscapes and the images, characters, characteristics, types, and representations that accompany them. These performances both "tropicalize"—"imbu[ing] a particular space, geography, group or nation with a set of traits, images, and values"—while they also direct our eyes and ears to the histories and maneuvers of a representation-making process that Aparicio and Chavez-Silverman designate as "tropicalization."[14] For Allan Punzalan Isaac, the particular case of American tropics—the shared "imperial grammar" crafted by related histories of U.S. martial and colonial rules—function as both a "geophysical designation" and "geocultural framing."[15] As these writers point out, the tropics simultaneously signify physical places, analytics, and historical practices through which meanings have been made. This book takes intellectual cues from these previous texts by paying close attention to sonic and musical figurations of and within these physical settings. Focusing on a diverse set of U.S.- and Philippines-based musical artists and sonic performances such as the turntablist-DJ group the Invisibl Skratch Piklz, karaoke and cover performances, Jessica Hagedorn's earlier poetry and music/theater performances, and Pinoy indie rock scenes in Manila, San Francisco, and New York, I show how each renders and reckons with the aftermath of U.S. imperialist tropes of the Filipino as primitive, child, mimic, and machine and how they help us re-imagine the tropical places of Filipino America as creative sites of musical life.

Tropical Renditions traces practices of voice and listening through a range of artistic and cultural forms, staged and everyday performances, taking place in "Filipino America"—places found in both the United States and the Philippines.

Chapter 1 of *Tropical Renditions* sets up an oscillating relationship between listening and voice that structures the rest of the book. Its remaining chapters follow the crafting of voice in Filipino America in diverse scenes of listening. They are voices that sing, speak, write, and perform on stage, in living rooms, along with the radio. These performances are captured on tape and in photographs; they flicker across film, television, and computer screens. Throughout this book, the Filipino voice is defined as a form of authorial presence, generic designation, place-making apparatus, and affective labor.

Tropical Renditions chronicles musical artists, practices, and events taking place (and sometimes, popularized) in the neocolonial era after the 1946 U.S. declaration of Philippine independence. This book begins in the late 1990s, at the height of centennial commemorations of the Spanish-American (1898) and Philippine-American (1899–1913) wars, to trace a longer discursive history of "Filipino listening"—back to early twentieth-century U.S. colonial photography and picture postcards. This genealogy continues on through related post–World War II cultural sites on both sides of the Pacific: the cultural politics of the Third World social/literary movements and the Vietnam/Cold War of the 1970s; U.S. government-sponsored multiculturalism policies of the 1980s, which were contemporaneous with the martial rule of Philippine president Ferdinand Marcos; the Internet/Dot Com boom and rise of an Asian American creative class in the 1990s; and the early twenty-first-century landscape of extranational politics. Each of these musical phenomena emerge at particularly salient moments and historical junctures during this span of more than one hundred years, when voice and listening resonate as political power, social legibility, transnational labor, and mobility.

Tropical Renditions, however, does not assume a comprehensive approach to popular music and performance in Filipino America. Nor does it memorialize a "who's who" of Filipino and Filipino American musicians since the end of World War II. There are a number of musical artists and genres that sing alongside yet remain absent from this book's pages.[16] I have chosen instead to turn my attention to musical artists working within popular musical idioms—experimental turntablist music, punk/indie rock, pop love songs/ballads, and even rock 'n' roll/ Motown—not readily associated, in popular and scholarly accounts, with race, popular music, and performance in the United States. Due to their affinity for the abstract and experimental, the emotional and sentimental, the artists in this book bear and subvert the burden of representation differently than those musicians working within genres and idioms more easily associated with racialized performance in the United States.

I demonstrate how these musicians and their tropical renditions function as performative approaches and reproaches to cultural and scholarly givens about listening, voice, and racialized performance. I argue that the music and performers of Filipino America do not maintain a singular relationship to disobedient listening practices. Instead, practices of listening against and beyond prescriptive discourses are integral to many other genealogies, musical and performance traditions, and forms of racialized insubordination.

Taking place during the late-twentieth century's long history, marked by neocolonial aesthetics and global multiculturalism, tropical renditions trouble simplistic notions of racial and cultural authenticity. In doing so, these musical phenomena challenge our notions of U.S. popular music and its genealogies. As staged and everyday sonic performances, tropical renditions evidence the always already mobile, migratory, and collaborative ways of popular music or what Sara Cohen describes as "musical 'routes' as opposed to roots."[17] This focus on musical production through pathways, rather than patrimony, recognizes the "translocal"—that each geographical place is composed of "processes always linked . . . to other places" by people and media technologies.[18] The analytic of translocal scenes accounts for the multidirectional and multisensorial quality of popular music's production, reception, and circulation.[19]

This book enters and extends ongoing conversations on the two-way cultural traffic between the United States and Asia. It brings together sites and concerns that are often divided between the fields of U.S. popular music, on the one hand, and ethnomusicology, on the other. This book aims to ask not only about the state of Filipinos in U.S. popular music but also about what is produced when U.S. popular music travels overseas. In this way, I take a performance studies approach to the musical aftermath of U.S. imperial cultures. I am interested in the small-scale and ordinary ways that Filipinos and Filipino Americans devise a musical life, as well as the ways of thinking and politics this musical life generates.

In the remainder of this introduction, I first turn to music as a way of thinking about Filipino history. This allows me to uncover intellectual approaches to the study of Filipino music and their political stakes. Then, I uncover the dominant discourse of cultural visibility (which also takes the forms of invisibility and hypervisibility) in Filipino America in order to propose instead a phonographic approach, one that attends to the sonic and musical with, as Fred Moten has theorized, an "ensemble of the senses."[20] With this phonographic method, I return to scenes within the U.S. colonial archive to trace a different genealogy of Filipino listening, a disobedient one that allows us to hear tropical renditions.

Filipino History in the Key of Music

As an archipelagic nation that has endured being occupied and colonized by multiple nations—Spain, the United States, and Japan, in particular—the historiography of the Philippines is often composed as disparate time periods brought together in a seamless fashion. In other words, Filipino history telling has taken the medley form. Before

Spanish explorer Ferdinand Magellan's landing on the shores of Mactan, Cebu, in 1521, the islands operated as diverse states of indigenous tribes, *datu* societies, maritime-oriented principalities, and minor plutocracies. With Miguel Lopez de Legazpi's 1565 landing and the crown's designation of the archipelago as "Las Islas Filipinas"—literally, the islands of King Philip II—the Spanish colonial period officially began, and the term *Filipino* emerged as a national and cultural moniker for the peoples of this heterogeneous archipelago. With Spanish colonization came Christianity and Catholicism, various codes of law, and the establishment of the oldest modern university in Asia, all in the service of the islands' political and cultural unification. As part of the Spanish East Indies, the Philippines were ruled as part of the Viceroyalty of New Spain and administered from Mexico City (1565–1821), then directly from Madrid (1821–1898, at the end of the Spanish-American War). Located in the middle of the Pacific Ocean, these Spanish colonial islands and their ports were key junctions along the Manila galleon trade's itinerary.[21]

During this Spanish colonial period, the Church became the main site of learning and instruction, especially in regard to music. Within the Church, as Antonio Hila writes, the *schola cantorum* (school of singers) and *escuela de tiples* (boys' choirs) introduced the island's inhabitants to otherwise alien Western musical forms. As Hila explains, "Totally strange to the native's ears was the unfolding of the new melody of the West, backed up with harmonic device based on a given scale. With no equivalent in native musical culture, the melodic sense of the new musical experience followed a regular, measurable ebb and flow. As a result of the interweaving of the horizontal or melodic and the vertical or harmonic, Western music's texture appeared thick in contrast to the thin, almost unilinear character of the ethnic musical tradition."[22] In his distinction between a "native musical culture" (read, pre-Spanish/indigenous) and "Western music," Hila enacts a popular discourse of Filipino music as ethnic and indigenous in contrast to Western classical forms.

Listening against such popular discourse, D. R. M. Irving instead proposes that we think of this initial colonial period, as well as the religious and secular forms it created, through the figure of counterpoint. Employing this musicological term as a metaphor for society, Irving writes, "Counterpoint within a colonial society involves the combination of multiple musical voices according to a strict, uncompromising set of rules wielded by a manipulating power."[23] Thus, for Irving, the *habanera*, *danza, polka,* and *marcha* not only influenced the development of native forms, such as the *balitaw, kundiman,* and *sarswela,* but coexisted alongside them as musical innovations. Meanwhile, the Church also found its way into and was changed by local folk expressions of religiosity such as the *pasyon, sinakulo, santacruzan, nobena, corrido, panunuluyan.* "Elements of musical encounter and negotiation such as these," Irving reminds us, "were entirely symptomatic of colonial societies in early modern Latin America and the Philippines," thus making a case for the archipelagic nation's musical affiliations under the Spanish empire.[24]

In the realms of both the religious and secular, while the Spanish mobilized music as a mode of education and political unification, various natives of the islands found ways of adapting these foreign styles into local forms, making them vernacular and part of what is now considered Philippine folk culture. One needs only to look as far as the *kundiman,* "a song which expresses the lofty sentiment of love, and even heroism, in a melancholy mood," or the *harana,* "a traditional form of courtship in which a young man woos a maiden through song," to note how these local adaptations of what had been deemed foreign musical styles are now considered traditional Philippine music.[25] These musical styles, as well as the performance forms of bands and *rondallas* that also emerged near the end of the Spanish colonial period, grew in popularity during the subsequent period of Philippine history.

The American period of Philippine history officially began in 1901, although the United States had arrived in the islands many years before, under the guise of military allies during the Spanish-American War and then later as enemies during the subsequent Philippine-American War. Issued on December 21, 1898, in the days immediately after the signing of the Treaty of Paris that ended the Spanish-American War, transferring political control of the Philippines from Spanish to U.S. hands and expanding U.S. military governmental powers from Manila to the rest of the country, and before the official start of the Philippine-American War in 1899, President William McKinley's doctrine of benevolent assimilation emphasized the altruistic tropes of friendship, protection, and filial affections. Deeming the Filipinos unfit for self-rule, McKinley and pro-imperialist factions framed U.S. imperial rule as a moral responsibility, to take up "the white man's burden" in order to civilize their "little brown brothers." This moral imperative was supported by the scientific findings of anthropologists such as Dean Conant Worcester and took shape in the establishment of U.S. educational, governmental, and public health systems in the Philippines and legal and trade policies of U.S. imperial rule. As this book claims, these sentiments and imperatives required sound and musical recordings, as well as their attendant technology, the phonograph, which played a crucial role in dramatizing McKinley's benevolent assimilation doctrines and upholding the turn-of-the-twentieth-century U.S. imperialist project.

During this time, anthropologists in the field recorded indigenous Filipino musical forms to substantiate popular scientific models of musical and human development while colonial subjects were trained in the martial form of the marching band, evidencing the cultural arm of U.S. disciplinary actions and the Filipino's capability to be cultivated and civilized.[26] These elements, prevalent throughout the period of U.S. colonial occupation, were on display at the 1904 World's Fair. As we shall see later in this introduction, anthropologists' photographed scenes of Filipinos listening to and interacting with phonographs depended upon and reinforced imperial tropes of Filipinos as primitive and childlike, dramatizing the Filipino's need for U.S. imperial supervision while also making a case for the archipelago's lack of a mature national musical culture.

The first half of the twentieth century in the Philippines also saw the spread of popular U.S. musical genres and performance styles through live shows, album recordings, and, later, radio, movies, and television. Local Filipino singers and musicians, mainly in the cities, learned "American sounds" to make a living performing in restaurants, clubs, and cabarets. In its early years, vaudeville was brought in to entertain U.S. troops and was dominated by non-Filipino entertainers. Yet, by the early 1920s, local performers such as former *sarswela* singer Atang de la Rama, Katy de la Cruz, and Borromeo Lou, as well as local theater venues, dedicated themselves to transforming the U.S. style into its Philippine vernacular performance form of *bodabil*.[27] Featuring a mixture of U.S. blues numbers, torch songs, ballads, and even the occasional *kundiman*, as well as sketch comedy and dance numbers, *bodabil* trained and showcased the talents of stage stars, some of whom would later make the transition to film, TV, and popular music recordings. When film and TV production halted during the World War II Japanese occupation, Filipino performers returned to the *bodabil* stages. During the wartime and postwar periods, *bodabil* helped to cultivate major Philippine singers such as Sylvia de la Torre and Pilita Corrales and comedians Dolphy and German Moreno. And, after the arrival of rock 'n' roll to Philippine shores in the 1950s, it was on *bodabil*'s stages that Eddie Mesa, the "Elvis of the Philippines," made his debut.

Despite these vibrant histories, there remains a dearth of scholarship, in both Filipino and Filipino American studies, on wartime and post–World War II popular music in the Philippines. This is due, in large part, to the particular tropes of Philippine nationalism favored since the 1960s and 1970s. Within this nationalist politics, folk and punk rock remain two preferred genres of protest music. All other late twentieth-century popular music forms—pop, new wave, disco, rock/indie rock, and hip-hop, for example—presumably fall under the tropical sway of the "miseducated Filipino." As Philippine historian Renato Constantino proclaimed in his important essay "The Miseducation of the Filipino": "The most effective means of subjugating a people is to capture their minds."[28] For Constantino, as well as many others, Philippine subjugation under the United States took the seemingly benign forms of colonial (re)education language (English-only) to unify Filipinos in the service of a U.S. imperialist project. His rendering of the far-reaching and long-term effects of linguistic colonialism and their impact on cultural values and references, as well as economic and social outlook, are true. But Constantino's theories depend on and promote a dominant nationalist discourse of "American culture" as one built from "a nation whose cultural institutions have developed freely, indigenously, without control or direction from foreign sources, whose ties to its cultural past are clear and proudly celebrated because no foreign power has imposed upon its people a wholesale inferiority complex, because no foreign culture has been superimposed upon it, destroying, distorting its own past and alienating the people from their own cultural heritage."[29] With such wholesale concepts of U.S. nationalism, one can miss out on the heterogeneity of American culture by misconstruing how "foreign sources" are what have shaped and created U.S. culture and music, in particular. This both points to the ways in which ideas of American nationhood are themselves imperialist imports and how the mere opposition of Filipino nationalism to a U.S. one forecloses opportunities for coalition and collaboration beyond simply nation-state formations.

Since that time, ethnomusicological studies continue to characterize Filipino national music through either of two musical modes:

the classical (read colonial/European) or the indigenous (read local minority/resistant). More recently, Christi-Anne Castro draws our attention to the ways in which classical and folk music renders the Philippine nation as modern and civilized and how Philippine nationalist sentiments and government policies animate the creation, performance, reception, and distribution of these musics.[30] Yet, her analysis unfortunately does not (because it cannot) include a sustained examination of Philippine popular music. Such omission further points to popular music's problematic relationship to Philippine nationalism. Moreover, almost any discussion of popular music and Filipinos or Filipino Americans is itself already precluded by what Kandice Chuh has aptly identified as a discourse of "about-ness," which "functions as an assessment of relevance" and both perpetuates and leaves unchecked systems of categorization that "manage minority difference."[31] A discourse of "about-ness" asks, "What is Filipino about Filipino popular music?" In this formulation, if popular music is deemed the domain of the West, then dominant tropes of Filipino popular music assume its objects, musical artists, and audiences are therefore derivatives and products of Western imperialism.

As the popular saying goes, the Philippines spent "four centuries in a convent and fifty years in Hollywood," lending the archipelagic nation both the backbeat of Latin-inspired rhythms and song forms and the heart of African American–derived beats, bass lines, and melodies (rock, soul, disco, and jazz). Yet, to make a case for a nation's modernity, one requires civilization logics that depend on the monumental and epic, not the borrowed and fragmented. Such logics undergirded the development and popularity of World's Fairs and museums, both of which were informed by the discourse and work of Western anthropologists. Some Americans can find their culture on display in museums as "art." Others have to scour specialized wings or natural history museums. Within civilization logics, Sarita See argues, "Filipinos cannot 'have' culture. Filipinos instead 'are' culture." Filipinos, she laments, have "internalized this colonial idiom and uncritically accepted the idea that [they] 'have no culture.'"[32] This idiom includes the dominant trope of Filipinos as "superb mimics of Hollywood actors and Motown musicians."

Rather than challenging Western anthropological and colonial discourses, ones that presuppose culture as the property and possessions of a certain class of people (those who "have" culture), while others merely stand in for culture (those who "are" culture), within Filipino American studies, this popular discourse continues to uphold simplistic notions of Filipino objectification and objecthood, offering no possibility for the object's resistance. In this popular discourse, the distinction between Filipino and Filipino American reenacts the cultural divide between homeland and diaspora, those forced to perform as cultural belonging(s) and those who need to possess cultural belonging(s).

Of course, mimicry also does not fit within civilization logics and its colonial idiom. Instead, it disrupts these logics. Rather than assume mimicry as not productive of culture, tropical renditions prove it as vital to the performance and proliferation of Filipino musical life. In the classical musical sense, rendition marks the expression or interpretation of an originating written composition. While this initial text, its own visual and written recording of the music, offers a template for the notes to be played, and directions on how they might be played, in the end, the (re)sounding of the music depends upon the performers themselves. Through a performer's renditions, the original is destabilized, unmoored from its fixed and entrenched position. By emphasizing performance as interpretative and transformative, renditions betray those desires for an origin or original.

Tropical renditions do not presume singular meanings, nor do they glorify the essentialist romances of cultural heritage or ancestry. Renditions are not inherited or passed down via lines of descent. They are not property to be protected, collected, controlled, passed on, or possessed by only a chosen few. Tropical renditions work against notions of musical forms and practices as wholly original and authentically indigenous. Instead, they are constituted in their own place and time, referring to past and contemporaneous performances while also signaling the potential and possibilities of future soundings.

Phonographic Approaches: Beyond the Kodak Zone

A powerful narrative of American exceptionalism rests upon the ability to make invisible the nation's war with and annexation of the Philippines at the turn of the twentieth century. As various scholars have suggested, this narrative obfuscates the neocolonial ties between the two nations that have continued beyond the U.S. declaration of Philippine independence in 1945. As literary scholar Oscar Campomanes noted in his well-known 1995 essay: "The invisibility of the Philippines became a necessary historiographical phenomenon because the annexation of the Philippines proved to be constitutionally and culturally problematic for American political and civil society around the turn of the century and thereafter."[33] Working from Amy Kaplan's formulation of American exceptionalism, whereby "the invisibility of the Philippines has everything to do with the invisibility of American imperialism to itself," Campomanes extends this "curse of invisibility" to various forms of forgetting. Whereas Campomanes identifies Filipino invisibility and its forms of forgetting as a problem of historiography, others such as Elizabeth Pisares define its impact as cognitive and perceptual. That is to say, the problem of invisibility lies in the Filipino's inability to be recognized (based on phenotype) as "looking" Filipino, and this problem is played out in the field of cultural representation. Pisares locates this absence of a Filipino American racial discourse by tracking how easily the look of freestyle music artist Jocelyn Enriquez transformed across her career and album covers.[34] These desires to make the Filipino body visible and legible in Asian American cultural politics seek to counteract the myriad ways in which U.S. educational, military, and government authorities as well as their opponents attempted to make the racial (il)legibility of Filipinos a perceptual concern, through their painstaking efforts to visually represent Filipinos, from the turn of the twentieth century until now.

"Far from rendering Filipinos 'invisible,'" as historian Vicente Rafael writes, "colonialism instigated the proliferation of Filipino bodies."[35] Photography therefore played a crucial role in depicting the Philippines as a society ill-equipped for self-rule through the recurring image of Filipinos as children, America's little brown brothers dependent upon Uncle Sam's benevolent tutelage. As the work of Benito Vergara and Laura Wexler underscores, it was specifically through the medium of photography that U.S. colonial government officials brought Filipinos into the Kodak zone. Coined by visual artist and writer Frank Millet in 1899, the Kodak zone defined the imperial circuits of knowledge formed by visuality and its concomitant forms.[36] Writing in the year before the Philippine-American War commenced, Millet opens his *Expedition to the Philippines* with the following:

Few persons had more than a very hazy idea as to the geographical position of the Philippines until the exhilarating news of Dewey's victory brought out the atlases. Manila was a familiar enough name. It suggested a short, thick cheroot . . . and was intimately connected with coils of bright yellow rope seen in every cordage shop. But the geographical position of this busy capital and of the group of islands of which it is the metropolis was about as vague in most minds as the situation of the last discovered irrigation area in Mars.[37]

Millet's observations exemplify the Philippines' figuration as "foreign in a domestic sense." While Commodore George Dewey's victory at the Battle of Manila Bay—one that marked the official end to the Spanish-American War and start to U.S. colonial occupation in the Philippines—made sure that Americans "brought out the atlases," the word *Manila* described objects already part of America's everyday life. At the same time, through an act of comparison, the Philippines were figured as Mars, rendering the Filipino as alien extraterrestrial. In the face of this turn-of-the-nineteenth-century U.S. imaginary's hazy ideas of the island nation, picture postcards and other photographic images of Filipinos listening to phonographs appeared in U.S. government reports, travel narratives, and historical documents, circulated nationally through popular periodicals and picture postcards, and "expand[ed] the aura of [a U.S.] imperialist state" in the Philippines as a benevolent presence and a political necessity. What is the afterlife of this collapse between the visual and visibility? And what might we move toward to go beyond the limits of this discourse?

If the colonial and ethnographic photo's power lies in its "domesticating" force, its ability to literally and figuratively fix individuals in a time and place, then *Bontoc Eulogy* and its opening sequence remind us of listening's creative potential to help us move from being stuck in a moment that we can't get out of. In his opening sequence, Fuentes offered us some guidelines on how to carefully and methodically listen to and for the past. They require our continual returns to the record. They require a type of listening that cues into different languages and voices. Throughout his film, Fuentes critiques the generic qualities of ethnographic film as "primarily observational in style (that is, it communicates an authoritative claim in relation to its 'objective' uninflected surface)." At the same time, he appropriates his presumed role as a "native filmmaker," the local subject given a camera by anthropologists as a way to capture the supposedly insider-only perspectives and to create something anew from the fissures and cracks in a record. If folklore and its modern successor, multiculturalism, desire and rely upon authentic visions of the Other, then *Bontoc Eulogy*—its opening sequence's staging of a listening practice and the subsequent interplay between the archival and the re-created—offers us an example of phonographies, ways of recording and transforming sounds that mean to inspire rather than prescribe.

Phonographies are practices that continually attempt to "write sound." They bear the traces of long-standing traditions of affiliation and distinction between sound as phonic substance and writing as language and a system of signs.[38] Referencing sonic phenomena and the processes and forms of representation (writing, recording, description) they enable, Alexander Weheliye argues, a phonographic approach reminds us that technologies are "vital elements" of popular musical performances "rather than supplementary to (their) unfolding."[39] The phonograph first captures sounds and then records, presses them onto a vinyl surface. We play back these sound writings and, through the aura of the device, feel both a connection to the past while reaching into the future. Through techniques of rhythm, meter, and the lyrical, poems translate and transform the sonic into literary and then, in the case of the spoken word, back again. Referencing both techne and technology, phonographies are a field of attempts to bridge the incommensurability of the sonic and literary. They also register the various forms and politics of difference enacted and engendered by this incommensurability. In today's U.S. popular music studies, the language of Enlightenment ideals and their divisions between the sensual and rational, aurality/orality and the literary, continue to dominate, most commonly appearing in the adjectival and descriptive modes of approaching sonic matter and musical structures. As "listeners and theorists of listening," a phrase given to us by Josh Kun, however, artists and audiences often offer us different ways out of oversimplified binaries.[40]

Written at the intersection of popular music, performance, and Filipino/Filipino American studies, this book is invested in a phonographic approach that pays attention to where the sonic, the literary, the visual, and the bodily intersect. In this book, a phonographic approach fleshes out musical recordings and other sonic artifacts, in the ways that Fuentes as well as performance studies instruct us. With this phonographic approach, I imagine and write about turntablist-DJs the Invisibl Skratch

Piklz's performance techniques of sonic abstraction and performed disavowals in interviews as alien articulations. They are performances that refuse to adhere to a politics of racial visibility while still reckoning with the bodily and human. With this phonographic approach, I imagine and write about karaoke as an artistic object and form, a dramaturgical web, and a pedagogical tool, not of mere or passive mimicry but instead of serious work. The serious work produced by karaoke connotes that its objects, scenes, and aesthetics can be simultaneously earnest and critical. With this phonographic approach, I imagine and write about Jessica Hagedorn's authorial voice, one often rendered as singular and hybrid, as bearing traces of the gangster routes she has traveled as a poet, musical collaborator, and performance artist. To claim musical routes, rather than roots, is to listen against notions of artistic lineage or heritage in order to hear the places of music and the circuits along which it travels. With this phonographic approach, I imagine and write about Pinoy indie rock not as a strictly bounded musical genre but instead as a translocal scene. This translocal scene consists of places, events, and relationships produced, in both predigital and digital forms, by the spread of both musical recordings and the attachments they generate.

This phonographic approach is deeply indebted to and moves alongside the important work of Fred Moten, whose theories of interinanimation help us recognize the ways that photography, sound, and performance work across forms and genres to enliven meaning. This approach is distilled into a theoretical image produced by Moten's own poetic line: "The phonograph is also a photograph of a movement and what it bears."[41] The machine of sonic recording and playback also inscribes, transcribes, and figures live events of the past and their "remains."[42] A phonographic approach helps us to consider the following: when brought into the present, what critical work do these photographs, as forms of musical recording, perform for the future? More precisely, when brought into the present, what do these photographs help us to hear? And what, in turn, does this hearing engender?[43]

In the next section, I return to earlier moments and histories of recording the Filipino—her voice, music, and ways of listening—to trace the important role that phonographs and photographs played in U.S.-Philippine colonial history, most especially in the ways they instilled tropes of Filipino listening and voice that we continue to carry.

Disobedient Listening

Introduced near the end of the nineteenth century, the phonograph was a technological revolution in sound and performance. Originally intended as a means for sound to travel across the miles (what Alexander Graham Bell's telephone achieved in 1876), Thomas Edison's invention instead inscribed sonic events onto tin-foil plates, creating a physical document and record of a live aural performance. Transforming aural ephemera into physical objects through the process of recording, phonographs allowed for the infinite and uncontrollable playbacks of past sonic events. These qualities of repetition and mimesis shaped the phonographic users' relationship to the machine and, in turn, its critical reception and corporate marketing. First marketed to businesses as a dictation device, the phonographic machine produced sound-objects for the professional and amateur listener's intensive and extensive consumption. Unlike their print media contemporaries, the newspaper and magazine, late nineteenth-century phonographs and records enabled audiences' repeat listenings to and personal collection of otherwise ephemeral and public musical performances.[44]

Among the U.S. colonial ephemera, a phonographic mise-en-scène of obedience and listening emerges. Titled "A Subuagane's first experience with a phonograph, Mountain Province, Island of Luzon, Philippines," the postcard illustrates a scene of intercultural encounter against a simple backdrop, emphasizing its three main characters: the improperly named Igorot, an American soldier, and the phonograph. The machine's function and the record's content are ambiguous. Is it recording or playing back? And, if so, what is it writing or sounding? The tribesman and soldier squat and gaze in each other's direction, a meeting mediated by the aura and presence of modern technology. In this postcard's imagery, the spectacle of primitive listening is tamed into a one-on-one pedagogical moment. The conjoined technological regimes of phonography and photography multiply what Susan Stewart has called a postcard's "domesticating force."[45] It encloses the primitive body in a scene of performed restraint—he obediently listens to the machine and, in turn, becomes an obedient machine—while the soldier's presence as U.S. military figure is muted by his benevolent role as teacher. Through their circulation within the U.S. nation-state's borders, picture postcards domesticated the Filipino within a U.S. popular

Figure I.I "A Subuagane's first experience with a phonograph, Mountain Province, Isle of Luzon, Philippines." From Jonathan Best's *Philippine Picture Postcards* (Bookmark, 1994). Courtesy of the author.

imaginary—as a radically and visually distinct body formed by the invisible structures of U.S. war and empire.

The transformative, civilizing power of a particular listening practice infuses the photograph. Reading the image as an evolutionary time line, the primitive on the left might transform and grow into the soldier on the right someday by moving through the modernizing effects of a sonic technology that teach him to listen properly.[46] Giving his ear and paying attention to the mandates sounded by U.S. imperial policies of benevolent assimilation, the Filipino is figured by this and other postcard images as "recipients, and therefore also carriers, of promises that emanate from a hidden and distant elsewhere."[47] Trained to properly hear a white man's voice and obey it above his own people, America's little brown brother is promised—through careful listening and faithful mimicry of his master's voice—the fruits of citizenship and belonging to a hidden and distant elsewhere. Predicated by these promises, obedient listening practices are part of the Filipino's miseducation process, leading him to forget his own national history, in favor of intimately remembering figures and events from a U.S. elsewhere, and to cultivate instead a musical culture of mimicry and cover songs.[48]

Figure I.2 "'A White Man's Voice' among the Igorrotes." From Jonathan Best's *Philippine Picture Postcards* (Bookmark, 1994). Courtesy of the author.

Yet, into the familiar sound tracks of historical violence, there are breaks in the record, imaginative spaces that provide room to improvise new movements and gestures across the seemingly smooth surfaces of historical time. Rather than magically falling under the spell of U.S. imperial technology and its promises, obediently listening to cultural imperialism's deafening silences, Filipinos visually and physically captured alongside phonographs instead listened apart, away, and against its colonial sound tracks, marking a genealogy of different listening practices in Filipino America. Broadly apprehending auditory phenomena, this practice of listening is a mode of reading or perceiving the underside of meaning through sound—tuning into tone as much as words, finding meaning in both words and feelings.

With a phonographic approach, I return to these snapshots as both evidence and performances of Filipino disobedient listening. They are sound records and performance documentation and, through them, I learn to read and listen differently. Like poems in Charles Bernstein's formulation, these photographs chronicle past soundings as well as help score future performances.[49] Though these images occupy the U.S. colonial archive on the Philippines, I would be remiss to leave them there. They have told us much about what and how U.S. colonial officials thought of Filipinos. Here, I want us to look and listen more closely to what these photographs stage. Doing so helps us not only reimagine the subjugating and disciplinary force under which these performances of listening took place. They also help us think seriously about how listening and music can take place in spite of the fact of everyday coercion and constraint.

Ironically, one of the most poignant displays of disobedient listening in Filipino America appears unexpectedly right in the heart of an early twentieth-century imperialist text. Published in 1914, the two-volume collection, *The Philippines, Past and Present*, remains a remarkable example of the U.S. colonial regime's reliance upon photographic mise-en-scènes—of benevolent assimilation and the Filipino's innate racial difference—in the name of its own expansionist goals. Part travel journal reportage and part legislative recommendation, the massive tomes chronicle the exploratory expeditions of Dean Conant Worcester (scientist and future secretary of the interior of the Philippines, 1901–13) into the Philippines' northern Luzon and southern Visayan regions, two areas specifically populated by non-Christian tribes. An American scientist and University of Michigan professor, Worcester's notes and letters from his first two excursions to the Philippine Islands, in 1887 and 1890 respectively, were published in an earlier book, *The Philippine Islands and Their People* (1898). One of the few Americans, at the time, with such extensive knowledge of the country's flora and fauna, Worcester was assigned to and played a key role in the Schurman Commission, a U.S. government-appointed body that reported on the social conditions in the islands—namely, the increased activities of the Filipino independence movement—and, therefore, recommended the need for further U.S. guidance in establishing civil government and educational infrastructures.

Chapters of Worcester's study are punctuated by the occasional photograph; unmarked by date or time of capture, the past and present are collapsed in these scenes and images. Nestled between Worcester's tales of narrowly escaped headhunting rituals, treacherous terrain, and first encounters with island natives, a portrait titled "Entertaining the Kalingas" illustrates an encounter between island savagery and Western modernity mediated by that ever-present colonial technology.

As the caption of Worcester's photograph informs his readership, "They are listening with great interest to the reproduction of a speech

Figure I.3 "Entertaining the Kalingas," from Dean C. Worcester collection. Photo courtesy of Bentley Historical Library, University of Michigan.

which one of their chiefs has just made into the receiving horn of a dicta-phone." In this scene of playback, the phonograph stands in for the tribal leader's body. Recording the native leader's speech, another transcript is added to the colonial archive. Recording and framing the Kalinga lis-tening audience, another version of "His Master's Voice" is performed.

Yet when one is tuned into the multiple loci of mediation—the phonograph, the photograph, even the paramilitary Philippine scouts (read native informants) surrounding the tribesmen—this document resonates differently. This photographed scene of subjection forces its viewer to reckon not only with the nature of Kalinga listening but, more important, with the colonial terror/regime of a proper response. Within an ethnographic imaginary, to render a "proper" response, tribesmen must re-cite the spectacle of primitives' reaction to modern sonic tech-nology, a display of childlike wonder and domesticated obedience. In a colonial imaginary, the proper response of attentive listening results in the colonized subject's fidelity to his master's word. The Kalingas' body language and facial expressions, however, do not affectively regis-ter such a response. Instead, ambivalence, even boredom, buzzes among eyes turned away from the scene's main stage; while defiant stares and self-aware smiles at the camera break the fourth wall and draw attention to the photographer's omnipresence by returning the gaze. Acutely aware of the camera's power to capture and the detrimental effects of exhibiting the proper response, these improper and disobedient subjects know enough to perform a version of not-caring by boldly staring down the master's gaze and selectively turning away from the command of his voice. These scenes of disobedient listening, with a phonographic approach, impress upon me at once as visual record, sonic recording, and performance stills. These scenes, staged and recorded within an imperial regime, allow me to craft a genealogy, a performance tradition, of Filipino insubordination.

A critical practice of disobedient listening not only aims to uncover some cultural truths or write against the wrongs of previous scholarship. Instead, it is a method that aims to denaturalize tropes surrounding Filipinos' relationship to U.S. popular music and, in turn, Filipino music. Armed with it, we can listen beside and beyond the stultifying tropes of domination, on the one hand, and resistance, on the other, to hear differently the places of Filipino America's musical life.[50] A critical practice of disobedient listening helps us to hear differently what popular music produces. Armed with it, musical performances previously dismissed as merely imitative, abstract, or multicultural unsettle dominant discourses of race, performance, and U.S. popular music. A critical practice of disobedient listening allows us to hear differently the burdens of representation and liveness that bear upon a politics of voice and listening. Armed with it, intimate scenes of musical performance and exchanges come alive and require that we recalibrate our default settings.

Outro: On Titles

I grew up raised by a mom who was constantly using things they were never intended for in the first place. Like when I ran out of glue to make the Arizona State flag for my social studies class and I was freaking out. And my mom brought out a bowl of cooked rice. I put the fresh soft grains between the sheets of construction paper and pinched. (It worked!) . . .

My uncle Charlie's house in the barrio of Santo Tomas is an amazing collage. There is concrete that he mixed and poured. There are the corrugated sheets he rescued from an unfinished construction project. There are shutters and doors he salvaged from multiple houses in the city that were demolished. Those particular pieces may be hundreds of years old—as they are in the Spanish style. The detail all about the house runs from tourist kitsch to the horns of one of his own field bulls. The thing about my Uncle Charlie is that when he made his house, he didn't think he was making a collage. He was doing what our family has been doing for generations. He was simply making.

—Patrick Rosal, "The Art of the Mistake: Breaking as Making"

I open this outro with two excerpts, substantial yet necessary, from poet Patrick Rosal's talk at the 2014 Remixed Media Festival. I hesitate to simply call it a talk because Rosal's writing style and oratorical performance betray what is commonly expected of an academic presentation. A performance poet, DJ, and former b-boy dancer, Rosal brings much of each form's techniques into his writing and its performance. Hearing him speak that day, I felt a sense of tropical renditions (and this book) come to life.

In "The Art of the Mistake," Rosal listens against the common segregation of the tropes of remix into the realms of *either* high art *or* popular culture, of either postcolonial or Western. He instead renders various scenes of performance, brings them together into one composition, in order to trouble these tropical divides. Emily Dickinson and John Keats's poetic lines. DJ Kool Herc's breaks and imported sound systems. Jun Jacinto's unplanned yet successful dance move during a 1986 Jersey City b-boy battle. The repurposing of turntables "in the basement of a maple split in Edison, New Jersey." The forging of bolos and machetes by the *panday*, blacksmiths, of San Nicolas, Ilocos Norte. "What is a remix anyway?" Rosal asks midway through his talk. "It's not just making; it's remaking. It's the joining together of two or more elements that wouldn't normally be joined." Through its writing and subsequent reenactments, Rosal's talk itself performs remix. It is not just a rendition of a written script of his making alone. It is a rendition of a written script that is always already a remaking of previous staged, recorded, and embodied performances.

Though more recently and popularly associated with hip-hop culture, the remix, as Rosal by way of Jeff Chang reminds us, is not just a product of local conditions (such as the everyday life and political conditions for blacks and Latinos in the 1970s South Bronx). It is also a product imported from tropical places like Jamaica, from where DJ

Kool Herc migrated, and other islands with long-standing cultural traditions forged from all kinds of survival in the face of all sorts of everyday violence. Like Rosal's Uncle Charlie's house or his immigrant mother's everyday remedies, these performances and traditions are often not deemed to fit under what Western art views and categorizes as remix or collage. Taking place in the realms of Third World, postcolonial, and immigrant quotidian life, these remix performances and traditions are often misrecognized, passed over, and unrecorded. Yet, as jazz pianist Vijay Iyer once asserted—everything he learned about improvisation, he learned from his immigrant parents—Rosal's piece helps us tune into the wide range of ways that artistry is learned and places where music is made.

To flip—to turn something over, transform and improve it. The beat—the accent (where emphasis is placed), the rhythm (that makes things regular, expected), the track (where the plural is combined into the singular). To flip the beat—to take a sample, a previous recording of a performance, and revise, rework, and adapt it so that it no longer sounds familiar and instead becomes your own, new thing. Flip the beat—as this book's introduction demands, urges, insists. As a performance studies scholar and writer, I aim to do more than merely uncover these musical performances and practices as simply working against previous tropes of Filipinos and Filipino Americans. As a fellow musician, listener, and fan, I am deeply invested in showing you, my reader, throughout this book, how these artists and their music produce new affiliations, politics, and ways of thinking.

FLIP THE BEAT. It's what Marlon Fuentes does when he takes sights and sounds from the colonial and anthropological archive, flips the beat, and requires that we reconsider our particular desires. It's what Pinoy indie rock and its bands, songs, fans, filmmakers, writers, bloggers, gigs, venues do when they take a musical genre, flip the beat, and come together to bring their stories, voice their sentiments, and sing their lives. It's what Jessica Hagedorn and her various collaborators (each traveling his or her own particular itinerary) do when they band together words and music and movement and images, flip the beats, the rhythms, where the accents are placed, and guide us in finding a place in music. It's what karaoke and cover performers in Filipino America do when they sing popular ballads—in English, Tagalog, Visayan, and

Ilocano—yet still [can] flip the beat, the key, the tone, the tempo, the timing, the meaning, and make the song their own. It's what the Invisibl Skratch Piklz do when they take previous sound recordings and discursive preconceptions, flip their beats, and tune into aliens through the channels that sonic abstraction provide.

By flipping the beat, the tropical renditions you are about to hear in the following pages are "simply making." And what they are simply making is musical scenes. Making a scene is about the potential for performance in everyday life: to act in ways that draw attention to oneself; to behave in a manner that is disruptive. Making a scene also connotes the concerted efforts of people gathering around common interests— important diversions, significant pursuits, passions that require the utmost attention. Musical scenes form around what is understood as personal preferences, individual tastes, one's sense of self. But they are also about deep attachments to places and people, songs and celebrities, bands and bars and clubs, looks and sounds.

In the following pages, making a musical scene takes on these multiple meanings—of being theatrical, on stage or in the everyday; of disturbing and unsettling the norms and discourses that have been made commonsensical; of the labors required, in concert, in listening, and in performance; of the places constituted by and constitutive of popular music; of the series of musical events shared by people in varying lengths of time.

The Invisibl Skratch Piklz make scenes in suburban garages, online and in competition in cities across the globe, and in the ways that one might imagine a discourse of visibility could and should work for racialized performers in the United States. Karaoke and its cover performers, including child stars such as Charice Pempengco and Josephine "Banig" Roberto, make scenes in living rooms, on cruise ships, and in hotel bars. They set the stage for Filipino American visual artists' pieces and get us thinking more closely about performances and practices, otherwise dismissed as merely imitative and reproductive. They require we take seriously what they actually produce. In her poetry, musical, and theater performances, Jessica Hagedorn made scenes, on the stage and page, in 1970s San Francisco and 1980s downtown New York, with other Third World and downtown musicians, writers, and performers. Looking back on these histories of scene-making shifts how we conceive of an authorial voice. Pinoy indie rock makes scenes in San Francisco, Manila, Los Angeles, New York; on stage, online, on the big screen, in festivals and one-off gigs and screenings; and in the ways we grasp how indie sounds, feels, and how it is made, in the United States and Philippines.

These musical scenes await our methodical and repeated listening. And so, we begin.

CHAPTER I

Sonic Fictions

When turntablists compose, they are theorizing tonally.
—Kodwo Eshun

At the end of the twentieth century, the San Francisco Bay Area incubated hip-hop culture's leading musical innovators. Defined by Los Angeles–based DJ Babu as "a person who uses the turntables not to just play music, but to manipulate sound and create music," turntablist-DJs reemerged from the shadows of hip-hop's commercial stages. With their symphonies of far-out sounds, these DJ-musician-composers stressed to global audiences their central role in the evolution of hip-hop's music and technology.[1] These turntablist-DJs, many of whom were former party or mix DJs, built upon a twenty-five-year-old tradition of mixing songs, looping break beats, and scratching or skillfully moving fingers across vinyl introduced by New York–based luminaries such as DJ Kool Herc, Grand Wizard Theodore, Grandmaster Flash, and Grandmixer DXT. Yet, in the 1990s, hip-hop's futuristic sounds resounded *not* from its cultural epicenter but, instead, from its outposts in California, namely, the northern "City by the Bay."

Within the tradition of DJing, turntablists work with extensive archives of sounds ranging from whole tracks of popular and obscure music (including films, video games, cartoons, television, and even radio shows) to sound effects (including lasers, human bodily functions, a variety of robot and spaceship functions) to break beats (full-length tracks either from previously recorded songs or produced simply for DJ albums). Similar to the role of a musician, turntablists utilize techniques of playing rehearsed and learned in collaboration with their instrument—the turntables—in order to produce sounds that are then arranged into compositions or tracks. Turntablists bring together the archival and technical to orchestrate sonic compositions of a symphonic quality, movements that contain within them a plethora of musical phrases and notes produced through encounters between a rotating album and a DJ's careful finger movements on his one hand with the added flicks of a fader in his other. To the unassuming eye, these gestures might read as the careless mishandling of records resulting in what can only be thought of as noise. But to the studied viewer, one armed with a phonographic approach, the utmost coordination is required to maneuver between careful scratch techniques, the proper placement of the needle to find the right spot on an album, the quick moves of the fader to produce the proper sounds back and forth between turntables one and two, moving with surgical precision to produce the right music while preventing the record from skipping.

Through these DJ-musicians' performative acts of scratching, or digital manipulation, turntables no longer stand as archaic technology for merely playing back commodified recordings of popular songs and tracks. Instead the turntables and performers together become instruments for slowing down the passage of real time and create sonic worlds and systems in the fragmented, yet holistic, breaks of popular songs.[2] Through this digital slowing down, turntablists defamiliarize popular song tracks and even sounds, troubling the affective value of songs, while simultaneously playing upon the audience's knowledge of certain songs to create a different system of listening. Turntablists disarrange the supposed divide between performer and machine—through full body tricks in competition, through the digital techniques of fingers that feel the physical grooves of vinyl and manage the clicks and flares of mixer controls.

As a set of musical practices, turntablism highlights the complex relationship between sound and sentience as well as between bodies and machines in live performance. We might think of turntablist performances and recordings as different ways to document the performing body. As these experimental turntablist-DJs' fingers inscribe new rhythmic patterns and other worldly sounds onto a record's smooth yet grooved surface, we are reminded of how time (through the record's archive) and space (whether it be the space of production, performance, or reception) are compressed in the present of a live performance. These performances expand the scope of our phonographic approach to include the gestural and bodily. How might we begin to listen and write about music, especially instrumental music, without leaving behind the musician's live performing body? How might we reenvision the politics that arise from the intersecting vocabularies of the sonic, literary, and sensational?[3]

At the center of a turntablist musical movement, the Invisibl Skratch Piklz (ISP)—a five-member turntablist-DJ group hailing from districts on San Francisco's outskirts (Excelsior and Daly City)—invented new scratch techniques, mastered the turntablist-DJ band arrangement, and dominated individually and collectively at national and international DJ competitions. Members of a California-based mobile DJ party scene, an active network of DJs, party promoters, and audiences from the mid-1970s to the early 1990s, ISP's QBert, Mixmaster Mike, Shortkut, and Vinroc earned their musical training at social functions (debuts, school dances, birthday parties, and house parties) in predominantly Filipino American cities and suburbs from San Francisco to Los Angeles. As Oliver Wang's work has shown, this California-based mobile DJ party scene carved out translocal spaces for Filipino American youth to socialize and build community, bringing them together around various kinds of music—freestyle, new wave, hip-hop, to name a few.[4]

In the early 1990s, San Francisco-based music producer David Paul brought together and distributed the first ever *Return of the DJ* compilations as a response to the lack of mainstream visibility to DJ culture. These widely popular collections ushered DJs back onto the main stage and featured mainly Bay Area–based artists, which set the stage for a shift from East to West Coast dominance in the national hip-hop DJ scene and ignited the emergence of turntablism as an international phenomenon.[5] By 1998, ISP's members were forced to retire from competing in international turntablist-DJ battles, such as the Disco Music Competition (DMC), because other competitors were intimidated. Rather than cultivate a cut-throat competitive spirit, however, ISP members have shared with other turntablist-DJs and audiences their off-stage personas and scratching tips through a pirate radio show (*Shiggar Fraggar*), online tutorial videos (*Turntable TV*), and an interactive website message board. In 2000, they organized the first-ever Skratchcon turntablist conference and, since that time, have built awareness of and community within turntablist culture.

With humor rather than bravado, flipping the beat of hip-hop masculinity, ISP's members—particularly DJ QBert (Richard Quitevis) and Mixmaster Mike (Mike Schwartz)—articulated musically a new genre of nerd boy culture with a particular focus on the sonic landscapes and alternative worlds of comic book hero cartoons, science fiction films, and video games. This reliance on futuristic tropes and figures is evident in their album titles (*Martian Breaks*, *Invasion of the Octopus People*, *Official Adventures of the Toad Man*), rehearsal locations (Temple Warplex and Octagon's Lair), and the space invading sounds of their recorded compositions. As the inscriptive and sonic qualities of turntablism congealed into possible extraterrestrial affiliations, DJ QBert translated this fixation into an artistic philosophy: "If you think of these sounds as a type of vocabulary, then you just imagine what types of sentences and things you could make up. I think of scratching as a form of communicating with aliens and other higher forms of being . . . and I wonder what types of scratches and things they would try to create."[6] The performative encounter between a turntablist-DJ's digital manipulations and the phonographic machinery of turntables plays an essential role in this shared musical language, this auditory kinship. As QBert later commented after the group's disbanding: "We'd always talk about how music would sound on other worlds and stuff . . . the Invisibl Skratch Piklz were definitely a sci-fi thing. A lot of it had to do as well with the sounds you can play with a turntable. You can just pick the weirdest sounds, and of course, that's going to sound alien."[7] Listening against technology's conventions of the turntable as merely a playback machine, for the last forty years, hip-hop turntablist-DJs like QBert have materialized and dematerialized sound—scratching words into notes and notes into noise.[8]

Listening against the persistent search for artistic intent, this chapter focuses on ISP's musical practices and performances. As tropical renditions, they highlight the methodological limits and pitfalls of racial visibility discourses, especially in regard to popular music and performance. Rather than marking the Filipino American turntablist-DJ as exceptional, ISP's members disobediently listen to these discursive demands. In the process, they resound familiar burdens of [in]visibility for racialized performers in the United States and the regimes of a proper response, especially from other Filipino Americans. By tuning into sonic abstraction (those turntablist techniques of digital and gestural moves across vinyl) I instead hear the labors of alienation—of estrangement, turning away, handing over, and crossing over—as a form of musical rendition that ISP performs. In this chapter, I take seriously what I am calling a turntablist methodology, the various practices—crate digging, scratching, beat-juggling, improvisation, and forming crews and collaborations—that have grounded and guided my own practices of archival research, close listening, phonographic approach, and writing.[9] Maneuvering with this methodology, this chapter begins in the translocal scenes—of the San Francisco Bay Area, suburban garages, and turntablist music—where the interplanetary messages of ISP and DJ Qbert's science fiction–inspired music first launched.[10]

Frisco Cantina

Released in 2001, Douglas Pray's *Scratch: The Movie* was the first ever widely distributed feature-length documentary on the history and evolution of DJ/turntablist culture. The film incorporated interviews with, behind the scenes footage of, and live performance recordings by DJs in order to present the most comprehensive history of U.S. hip-hop DJ culture to date.[11] While the film largely pays tribute to the predominantly New York–based African American and Afro-Caribbean male innovators of DJ culture, an interlude in the film's East Coast and urban-centric vibe takes place immediately after the title shot "Turntablism" appears.

Fast-motion shots of driving along Northern California's Highway 280. The camera zooms in on freeway signs for Daly City. They flash on the screen and situate the audience for the documentary's next set of interviewees. Dubbed the "adobo capital" of the United States, Daly City is home to the largest population of Filipinos outside the Philippines. As the familiar joke goes, "You know why it's always foggy in Daly City, right? Because all the Filipinos turn on their rice cookers at the same time." In the Filipino imaginary, Daly City is shorthand for suburban Filipino America.[12] In the turntablist-DJ imaginary, Daly City is shorthand for one of its most famous crews—the Invisibl Skratch Piklz (ISP).

Two of the more commercially successful members of the now-defunct San Francisco–based turntablist-DJ group, both Mixmaster Mike and DJ QBert provide the film's comic relief by recounting how their musical approaches were inspired and informed by aliens and outer space.[13] Most widely known as the touring DJ with the rap trio of the Beastie Boys since 1998, Mike recalls an evening when he witnessed the bright lights of spaceships landing on an open field across from his Daly City childhood home while he rehearsed his scratches and cuts. Surely, he surmised, his music had summoned these interplanetary visitors. Set alongside this narrative, *Scratch* quickly cuts to scenes of Mike performing in his bedroom. First showing off the song's original album cover, he then plays enough of a snippet from the chorus of Delta blues musician Robert Johnson's "Ramblin' on My Mind" to situate the listener. From there, and on the opposite turntable, he drops the beat to Dead Prez's anthemic "Hip Hop," which sets his performance's meter. He then flips the Johnson sample, distilling Johnson's sung melody and voice into tonal notes through the sharp, quick flicks of the fader, with his left hand, in rhythm with his right hand's fingers as they stab, chirp, transform, and warp across the LP's vinyl surface. His gestures produce an otherworldly symphony, both the stuff of science fiction movie sound effects and a form of musical intergalactic communication, the kind that reaches out to other worlds as it did that one evening in a Daly City apartment.[14]

To be clear, not all of ISP's members are from Daly City. DJ QBert himself grew up in the Excelsior District, right outside San Francisco's Outer Mission neighborhood and birthplace of another Bay Area musical genius, The Grateful Dead's Jerry Garcia. So, while they often "repp'ed" (represented) Daly City hats and T-shirts at international DJ competitions, they also paid homage to San Francisco and the Bay Area more broadly. In their 1998 *URB* magazine cover story, when asked if the Bay Area "spawn(ed) the world's sickest DJs," QBert immediately replied, "I don't think that's true. There's a lot of good DJs everywhere." But when pressed to account for the leading role of Bay Area turntablists in the emergent scene, he explained: "I think that our culture itself, in San Francisco's history, is known to be really open-minded. It's like a melting pot of friendliness. . . . [Yeah] everyone's cool out here, everyone's open-minded, exchanging ideas. It's like a marketplace for ideas."[15] At this point in their interview with hip-hop critic Dave Tompkins, Mixmaster Mike chimed in, "Kinda like what the aliens do," and QBert instantly followed up with, "Yeah, Yeah . . . You ever seen in Star Wars that cantina scene, with all the aliens going in there and everyone's interacting? That's Frisco." The conversation quickly devolves into theories of aliens designing the City as their "trading base" and the pyramid-shaped Transamerica building as their telephone tower ("aliens' AT&T"). While all of this might appear as far-out, perhaps far-fetched, and definitely science fiction–inspired, it also suggests the notion of San Francisco as a translocal interplanetary scene, a place within a network of places connected, in this particular case, through artistic and cultural exchanges and encounters.

In most narratives of U.S. hip-hop history, the San Francisco Bay Area functions as a minor place in comparison to the genre's capital, New York City. Furthermore, despite its demographics, history, design, and planning, Daly City is often characterized as a suburb in comparison to "the City" proper. Rather than continuing to uphold hip-hop and urban studies' well-established and prescriptive binaries of East Coast/West Coast and center/periphery, the figures of "cantina scene" and "trading base" suggest another way of imagining the relationship between popular music and place. Within the framework of translocality, places such as San Francisco and Daly City are conceived as "processes, always linked by people to other places."[16] This reframing, in turn, reminds us that the portability and reproducibility of popular musical forms have always allowed for other, oftentimes unauthorized, modes of sharing, exchange, and circulation. In the history of popular music scenes, cities such as San Francisco, New York, Manila, Detroit, Liverpool, and London, to name a few, have functioned as nodal points and convergence sites in the cultural traffic of musical styles and objects, musical performers and fans. These ideas are further explored in later chapters, as I discuss Jessica Hagedorn's poetic and performance collaborations in the translocal scenes of 1970s Third Worldist San Francisco and 1980s downtown New York and as I remap Pinoy indie rock's itineraries. But, for now, I want to follow QBert and Mixmaster Mike's leads to reimagine the scenes where popular music's making takes place.

First, San Francisco and Daly City. Then, the suburban garage. For, as legend goes, it was a car accident that actually prompted the change in DJ QBert's musical approach and DJ style:

HOW A SERIOUS ACCIDENT ALTERED QBERT'S STYLE OF DJ'ING. Back in 1989 QBert had a very serious accident as a pedestrian in San Francisco's Excelsior District that changed his whole style of DJ'ing. "It meant I couldn't walk around and stuff and I couldn't do anything really, jog, run, whatever," he recalled of the accident's initial impact. "But it kind of turned my career around. . . before my accident, I would do all these turntable tricks like behind the back and under my legs and skratch with my feet and all this flashy stuff. So there's two ways that the music could have gone: toward the more flashy side or toward the more musical side . . . and because of the accident it made me sit down at my turntables and work on just the musical side of it."[17]

Confined to a wheelchair for months, QBert moved from the "flashier" side of party DJing to focus on the more musical side of scratches — developing new ones such as the crab and perfecting old ones such as transformers, chirps, and tweaks. In the living space and work space of his parents' garage, QBert became one of the forerunners of turntablism taking a decisive musical break from the pattern-based blends between two discrete songs of hip-hop party DJing into the realm of formal musical phrases filled with layers of polyrhythms and alien sounds. As illustrated in hip-hop films and books, the domestic space — from garages to bedrooms, attics to basements, and everywhere in between — has functioned as studio, rehearsal space, and even performance stage for many emerging artists and producers.[18]

Without the institutional curricula of today's DJ academies, workshops, and even classes at Berklee College of Music, QBert, like many of his era's turntablist-DJs, was self-taught. "Self-training," as Alexandra Vazquez has written, "requires an innate talent for improvisation: one has to assemble a motley combination of teaching aids, be they handed down from family or other formative babysitters like record players. . . . [Nevertheless] it is an astonishing thing to imagine all those makeshift exercises when formal lessons were out of reach."[19] Writing about freestyle artist Judy Torres's "makeshift exercise" of lying on her living room floor to "get vibrato," Vazquez also reminds us of the surprising locations in which musical learning takes place. The backyard parties where street dance team Culture Shock's Michelle Castelo watched and learned, from sisters and cousins, how to dance the latest moves.[20] The garage in Moreno Valley, California, where a bored Kid Rainen (Rynan Paguio) of the Jabbawockeez dance crew practiced head spins all day. Or, of course, the Daly City garage where a handicapped QBert perfected his musical techniques.

Generally configured by urban studies as unsightly and reminiscent of airport hangars, the suburban home's open garage doubled as the scene for QBert's artistic (and historic) shift among other everyday musical and performance events in Filipino America's musical life.[21] Deemed neither inside nor outside the home, garages have often been transformed into makeshift stages for the rehearsal, performance, and proliferation of youth subcultures. Think garage bands, garage parties, and a teenager's playroom. Still part of the home, garages allow parents the luxury of their children at proximity while relegating their noise production outside of the enclosed quarters of the domestic sphere.[22] Thus, as a side note or even counterpoint to the internal domestic atmosphere of the Filipino immigrant house party, an event I further describe in chapter 2, in the garage, Filipino American youth learn new skills and further hone their artistic styles—choreographing dance routines, perfecting break-dancing moves on cardboard *balikbayan* boxes, freestyling rhymes, trying out the latest scratch technique, and making mix-tapes. The Filipino American house party DJ not only pollutes the air by disseminating sounds not welcomed by suburban ears, he also creates the sight of an unmanageable crowd of young bodies in motion. In the garage, the turntables join other machines, tools, and symbols of material accumulation normally housed in this liminal space—midsize sedans and family vans, power tools and lawn mowers.

By turning our ears toward the suburban garages of Filipino America, we begin to hear how genre cultures, ways of life that coalesce around a particular artistic category, are also evidence of translocal networks of affinity as much as alternative musical genealogies. Some turntablist history time lines start, at the turn of the twentieth century, with Thomas Edison and others' turntable inventions. Turntablist performance, others argue, began in 1939 with John Cage's *Imaginary Landscape #1* (which combined recorded sound on two turntables, percussion, and other noise) and continues with his performance of *Imaginary Landscape #4* (on twelve radios) in 1951. As writers such as Caleb Kelly remind today's listeners, hip-hop turntablist-DJs were not the first to experiment with phonographic technology and sound. They instead find themselves akin to performance and sound artists such as Cage, Pierre Schaeffer, Nam June Paik, and Christian Marclay, to name a few.[23] However, as artist and scholar Kodwo Eshun notes, "What John Cage did was restricted to a few people in New York, a few people in London, a few people in Berlin, etc. But people like Grandmaster Flash and Grand Wizard Theodore invented not just a new operation of sound, but a whole new conceptual attitude toward sound: The idea that every record is open to misuse and can be combined with a second record."[24] Thus, the mass appeal of hip-hop turntablist-DJs' phonograph effects, so aptly termed by Mark Katz, far surpasses their avant-garde predecessors.[25] Turntablist-DJs harnessed more of what Katz outlines as the phonograph's capabilities—its portability and tangibility, its openness to manipulation and repetition, the ways it captures music's ties to temporality and (in)visibility. These last two points are crucial in making sense of how ISP's techniques and performances challenge and broaden conversations about turntablist-DJ culture. For while all turntablist-DJs play with musical time—the pasts of album's recordings, the presents of live and improvised performance—and take pleasure in perhaps being unseen but still always felt, the InVisibl Skratch Piklz's music helps us begin to articulate a Filipino futurism that still always needs to grapple with the history of a Filipino condition in the United States.

Perhaps bebop jazz artists better instruct us since, like them, turntablists made a decisive break from their musical predecessors (hip-hop's party DJs), moving away from the hip-hop party DJ's style of pattern-based blends and seamless transitions between two discrete songs and into the realm of musical phrases filled with polyrhythmic and alien sounds. In the words of DJ D-Styles: "There is a whole other breed of DJs today that wouldn't even label themselves a DJ. They think of themselves more as musicians and composers, and don't worry about whether people can dance to what they're doing. Some music we make is just listening music, very similar to the jazz movement in the 1940s when bebop moved away from the traditional jazz dance band."[26] African American musicians such as free jazz/hard bop legend Sun Ra looked to science fiction to invent alternate identities and narratives of liberation. With its logics of madness and insanity, in the affective key of alienation, and in order to signal extraterrestrial spaces of sociality through music and sound, the genre culture of Afro-futurism has proliferated due to the work of its musicians, writers, digital/media artists, filmmakers, and critics. They have worked through the generic conventions of science fiction as it "reference(d) a past of abduction, displacement, and alien-nation, and inspire(d) technical and creative innovations."[27] In line with turntablism's broader cultural traditions, QBert and ISP draw artistic inspiration from experimental jazz, Afro-futurism, and science fiction—genres rendered as part of the musical form's artistic lineage.

The emergence of science fiction in the 1940s corresponded with the demise of the freak show tradition. No longer able morally or scientifically to justify live and spectacular displays of deviant bodies, as cultural historian Jeffrey Weinstock observes, "a psychic need for freaks found expression in SF (science fiction) fiction and film."[28] U.S. popular culture turned to SF in order to talk about the human condition through its close encounters with alien others, advanced technologies, and time travel into the primitive past and the extraterrestrial future. Yet, for just as long, countertraditions within SF culture, such as Afro-futurism and Asian futurisms, have evolved by mobilizing the genre's most famous characters (aliens, cyborgs), story lines (escapology, abduction, exploration), and tropes (technology, extraterrestriality, outer spaces) to "allegorize (racial) tension and exclusion" and articulate radical and liberatory politics.[29] While earlier American writers (such as Jack London and Sax Rohmer), as well as contemporary cyber-punk texts (*Blade Runner*), preyed on and propagated discourses of "yellow peril" and "techno-Orientalism," since the second half of the twentieth century, Asian and Asian American writers, filmmakers, musicians, and critics have also turned to the metaphor of the "alien"—"from the extraterrestrial being who seems to speak in a strange, yet familiar, accented English to the migrant subject excluded from legislative enfranchisement"—as a means to critique characterizations of Asians as hordes of unfeeling automatons and inscrutable foreigners.[30]

Afro-futurism, as Kodwo Eshun reminds us, is "a *possibility space* which leaves behind or moves away from traditional notions of Black culture as based on the street, for instance, based on traditional notions of masculinity, based on traditional notions of ethnicity."[31] This critical and utopian thread of Afro-futurism, in the words of Juliana Snapper, "extends" into the sonic fiction traditions of turntablist music with its proclivity for sci-fi film voice-overs and sound effects, alien and robotic imagery, and other "alternative means of perceiving heroism and history."[32] As Snapper clearly outlines: "The way turntablists play with time draws inspiration from science fiction and comic books—media equally obsessed with time travel and conceiving new narrative and social networks. Robots, monsters, and aliens cover record labels and T-shirts. Voice-overs from science fiction films and sounds from laser guns saturate scratch routines. QBert's animated film *Wave Twisters* is a sci-fi mini-epic."[33] Although I agree with Snapper in the potential for alternative history-tellings and hero-worship than traditional masculinist subjectivity, I would argue that male turntablists are not completely devoid of misogynistic tendencies and particular homosocial relationships (as noted through their album covers, sound samples, and website illustrations).

These types of tendencies and relationships fully color as well their particular gendered and racialized relationship, as Filipino American male cultural producers, to the Afro-futuristic tropes of alien-ness and madness. Not easily falling into the either/or categories of the "Oriental" or "Primitive," these turntablist-DJs bring to the forefront the peculiar situation of Filipinos in the United States.

Therefore, drawing on the critical foundation that Snapper's work lays out, I want to think further about QBert's articulations of the links between his music and aliens as they dramatize the outer-spatial or extraterritorial experiences of Filipinos in America. The figure of the alien has served as a metaphor for Asian immigrants and, by extension, Asian Americans. As forever-foreigners, in the U.S. popular imaginary they are both diametrically opposed to yet constitutive of American history and culture, a relationship that performance studies scholar Karen Shimakawa has designated as national abjection.[34] Since the days of U.S. imperial rule, the social and legal status of Filipinos in America has oscillated between uncivilized natives or little brown brothers and U.S. nationals or military allies. This intimate yet forever-alien status of being "foreign in a domestic sense," as Sarita See has underscored, is what prefigures the decolonial imaginary of Filipino American visual and performing artists.[35] Thus, the language of alien kinship and extraterritoriality, formative to the discourse of the U.S. exceptionality and imperialism in the Philippines, finds a place in Filipino American cultural criticism. Through our disobedient listening to the "weirdest sounds" and styles of DJ QBert and the Invisibl Skratch Piklz, we can and should take seriously the political and aesthetic alliances made possible by the identity category of alien, as both a recuperation of previous histories and a signaling toward other forms of extraterrestrial intelligence. Extending from Afro- and Asian-futurist artistic traditions, ISP's musical and everyday performances disobediently listen to codes of masculinity as well as discourses of racial visibility.

The Burden of Being Invisibl

Though some of the most widely recognized Filipino American musical artists in U.S. popular culture, DJ QBert and the Invisibl Skratch Piklz have repeatedly and purposefully avoided responding to questions of how race and ethnicity inform their music. At the height of their fame in 1998, ironically the same year that Filipinos in the United States commemorated the centennial of the end of the Spanish-American War and beginning of the Philippine-American War, DJ QBert stated in an interview: "We're not Filipino artists, we're artists."[36] This sentiment was further reinforced, musicologist Juliana Snapper points out, on the turntablist collective's website: "Q. What race are the Invisibl Skratch Piklz? A. Same as everyone else, the 'Human Race.'"[37]

DJ Qbert and ISP's adherence to humanist discourses, for critics like Dylan Rodriguez, indexes a particular Filipino American "common sense," constituted by "political ambivalence" and "arrested raciality," which "works to reproduce the fundamental tenets of Filipino Americanism as a deformed nation-building project."[38] Averting racialized/nation-based figurations and purporting racial transcendence, within Rodriguez's formulation, the improper responses of these prominent artists instead dangerously reiterate multiculturalist problematics of abstract liberalism. Here, we might take a moment to hearken back to the colonial terror regime of an improper response staged in Worcester's photos as discussed in this book's introduction. By doing so, we deepen our understanding of how containment discourses of political resistance are just as limiting and prescriptive and learn to disobediently listen to them, as well.

At the very least, these political imperatives underscore and uphold a popular and contradictory language of visibility for (and multiculturalism's paradoxical demands on) Filipino and other racialized artists in the United States. For Asian American and, particularly, Filipino American musical artists, the state of being everywhere and nowhere in the U.S. recording industry constitutes what Allan Pineda (Apl de Ap of the Black Eyed Peas) terms a "quiet storm."[39] The most famous Asian Americans still serve in the background of U.S. popular music and remain, in Josh Kun's terms, "the most visible yet invisible pop figures" as back-up singers (Justin Bieber's Legaci), producers (such as The Neptunes' Chad Hugo and freestyle music producer Glenn Gutierrez), and

DJs (Jay-Z's DJ Neil Armstrong and the Beastie Boys' DJ Mixmaster Mike). Asian American musical artists who have managed to land center stage in U.S. popular music must still withstand the industry's demands for particular exposure.

Within the U.S. music recording industry, *Filipino* as musical descriptor (that is, a "Filipino" artist) signifies struggle, proving detrimental to one's artistic and professional development. In the sense that artists want to be both seen and heard, Filipino as musical descriptor is neither legible nor marketable according to industry standards. Returning to QBert's quote and placing it within its longer, original context: "We're not Filipino artists, we're artists. We're not from the Filipino race, we're from the human race. Ever since we started, race didn't matter to us. As soon as it does matter, there's something wrong. It never occurred to us that being Filipinos would *hinder* us in doing what we love. It never crossed our minds" (emphasis mine).[40] QBert's quote, itself a performance of refusal in the setting of an artist interview, illuminates two popular discursive streams within U.S. racial politics: first, a nation-based political project where historical injury renders a group's visibility in a multiculturalist landscape (one where the matter of race is marked by hindrance and wrong) and, second, this project's relationship to art-making and aesthetic practices (those things that one loves).[41] As turntablist-DJs, QBert and the other ISP members instead aligned themselves with their musical genre, one that often sidesteps the visibility paradox of mainstream hip-hop recording industry and cultural narratives by the casual yet false claim that DJs are heard but rarely seen.[42]

Beyond these paradoxes, QBert's improper response also offers the opportunity to examine the limits of racial visibility discourse. It performs a refusal that even forces us to rehearse listenings beyond such discourse. Attentive to the "principle of compulsory visibility," in Foucault's terms, we are compelled to remember its implementation through systems of surveillance and disciplinary actions and its particular historical impact upon racialized bodies. As discussed in this book's introduction, for Filipinos and Filipino Americans, this principle resonates with a particular history of U.S. colonial and anthropological ventures whose politicized efforts depended upon the form and aesthetics of photography. Despite these critical reminders, however, many still adhere to a politics where "visibility equals empowerment," a project that aims to fight against invisibility within U.S. popular culture rendered through acts of racial misrecognition or lumping. Filipino American literary studies scholar Elizabeth Pisares's writings on Filipino American popular musical artists, such as ISP and freestyle artist Jocelyn Enriquez, espouse such politics by arguing that perceptual absence—the product and process of Filipino American racial (mis)recognition—accounts for their invisibility within U.S. popular culture. Put simply, this condition of invisibility is due to the Filipino American's quality of scrambling America's practices of reading race through *inference* and *interpretation*—"if she 'looks Asian'" but "she has a Spanish last name"—through "the confluence of several factors: preconceived notions of race; immediate context; and perceived information such as skin color, facial features, dress, hair, accent, name, social class background, education or neighborhood."[43]

Moving her attention from close readings of Enriquez's album covers and her decision to include Spanish-language versions of her songs, Pisares seems to reach her methodological limit when she approaches ISP and DJ Qbert's music. "Devoid of inherent semantics, especially as a song's cumulative elements are isolated," as Pisares describes ISP's music, "ensembles broken down into discrete instruments, bars parsed into phrases into notes and beats and shouts." For her, these turntablist compositions "are not a music identified as Filipino American [since] the condition of perceptual absence forecloses their racial categorization." Instead, she argues for ISP and DJ QBert's cultural legibility by turning to their artistic practice as metaphor. "It is the reconstructive process— to select samples from disparate sources, to decompose them through any of the hundreds of turntable techniques, and to re-sequence the discrete elements—that offers a model of Filipino American representation."[44] Endeavoring toward a formalistic analysis, one that turns to reconstruction rather than deconstruction and abstraction, Pisares remains entrapped in a discourse of racial visibility, one that works in tandem with multiculturalism's call to identify and market objects and performances as authentically belonging to and indicative of a single culture.

Asking questions in line with the "about-ness" discourse (that is, "what is Filipino about ISP and their music?" rather than "what *makes* ISP and their music Filipino?"), Pisares and other scholars miss the opportunity to discuss in detail the actual sound of the music, its performance, and what each of these things *do*. Rather than simply reflecting realities, music and its performance bear performative power. That is, through their enactment, they are able to make social realities and worlds. Shifting our focus from categories (Filipino American music) to processes (Filipino Americans making music), we begin to understand music in the way that QBert's earlier quote suggests—not as a form antithetical to writing and language ("devoid of inherent semantics") but instead its own "type of a vocabulary," one based on the various meanings invoked by the phonographic. In this way, music is never simply a singular object, recording, or event but always-also all those things that its production, performance, and reception make possible.

I never want to miss an opportunity to listen closely to ISP and QBert's music because listening to their technically virtuosic performances, for me, is an intellectually invigorating endeavor. Their performative manipulations of recorded sound challenge listeners to focus on sound's formalistic qualities and, therefore, move away from simple notions of content-based representational practices. The genre of turntablist music listens against popular musical demands for a song's lyrics to be the overarching narrative structure. Just as the category of Filipino helps us listen against the discursive regime of racial visibility, so too does ISP disarrange the holistic ideal of a song's structure, from the narrative logic of lyrics to the disintegration of musical phrases into the sounds and rhythmic patterns of triplets and sixteenth or thirty-second notes. This technique, I would argue, is related to an approach that historian Vicente Rafael identifies among Filipinos: "the 'minor' style of the episodic narrative" that "digresses, circling around recurring motifs and recalcitrant obsessions."[45] Rather than an "epic" style of mixing that moves and transitions smoothly from one song to the next, a turntablist's episodic mode of performative critique disassembles musical structures in order to create new layers of sonic meanings through the violent yet carefully precise gestures of scratching. In turn, by separating and then recombining recorded sounds (musical notes, break beats, sound effects), artists working within the genre of turntablism sonically express aesthetics of abstraction. As racialized artists in the United States, such a move squarely places them "between being praised for producing abstract art that transcends identity and achieves universalism and being condemned for art that is 'too abstract' and disavows identity."[46] In these terms, Sarita See describes the work of Filipino

American visual artists Paul Pfeiffer and Reanne Estrada, whose minimalist pieces are "void of unambiguous, overt signs of things Filipino" and thus often "perceived as having nothing to do with being Filipino." Yet, as evidenced by Pisares's reading of ISP and QBert's work, the same can be and has been said about abstract (read instrumental) and experimental music by musicians of color.

Invigorated by See's cue to remember that the artistic process of abstraction can be its own political practice, I want to return to ISP and QBert's abstract and experimental music as a way "to think about identity as a politics of evading rather than securing visibility and legibility."[47] Mobilizing "shape-shifting tactics," See argues, these artists create works that "do not lend themselves to memorialization" and, by doing so, disobey the rules of visibility politics.[48] Like performative gestures ephemerally moving across vinyl, the art-objects of Pffeifer, Estrada, and others are not celebratory, feel-good events or impermeable, spectacular structures. Rather, these pieces, performances, and practices strive to resist and challenge racial visibility's limits and demands. In staging a "politics through form rather than merely content," they offer their audiences the possibility to imagine other forms of affinity and affiliation.

The Labor of Alienation

Abstraction, when figured as disembodied and immaterial, is chided as apolitical in the face of nationalist and, in turn, multiculturalist demands for epic and memorial forms. Rather than attempting to reconstruct or revive seemingly forgotten historical and, therefore, representational bodies, abstraction deconstructs fragments of these (whole) bodies and narratives, alienating them from their sources in order that audiences might see, hear, feel, and imagine otherwise.[49] Contrary to popular belief, abstract artworks require bodies for their production and often centralize themes of the bodily and material. Grandmaster Flash, innovator of the scratch, "clearly regarded the technique's expression of physicality—the virtuosity of the body—as a major element of its meaning."[50] Working in collaboration with the turntables, turntablist-DJs' bodies—ears, eyes, fingers—are fully activated then in the service of sonic abstraction.

Sonic traces electrify the thin line between the turntablist-DJ's performing body and technology's machine. In this intimate zone of musical touch, the phenomena of sensation not only invoke the fantasy of an unmediated encounter between bodies and machines but also call up the troubling yet inescapable phenomena of movement. Sensation, gesture, writing, and sound collide in a popular form of performance as turntablist-DJs pull back, vibrate across, and sometimes simply tap a record's surface (drags, scribbles, and swipes), scratching while rhythmically clicking a mixer's fader to create sharp, accented notes (baby scratch, twiddle, and crab) and even new sounds (transformer, chirp, and marches); slowing a performance's roll, a type of turntablist composition break, through the initially languid, then simply funky beat pattern devised by the coordinated movement between two records on two turntables, each playing the same break beat, and the fader's sound channel-opening effects (beat juggling). As Brian Massumi writes, "When positioning of any kind comes a determining first, movement comes a problematic second. After all is signified and sited, there is the nagging problem of how to add movement back into the picture."[51] Instead, turntablist-DJs physically bear on an already moving record with the added velocity of their scratches. Our phonographic approach accounts for this music as sonic frictions, sounds produced in the moment and after the fact of these gestural movements.

As live musical gestures, scratches "return a record to a specific moment and place" of audition and performance.[52] As audible inscriptions, turntablist-DJs' scratches expand a record's dimensions by "transmuting [these] electronically transmitted (semi-identifiable) traces [of music] into furred and splintered drum noises . . . the richness of tone spiked with percussive impact." Touching music, turntablist-DJs share felt sounds. With their "entrancing elaborations and variations on repetition" on otherwise familiar musical breaks (now made alien by their human hands), turntablist scratching exposes the break's scaffolding only to sonically resignify and redesign interiorly, not in order to domesticate it but, instead, to map the expansive inner space of sound. Just as quickly as it settles into a groove, however, the music, in the hands of a turntablist-DJ, is shuttled back into transit. The break is revealed to be that other musical structure—the bridge—"to another world, revisiting the past, suspending time, and transforming the familiar into something unrecognizable."[53] Contemporary turntablist-DJs invoke genealogies of the phonograph as a device of "crossing over." At

Figure 1.1 Invisibl Skratch Piklz. Courtesy of Brian "B+" Cross, Mochilla.com.

the same time, however, through their digital manipulations of sound, turntablist-DJs alienate audiences from familiar and expected musical breaks, patterns, and rhythms. These new phonographers insist listening ears travel through the inner spaces of music with out-of-this-world sounds created by encounters between humans and machines. This is the stuff of science fiction, as well as the postcolonial and postmodern, where and when shifting temporalities create spaces to flip the beat and reimagine the future.

On the February 1998 cover of URB magazine, five boyish Filipino American faces were framed by the question: "Are these the best DJs on the planet? in the universe?"[54] Four years after the Disco Music Competition (DMC) judges' decision to ban DJ QBert and Mixmaster Mike from the international DJing competition's championship round, the hip-hop cultural magazine's feature article, "Science Friction," brought together the turntablist crew's virtuosic skills and their self-crafted extraterrestrial associations into the tale that "somewhere in the San Francisco Bay Area 51 resides a small group of Earth-spawned aliens known collectively as the Invisibl Skratch Piklz."[55] The influence of science fiction tropes and characters on the crew's sound and image, on one level, references a nerd boy/geek culture replete with video games, afternoon cartoons, comic book characters, and action figurines. By tracing a genealogy of alternative masculinity and mapping extraterritorial spaces for racialized subjects in the United States, the Piklz herald turntablism as a contemporary aural sector of longer science fiction traditions.

By the height of turntablism's musical prominence in the late 1990s, DJ QBert and ISP propagated their artistic philosophy of "Science Friction" with musical techniques and personal mythologies crafted from and inspired by science fiction's tropes, practices, and styles. Highlighting even further their connections to outer space, over the years QBert and ISP have bestowed their performance recording and break beat albums with titles such as *Wave Twisters Episode 7 Million: Sonic Wars within the Protons, Cosmic Assassins*; *Horny Martian Breaks*; and, most recently, *Extraterrestria/GalaXXXian*. Capitalizing upon ISP's brand of "Filipino futurism," in 2001 DJ QBert premiered his animated feature film *Wave Twisters*, a science fiction–inspired adventure set to turntablist-DJ music.[56] Reformulating turntablism's foundational techniques for the purposes of filmmaking, *Wave Twisters* utilizes the technology of visual scratching (moving scenes back and forth in sync with the musical score) and sampling (integrating diverse sources such as photo collages, live action, and 3-D animation) to tell the story of its hero, Inner Space Dental Commander, and his band of comrades, a droid named Rubbish, and his lovely assistant Honey Drips, on their journey to save the "Lost Arts" (aka the four pillars of hip-hop—break dancing, emceeing, graffiti art, and DJing) from the evil forces of Lord Ook. In *Wave Twisters*, as with ISP's musical recordings, the adolescent (nerd-boy culture) and the avant-garde (sound and film technologies) comfortably coexist. Drawing from and manipulating a popular archive of filmic and video game–inspired sounds (lasers, spaceship beams, and warp speeds) as well as undoubtedly human-made ones (flatulence, female moans, and the ubiquitous "Ahh" of hip-hop scratching), QBert composed a sound track for travels through the inner-worlds of actual bodies, including the Inner Space Dental Commander's patients, and of Lord Ook's dominion.

The film opens with a black-and-white scene of DJ QBert in a three-piece suit, baseball cap, and bizarre glasses playing and then scratching a musical break that announces, "Turntable TV." With this opening performance and commercial breaks from fictitious sponsors, the film plays with the form of a television show episode while it brands itself under the broader title of *Turntable TV*, a series produced under QBert's company, Thud Rumble.

The episode quickly sets the viewer in a world cultivated by and for geek culture: jokes about drugs and sex ("nitrous visions" and "Red Worm"); humorous takes on everyday interactions with technology ("Wahoo maps," 1980s video game design, and "Disc Doctor"); and comic-book storytelling conventions (visibly sexualized female bodies, heroes and villains, inner and outer space battle-journey). Throughout the film, QBert plays with and on sounds—lasers, farts, spaceship beams, and warp speeds—to create a soundtrack for travels through outer space, bodily inner-spaces, and time.

In the first sequence of the animated saga, "Enter the Inner Space Dental Commander," the audience is bombarded by an underlying yet heavy driving beat, the sounds of an approaching bass army marching forward. QBert transitions into the song with the sounds of a villain spaceship dropping shots à la the 1980s video game Galaga. As the track begins, a male voice sounds the expression *Aaahhh*, which is then broken into sixteenth notes by the pushing forward and pulling back of QBert's fingers across the rotating vinyl. Taking the simple sound one makes in a dentist's chair, the next segment of the track includes a variety of other "Aah" responses—in robotic C-3PO-style voices, ecstatic female voices, and male voices in lower registers—to the repeated call of the word *Say*. Each sounding of these two words is manipulated into a variety of thirty-second notes and triplets, all through the delicate movements of the turntablist's fingers across vinyl albums. The track ends with a sound similar to walking through the rubber banding of reality, a furry version of the noise made when one grabs one's cheeks and jiggles them side to side but, this time, made by a DJ's digits scribbling across a rotating disc. Throughout the rest of the film, QBert assembles snippets of common science fiction film dialogue and sound effects to sonically dramatize a scene of encounter between the ship's crew and outside visitors. "Who are you?"; "Where do you come from?"; "Intruder!"; the sound of a ship's alarm; the approaching villain's pronouncement, "I am the Red Worm." These phrases are manipulated into notes for emphasis through dramatic pauses created through a pulling-back of their sounding by the record's forward movement.

Alongside these more explicit examples of science fiction forms, DJ QBert and the Invisibl Skratch Piklz—as culturally visible Filipino American turntablist-DJs who both disobediently listened and performatively abstracted sounds at the end of the twentieth-century—suggest to their audiences a different set of outsides and beyonds, extraterritorial spaces often invisible from popular view: the suburban garages where they honed their sound; San Francisco as an outlying city within a U.S. hip-hop cultural imaginary; and other translocal places within Filipino America (to be discussed in future chapters).[57] At the same time, they offer critics and scholars a turntablist methodology—one intimately aware of diverse archives but unafraid of juggling between disparate historical moments in order to experiment with and explore the contours of particular themes and possibilities. ISP and other turntablist-DJs reshift contemporary discussions of technology, race, and performance in the United States by staunchly recalling the phonographic machine's magical, even otherworldly underside. Disobediently listening to different forms of imperializing scripts and, instead, playfully handling sounds and other forms of sense, turntablist-DJs proffer new languages and spaces of political possibility through otherwise degrading identity categories—nerd, alien, extraterritorial. With their techniques of sonic abstraction and calls for extraterrestrial communication, ISP invokes the spirit of other speculative genres—hearing and feeling in the present, revisiting the past, in order to imagine some still invisible futures.

Turntablist-DJs like QBert and ISP disobediently listen to the standards of playback technology. Unruly and unrefined, they instead sonically summon an unforeseen lineage of disobedient listeners throughout Filipino America's recorded history. At its very core, the art of turntablism demands sedition to the Golden Rule of phonographic technology—do not touch the record.[58] Through the performative gestures of scratching and other musical forms of abstraction, turntablist-DJs disrupt smooth tracks and alienate even the most familiar melodies in order to render and turn our attention toward other worlds and ways. Deeply learned in and proficient with records from diverse musical eras and sonic sources, ISP stages promiscuous conversations between otherwise unrelated sounds and songs. But they do so in an effort to communicate beyond this terrestrial life. Unlike cover performances, the genre of turntablist-DJ performance aims to create new sounds from the sonic shards of abstracted songs and, in turn, symphonic compositions from these new tones. All turntablist-DJs perform the labor of alienation through performance techniques (of cutting, scratching, beat juggling) that disrupt smooth musical tracks and make foreign otherwise familiar songs and sounds. For listeners unaccustomed to turntablism's styles of sonic manipulation, these cuts and scratches might sound indifferent or even hostile to a pop musical original. Heard from afar as chaotic and without structure, these turntablist-DJs, upon closer inspection, perform mind-boggling and virtuosic techniques—scratches, cuts, and transitions that happen so fast and flawlessly, they are rendered unthinkable and sometimes even unseen to the human eye.

ISP and QBert's improper responses to the burdens of racialized representation, as exemplified in the scenes of the artist interviews, are their own unique performances of listening against the limited discourses of racial visibility. A mode of performance akin to the Kalingas' performances of disobedient listening, through disinterested glances in the colonial/anthropological photograph, I hear ISP and DJ QBert's improper responses, in the setting of the interview, as their own laborious acts of alienation, ones that work through the mode and moods of disaffection and, therefore, form part of a longer history of Filipino insubordination. This mode of performance, however, does not (and cannot) fall on one side or the other of the resistance/domination binary. Instead, these disobedient practices, enactments of refusal within colonial and colonizing mise-en-scènes, resonate the tense intimacies of U.S. imperialism and its aftermath.

Through their alien symphonies and their side stepping responses, ISP and QBert guide us toward a listening that is not merely in opposition. A disobedient listening practice does not limit itself to face-offs or direct confrontations. Like the Kalinga men's disinterested glances, forever captured in those anthropological photographs, ISP and QBert's performances of refusal, their artistic moves away from the human and toward the extraterrestrial, also require our eyes and ears to slant in different and sometimes unknown directions. I am thinking through all of this along the conceptual line that Fred Moten has previously laid out. Through the figure of painter Beauford Delaney, Moten describes a long-held distinction evident in the seemingly oxymoronic term *the black avant-garde.* That is to say, as Moten argues, blackness and avant-garde as always already defined as if "each depends for its coherence upon the exclusion of the other." These exclusions congeal in the tropes that foreshadow the places of encounter—Paris, Greenwich Village, Harlem—and that anticipate how Delaney's paintings would be "read." Moten writes:

> (In spite of the uncountable instances of such geographic activity) this encounter is most often conceived of as driven by an agency that moves in only one direction. Whereas a powerful strain of post-colonial theory structures itself as the reversal of that direction and its gaze, I'm interested in the discovery of a necessary *appositionality* in this encounter, an almost hidden step (to the side and back) or gesture, a glance or glancing blow, that is the condition of possibility of a genuine aesthetic representation and analysis—in painting and prose—of that encounter.[59]

By moving along the ways that Delaney "alternatively called voices and forces, the painted sounds of the thought of the outside," Moten re-directs us to the "merely gestural" as instead "the *appositional* force that manifests itself in Delaney's paintings and texts as irreducible phonic substance, vocal exteriority, the extremity that is often unnoticed as mere accompaniment to (reasoned) utterance."[60]

In their performative acts of refusal (actions that seem to convey their feelings or intentions in a transparent manner) and sonic abstraction, ISP and QBert also wield the appositional force of the merely gestural. Through the science fiction tropes of aliens and outer spaces, their music and performances shift us toward extraterrestrial as its own oxymoron. That is to say, the alien is not outside, not beyond, "not 'other' than earthly but acts back on and unsettles assumptions about commonplace brands of knowledge."[61] An E.T. methodology remobilizes a science fiction lexicon to describe the experiences and effects of slavery, colonialism, and empire—the ethics of visitation and trauma of abduction, the epistemological shocks and new modes of belonging and knowledge, the outer spaces of anthropology and the interplanetary, as the Philippines was once imagined.

In turn, while QBert and ISP's other members have originated certain scratches and musical techniques, they cannot necessarily claim ownership over them. These musical gestures are performative yet ephemeral. Their scratches and other musical techniques are forms of what Marxists term alienated labor. Many of these sonic innovations are produced when one DJ observes, then flips another's technique and style. Therefore, turntablist practices of rendering and rendition capture an artist's signature only if and when a performance is recorded (be it in the memories of other turntablist-DJs, on tape, or record.) These conditions require us to ask: What is the afterlife of the musical gesture? What type of trace does it leave and, even in that trace, who can claim to possess it? How does performance allow us space to reckon with the improvisatory and unscripted qualities of the merely gestural as well as the merely mimetic? These questions will be taken up, in chapter 2, through an examination of karaoke and cover performances in Filipino America. For, while both musical practices of rendering offer the promise of "making a song your own," there still remain a set of historical and political realities that circumscribe which songs can be "yours." Moving beyond the desire for musical ownership, chapter 2 listens instead to what karaoke's practices, performances, and scenes—centered on repetition and replication—actually work to produce.

....

CHAPTER 2

The Serious Work of Karaoke

Thus was I initiated into the joys of Filipino music. And thus I absorbed one of the Orient's great truths: that the Filipinos are its omnipresent, always smiling troubadours. Master of every American gesture, conversant with every Western song, polished and ebullient all at once, the Filipino plays minstrel to the entire continent.

—Pico Iyer, *Video Night in Kathmandu*

"Sinatra Song Often Strikes Deadly Chord" declared the February 7, 2010, *New York Times-Asia* edition headline. Claiming almost a dozen civilian lives over the previous decade, the "My Way" killings were dubbed a new subcategory of crime by Philippine authorities. How and why, the article mused, had the American crooner's signature tune provoked a flurry of violence in an island nation thousands of miles away? According to scholar Roland Tolentino, the "triumphalist nature" of the song's lyrics tapped into the country's masculinist vein. "Awash in one million illegal guns," the University of the Philippines professor observed, "the Philippines have long suffered from all manner of violence, from the political to the private." Penned by singer-songwriter Paul Anka as an ode to Sinatra's diminishing career in 1957, the ballad's victorious and fatalistic tones make musical a male will to live among the violence of Philippine everyday life. For others, the ubiquity of karaoke, as technological device and everyday practice, was to blame. "Social get-togethers invariably involve karaoke," journalist Norimitsu Onishi wrote. "Stand-alone karaoke machines can be found in the unlikeliest settings, including outdoors in rural areas where men can sometimes be seen singing early in the morning. And Filipinos, who pride themselves on their singing, may have a lower tolerance for bad singers."[1] Whatever the case may be, the "My Way" killings phenomenon beckoned attention toward the serious relationship between Filipinos, U.S. pop songs, and karaoke.

This article was not the first modern-day journalistic rendering of the "Filipino voice." In his 1989 *Video Night in Kathmandu: And Other Reports from the Not-So-Far-East*, travel writer Pico Iyer aimed to chronicle what he termed the cultural anomalies that occur when East Meets West.[2] Sparked by an interest "to find out how America's pop cultural imperialism spread through the world's most ancient civilizations," Iyer went forth as an observer of "low-intensity" conflicts of late twentieth-century globalization. While traveling throughout Asia, he aimed to find local resistance and "counter-strategies" to America's "Coca-Colonizing force," a force created and aided by increasingly portable technology and mobile tourists. Upon his arrival in the Philippines—"not just the site of the largest U.S. military installations in the world" but "also perhaps the world's largest slice of the America empire, in its purest impurest form"—his cultural visions began to blur. Instead, he tuned in to Manila's sonic and musical landscape and, in his listening, observed the archipelagic nation as culturally empty: "And all day long, from dawn to midnight, music buzzed through the streets of Ermita . . . Sometimes the songs were played in the original recording, sometimes reproduced live, but with such high fidelity that it was impossible to tell if the sound came from jukebox or human voice. Either way, the sound was sunny and intoxicating. In Ermita, I felt as if we were living inside a Top 40 radio station."[3] Despite the lure of these "sunny and intoxicating" sounds, Iyer expressed further sadness upon realizing that Filipino singers' adept mimicry extended to a broader national affect. Through voice and gesture as well as album covers and song titles, Iyer argued, the feelings of Filipino music and musical performance—romance and "lush sentimentality" (traits seemingly shared with Latin culture)—are "borrowed" from its former colonizers, both Spanish and American. With its "brilliance at reproducing his master's voice," the Filipino voice, in particular, and Filipino music, more broadly, functioned for Iyer as musical mannequins—objects animated by always already outside forces, hollow reproductions derived from an American original—despite the nation's regard for "its musical gifts as a major source of national pride."[4]

In its unthinking and yet brilliant reproduction of American popular music, the Filipino voice indexes the slippage between human voices and their machine-like abilities. As musical mannequins, mere objects or figures for the display of U.S. popular music, Filipino voices, and, in turn, Filipino musical culture are, according to this discourse, "hollow reproductions" animated only by outside (read colonial and colonizing) cultural forces. Like many other studies of U.S. popular musical forms in non-Western countries, this popular discourse of the Filipino voice preys upon notions of U.S. musical originality that depend upon non-U.S. popular musical cultures as merely derivative. These characteristics of the Filipino voice and Filipino music generally have been naturalized through the historical fact of Filipino overseas performing artists and transformed into cultural givens about Filipinos and Filipino Americans. The prevalence of Filipino American contestants on U.S. television singing competitions, such as *American Idol* and *The Voice*, and the star narratives of Journey frontman Arnel Pineda and child star Charice Pempengco only strengthen these beliefs.

Before continuing, I need to clarify that despite placing my critical attention on Iyer's formulation of the Filipino voice as imitative, it is by no means an exceptional one. According to Lucy Burns, as early as the mid-nineteenth century, Jesuit priest Jean Mallat commented numerous times in his study *The Philippines: History, Geography, Customs of the Spanish Colonies in Oceania* on the Filipino "Indio's distinguishing talent for/of imitation."[5] In his acknowledgment that "this [talent] does not exclude, up to a certain point, genius and invention,"[6] Burns argues that "Mallat does not foreclose originality or uniqueness despite his conclusion that mimicry is the distinguishing ability of the Indios/Filipinos," and thus "provides inspiration as it underscores the dynamic labor of imitation."[7] In the same time period as Mallat's study, Filipinos, already "trained to provide western music at official and social occasions," started finding opportunities to perform abroad. As Lee Watkins writes, "In Shanghai, Filipino musicians were involved in the entertainment industry since 1881, when a Spanish conductor formed a municipal band with musicians who were all recruited in Manila."[8] These historical records point to the fact that Filipino musical imitation did not develop solely in relationship to U.S. popular music but to Western music more broadly, especially during the period of Spanish colonization in the Philippines.

In turn, early twentieth-century U.S. colonial occupation of the Philippines, and the educational systems it implemented, only worked to further the economic need for Filipino performers and their skills of musical imitation. In the 1920s, during a time when "U.S. investments dominated business and commerce" in the Philippines, radio was introduced. As Elizabeth Enriquez writes, "The first Filipino broadcasters learned broadcasting through imitation of the Americans and their language, the manner of their speech, their music, their witticisms, their humor, and the way in which they organized radio programs and conducted business in a radio station."[9] By the end of World War II and official U.S. colonial occupation, Watkins reminds us, "Filipino musicians helped entertain the local Chinese and the large population of ex-patriates with jazz music from the United States, which they learned to appreciate and perform in the Philippines."[10] More contemporary examples of overseas performing artists, "Saigonistas" or "Filipinos [performing] in *Miss Saigon*," Lucy Burns notes, "are the embodiment of a colonialist genealogy of performance training—of imperialism through education. Once again, we encounter Filipinos' splendid dancing, angelic singing, and natural acting as visible and embodied evidence of the success of colonial education."[11]

However, as both critical and everyday commentators note, many of the Filipino musicians who have constituted the OPA labor force have not received formal musical education. Instead, they have developed their musical skills through the practice of "wido," a Tagalog version of the Spanish word *oido* (heard). As Jackson Gan, director of marketing for the Philippine-based company JS Contractor and manager for Filipino "house band" exports, noted in a 2005 *New York Times* article, "By listening to a song once on the radio, they can play it. They can copy anything. This is their real talent. It's inborn."[12] This Filipino musical attribute is naturalized; it developed despite the lack of musical training but with obvious potential for economic opportunities from musical performance. It has found its most spectacular display in the case of Pempengco, who will be discussed later in this chapter. For what it is worth, at the intersection of social commentary and reportage, Iyer's writing has been the most detailed and therefore critically cited study on the Filipino voice and mimicry.

Despite the work of scholars such as Burns and Watkins writing that aims to reveal the performative labor history of Filipino cover singers and musicians, the popular racialized discourse that figures the Filipino voice as sadly attempting to move toward Americanness and modernity, through its replications of its master's voice, has remained unchecked. These dominant tropes reverberate throughout broader attitudes toward karaoke and other cover performances as inauthentic music making and entirely derivative musical performances, ideals always tinged with ironic and emotional distance. In Iyer's and Onishi's writing, there is an added irony—that these skills or Filipino "musical gifts" of mimicking are regarded as a source of national pride and, in turn, the basis of cultural low tolerance for "bad singers."

Such commentaries operate as forms of "irony as critique," as Neferti Tadiar has brilliantly identified, approaches that "create an interpretive boundary between dreamers and analysts."[13] To "be ironic," Tadiar argues, is a deliberate act. "Being in an ironic condition," however, is an unwitting state. With this critical distance, journalistic and popular renderings uphold a "fantasy-production" of the Philippines, as a "place of ironic contrasts and tragic contradictions" and a "country dominated by misplaced dreams." These fantasies should not be confused, however, with dreams (both "actions and wishes") and imagination, a "social force" and practice that is and has always been a part of everyday life. Disobediently listening to a belief in the "newness" of imagination, one that would argue that "they—we—have only been collectively dreaming the dreams of others," Tadiar instead renders this "newness" as the product of the "autonomization and privatization of imagination."[14] Instead, she argues that we move "beyond the one-sided story of global 'Americanization'" in order to hear how these dreams work and operate within a larger political economy.

In her ethnographic study of contemporary Filipino overseas performing artists (OPAs), Stephanie Ng precisely listens in this way, focusing on the cultivation of performance skills that enable dreams of migration and economic opportunities. Ng pays close attention to elements of these musicians' live performances—their vocal timbre/style, gestures, facial expressions, dance movements, audience interaction, and relationships with employers—rather than simply their song repertoire. Less a national designation, the term Filipino, Ng writes, "constitutes a musical category or [rather] a category of traveling musicians," figuring a diasporic history of labor migration and a set of performance skills defined by musicians, booking agents, and hotel audiences.

Like Burns in her work, Ng's essay challenges popular ideas of Filipino entertainers as mere "'clones' of western pop stars." By taking into account their lives and labor as performers, she proposes that "their singing of mainstream pop and rock, communicating in English, general demeanor during performance, and constant perpetuation of their performed identity are all part of their adoption and packaging of a transnational work culture or third culture."[15] In interviews conducted with "Filipino" singers, she "listened closely as they expressed their feelings of pride about the fact that they are able to 'sing like the original singer.'" This ability to sing "like" the original singer is precisely what distinguishes "Filipino" entertainers within these tourist economies and circuits. Yet, more than just national pride, it is a source of pride in one's craft. As Ng writes: "Copying entails a high degree of accuracy, achieved through much effort. Singers often spend hours listening to the recordings by the original singers, in order to capture every inflection. The burden of exacting imitation is compounded by the burden of performing this life, creating a double burden of labor. It places a great deal of pressure on 'Filipino' musicians who know that they are being judged not only by how well they sing or play an instrument but by how well they sing and play like so-and-so."[16] Behind the sunny disposition and demeanor of these cover singers and performers remain the burdens and realities of the various forms of affective and intangible labor that they enact within this post-Fordist service industry. Against common tropes of the Filipino voice, as thoughtlessly or mechanically rendering U.S. original pop music, Ng's study reveals this transnational work culture's techniques of musical listening, affective manipulation, flexibility and fluidity (in song, performance, and movement), producing feelings of "home" and "community" through musical performance.

Guided by Burns's and Ng's work, this chapter disobediently begins from the tropical view of the Filipino as mimic. That is to say, it listens against common discourses and approaches to karaoke in order to undertake writing and thinking about what these tropical renditions produce. Listening disobediently to karaoke, we hear the ways that Filipino America's karaoke and cover performances re-sound U.S. popular music not simply as what Arjun Appadurai has identified as a "nostalgia for a past that is not one's own."[17] Instead, the tropical renditions of karaoke in Filipino America help us map pop songs' alternative genealogies in the aftermath of U.S. wars and empire in Asia and in ways that move away from notions of voice as origin and original. In the flickering afterglow of karaoke's video screens, we are left not only to question voice as a marker of ethnic authenticity but also to reckon with what is produced by voices emanating from certain performing bodies.

Against the view that, as Burns has described it, "racialized bodies that inhabit hegemonic forms of performance can only produce forms of unoriginality or inauthenticity," this chapter demonstrates karaoke and cover performances' ability to produce new meaning.[18] As a form of technology, artistic practice, and musical scene, karaoke has offered its audiences, and other artists, a set of theoretical images, cultural forms, and analytics through which to create their own critical renderings. At once artistic medium and expressive act, karaoke lives at the intersection of the visual, the sonic, and the performative.[19] Its study therefore requires a phonographic approach. Unlike the important ethnographic work of Rob Drew, Deborah Wong, and Casey Lum, this chapter considers karaoke beyond everyday public scenes of performance, moving it into the realms of visual arts, transnational domestic spaces, online platforms, and daytime television.[20] By doing so, it draws our attention to karaoke as a set of visual aesthetics, its dependence on participation (or call/interpellation of potential singers), and its place within a larger cultural landscape of musical training.

I begin this chapter with a turn toward two Filipino and Filipino American visual art works: the installation work of Manila-based artist Louie Cordero and the karaoke videos of the California-based trio Mail Order Brides/M.O.B.—Eliza "Neneng" Barrios, Reanne "Immaculata" Estrada, and Jenifer "Baby" Wofford. Their visual art pieces tune us into karaoke as an artistic object and form of secondary orality, one with the potential for playfully serious critique. I then turn my attention to karaoke as performed in the scenes of a Filipino house party, in order to consider the form's theatricality and dramaturgy as a means for maintaining translocality in Filipino America. Here, I follow the intellectual lead of previous scholarship that has focused on karaoke as a means of social exchange, for both immigrant and U.S.-born Asians in America, as well as critical enactments of temporal critique and placemaking. Attentive to karaoke as an alternative form of musical pedagogy and training, this chapter closes by focusing on the role of karaoke in preparing Filipina child star Charice Pempengco for the stages of U.S. afternoon talk shows and concert halls. By pursuing the trajectory of

Charice and other young stars' narratives in the United States, we can observe the ways in which their singing voices and performing bodies authenticated a certain affinity with U.S. viewers through the trope of the Filipina child. It is a relationship of reception that is easily activated but inevitably outgrown.

"Feelings, Nothing More Than Feelings": Karaoke as Performative Objects

Commissioned by the 2011 Singapore Biennale, painter and conceptual artist Louie Cordero's "My We" also takes part in re-presenting the violent events of the "My Way killings." Staged in a room with hot-pink walls, the installation includes four fiberglass cast figures and the centerpiece of a videoke machine—an all-in-one karaoke, TV, and speaker system. Each cast figure has been impaled with everyday objects like toilet plungers, kitchen knives, scissors, rulers, brooms, a bedpost, and small axes. Their wounds appear gruesome yet comical; deep cuts expose bright pastel guts and innards that look more like candy than bloody gore. Dressed in a D.A.R.E. T-shirt, one figure has been pinned against the wall. Another lies on the ground, one bare foot extended while a Nike tennis shoe hangs off his other bent leg's foot. A third figure, shirtless and barefoot, remains on his knees. Groveling, he reaches out one hand in a form of pleading. Dressed in an aloha shirt and khaki pants, the final figure bears an uncanny resemblance to Cordero himself. A gold chain encircles his wrist, like a leash, and yet is attached to nothing. "Generously coated in candy-colored skulls and psychedelic scenes of suffering," the videoke machine, as Manila-based pop critic Alice Sarmiento describes it, plays a loop of a "muzak rendition" of Sinatra's anthem, its lyrics superimposed over video and tabloid headlines about the killings "with the words going up in flames as the song played."[21] "My We" manifests Cordero's trademark "scatological humor and fluorescent hues" and his indebtedness to comic books, kitsch, heavy metal, and 1970s horror films.

Associating the biennale's title ("Open House") with the idea of a party, where, as Sarmiento writes, "videoke is ubiquitous and 'My Way' is a fixture on every playbook," Cordero found inspiration while bike riding past a rowdy group of guys outside his neighbor's house one night. Yet, the piece does not aim toward reportage. Instead, it listens against a fantasy-production of the Philippines, as "a place of ironic con-

Figure 2.1 Detail from "My We," Louie Cordero.
Courtesy of the artist and Singapore Art Museum.

trasts and tragic contradictions," in order to stage its macabre and irrev-
erent humor. "The word 'visceral' has been used to describe his work,"
Sarmiento notes, "hinting at how Cordero borrows from 70's horror
and cult classics." As a tropical rendition, "My We" also performs the
visceral as the deep-seated cultural vestiges of the Philippines' colonial
pasts and neocolonial present. The piece requires us to imagine affective
responses, other than irony, to the case of Filipinos and karaoke performance. Through the videoke machine, it not only underscores the ability
of karaoke technology to create a scene but also the aesthetic qualities
of the machine's components.

Karaoke videos function as a secondary orality, what media theorist
Walter Ong famously termed contemporary "high" technology forms
(such as telephones, television, the Internet) that require and expand
the uses of earlier technologies (namely, writing and print).[22] Accompanied by simple musical tracks, song lyrics, as they appear on-screen,
both enliven and are enlivened by karaoke singers. Sung out loud and
in public, whether at a local bar or in a domestic living room, karaoke
renders the singing of pop songs a musical speech act whose enuncia-
tion produces social and personal meaning. The notion that karaoke's
shoddy aesthetics might facilitate anything more than a mind-numbing

Figure 2.2 Detail from "My We," Louie Cordero.
Courtesy of the artist and Singapore Art Museum.

listening experience often amuses and disturbs the average individual. In turn, every karaoke aficionado can recall at least one episode where too many hours of one's life were squandered in front of a glaring television screen. Even the best quality karaoke machines are capable of misspelled and incorrect lyrics.

With their "Karaoke Trilogy" project, Filipina American art collaborative Mail Order Brides/M.O.B. tune audiences into these particular aesthetics of karaoke videos—the intersecting layers of meaning produced by the video's image/narrative, text, and music as well as how the video itself both sets the stage for and corresponds with a live karaoke singer. With their karaoke video renditions of Engelbert Humperdinck's "What Now My Love" and Madonna's "Holiday" filmed and edited in San Francisco in 1997, their "Mail Order Bride of Frankenstein" (set to Joan Jett's "I Hate Myself for Loving You") filmed and edited in 2002 while they were artists-in-residence at the McColl Center for Visual Art, M.O.B.'s project's song selection gestures toward karaoke as a popular song archive, one with intergenerational appeal and diverse pop music genres. In the case of "Holiday" and "What Now," the original karaoke instrumental and backup vocal tracks remain while the narrative-based music video and its song lyrics, appearing at the bottom of the screen, are altered.

"What Now My Love," a standard popularized by Humperdinck, provides the soundtrack to M.O.B.'s fictionalized "love-lorn tale of betrayal and revenge in and around a suburban hot tub."[23] The video's plot revolves around the love triangle of Wofford, a white male lead, and a tattooed female temptress. It opens with a close-up of Wofford: her mascara-smeared eyes look forlorn and tragic, her mouth contorted into an exaggerated frown, and a white swim cap and white swimsuit framing her face. With a jump cut, we are brought back to "happier times" as she and the video's male lead campily make out while seated in a hot tub situated in front of tall, well-manicured shrubs, both markings of suburban style. As they toast each other's red plastic cups, amid splashing hot tub waters, a robed woman enters the scene and seductively walks in front of the couple, catching Wofford's lover's eye. As the temptress enters the hot tub, the camera zooms in on her tattooed legs—the first marked with the emblematic heart featuring a sash that says "Dad," the second marked with a similar heart featuring an empty sash, one in

Figure 2.3 Still from "What Now My Love" karaoke video, Mail Order Brides/ M.O.B. (Eliza Barrios, Reanne Estrada, Jenifer Wofford). Courtesy of the artists.

Figure 2.4 Still from "What Now My Love" karaoke video, Mail Order Brides/ M.O.B. (Eliza Barrios, Reanne Estrada, Jenifer Wofford). Courtesy of the artists.

search of a name to feature. Intrigued by this harlot, the white male departs from the hot tub, leaving Wofford confused and saddened.

Yet, in a transformative montage, Wofford removes her white swim cap while Barrios and Estrada immediately join her in the hot tub. The trio's eyes and facial expressions quickly turn maniacal as the wheels in their minds begin to churn. In the next and final shots, the camera takes on what we may assume to be the trio's point of view, spying on the new couple, their robes opened suggestively while they sit on a deck, feeding each other mangoes. The scene quickly turns psycho (à la Norman Bates), but all we see are the temptress's coconut bra and the white male lead's robe flying up into the air, suggesting that a confrontation is taking place down below.

As the video's narrative progresses, the song's lyrics, appearing at the bottom of the screen, begin to take on a life of their own. Extra words, both in proper English and Tagalog, appear between actual song lyrics. These added words call to mind the all too real possibilities of karaoke singers' accidental addition of words into original pop songs or changing lyrics to alter their meaning. M.O.B.'s videos open our ears to pop songs' multiple meanings, especially as they are emphasized in improvised karaoke renditions. M.O.B.'s video takes on an additional layer of critique, forcing viewers to question not only the veracity of karaoke video lyrics but also the power they wield in somehow mandating what a karaoke singer's eyes follow and what she then actually sings. Throughout their videos, the original (sometimes mistaken) lyrics are sometimes phonetically spelled to capture how they would sound if sung with a Filipino accent. Written in this manner, M.O.B. helps their audience imagine the different types of performances these lyrics might bring forth—ones accented in a particular manner—while they also force, ask, allow the karaoke viewer/singer to inhabit the sonic space created by singing in this particular way.

With their higher video production value, M.O.B.'s experimental karaoke art objects resemble an earlier generation of karaoke videos. In contrast, today's karaoke video is more minimal in style and production cost, featuring computerized stock images of foreign and tropical landscapes or simply single-colored backdrops. These images are accompanied by tinny Casio-produced semblances of melody and rhythm lines, sometimes a canned backup vocal track, just enough to jog a karaoke singer's memory and guide her through a song's structure.

Figure 2.5 Still and exhibit image from "Holiday," Mail Order Brides/M.O.B. (Eliza Barrios, Reanne Estrada, Jenifer Wofford). Courtesy of the artists.

Unlike their original recordings, popular songs' karaoke renditions offer the bare minimum in terms of a musical experience. With tinny Casio melodies and mechanical mono-rhythmic drumbeats, most karaoke videos merely serve as degraded versions of original, professional recordings. Rarely produced in the song's original key, a karaoke track's opening notes are often deemed unrecognizable even by the most avid fan. Today's more popular karaoke videos serve as a glorified lyric sheet with a scratch (or rehearsal-style) musical track.

Guided less by a listening public's mandates for layered audio recording processes, karaoke's empty or canned soundscape is composed of instrumental and visual elements that serve to bring (all types of) singing voices to the fore. This objective materializes in a potent symbol—the microphone—an instrument that holds the promise of karaoke (and popular music, in general): "To have a voice and be heard. To delight myself and thereby delight others. To make a song my own and dispense it as a gift."[24] In the style of post–World War II pop crooners such as Frank Sinatra and Bing Crosby, seasoned karaoke and cover performers apprehend the power of a microphone not merely to amplify one's voice but, more so, as the means through which a song's range of emotional meaning is uniquely expressed by the manipulation of one's voice—making a song your own.

Since its humble beginnings, the karaoke machine has evolved through a variety of sizes and formats—Minus-One cassette tapes, laser disc/video CD machines, and, more recently, Magic Mics, or microphones housing chips loaded with more than three hundred songs— so that, over time, machine and microphone become one. Storing such large song selections on either discs or chips, the technological object of karaoke serves as its own digital library, a pre-iPod/iTunes repository of popular music with songs arranged by broad genre-based categories (such as pop/rock, standards/Broadway musicals, rap/hip-hop) as well as language (Spanish, Japanese, Tagalog, etc.). Through such technological streamlining, karaoke machinery has made itself even more mobile—finding its way into automobiles and onto cellular phones— while karaoke's users have expanded the reaches of karaoke as a performance/event—singing with others in remote places through multiplayer platforms online and through Xbox video game consoles. As a technology both networked and "on the go," the possibilities for spontaneous and expansive karaoke performances have increased beyond the traditional weekly bar event or private rooms of *noraebangs* and other karaoke businesses.

Against the will of Western music criticism, with its preference for composition and its norms of classical training, karaoke revels in popular music's preference for, and oftentimes fetish of, what Rob Drew has described as, unique voices: "those shouts, moans, wails, and squeals that, stifled by classical training, are vital components in the expressive repertoire of the human voice."[25] Since its inception, the U.S. recording industry's star system has depended upon sound recording technologies' ability to capture the unmistakable sound of a singer's voice. At the same time, the industry maintained its power by distancing listening audiences from the act of making music. Karaoke singing, instead, emplaces pop music's fans and amateurs into an everyday scene of music and meaning making.[26] As ethnographer Rob Drew astutely points out, the everyday performance form of karaoke is "receptive to as wide a range of voices as speech itself, and defined as much by quotidian social skills as by formal musical skills. Vocal ability is ultimately less important in karaoke than the ability to feel others out, humble oneself, laugh at oneself, and think on one's feet."[27] Here, as for other cover performers, a karaoke singer's performance ability is underscored in two ways—first, in the process of learning not only a song's lyrics but the song's emotional meanings and messages; second, in the process of performing in front of an audience, selecting songs suitable for the crowd's mood and being able to improvise with limited technology, cramped spaces, and (more often than not) a distracted audience.

If karaoke is a form of what sociologist Erving Goffman designated as "keying," "the transformation of a preexisting activity into something patterned yet different from itself," then, as Drew reminds us, "a karaoke performance is a complex, multi-layered sort of keying, for its template is not a written set of lyrics, nor even a song composition, but a full-blown, prior performance—a popular recording."[28] One is reminded of this template every time she punches in the numbers corresponding to her selected song and a title page image appears on screen listing the song title, song writers, and (very often) "the style of" a particular recording artist. With a phonographic approach, we remember that this template is a composite of not just sound recordings but also previous visual recordings and live performances. Tuning us back into the scene of karaoke performance—be it in a bar or living room—Drew also serves up a worthy reminder of karaoke's performative power: "People use songs in karaoke to define themselves and influence others, yet just as often, songs seem to use people, putting words in their mouths and voices in their heads, some of them apparently meaningless, others terribly meaningful. Songs *do things* in karaoke bars, they seduce and repulse, embolden and embarrass, connect and divide" (my emphasis).[29] If the musical structure of lyrics, melodies, and rhythm operate as a song's written law, then karaoke is the courtroom of recorded popular music where various interpretations of the law take place but, in the end, accede to its most "popular" rendering. While the karaoke singer, with the microphone in hand, commands attention and takes center stage, in the end, it is the audience (that is, everyone except the microphone-holder) who decides the "success" of the performance based on, at best, rapt attention, thunderous applause, and postperformance cheers or, at worst, distracted presence and polite clapping. Disrupting notions of the "who" and "where" of music's creation, karaoke is also a potent reminder of how popular music functions in people's everyday lives and the radical possibilities it engenders.[30] If mainstream

America's aversion to karaoke rests in its vexed (read private) relationship to musical recordings—consuming music individually, even in a crowd, and singing in places away from public view (such as showers, cars, bedrooms), then this next section considers how karaoke functions within the various publics of Asian America and Filipino America.

"Take Me Home, Country Road"

[Karaoke performers] risk failure in the most intimate, diffuse performance contexts, where failure can feel very personal. Performers willingly shoulder this burden on behalf of the radical notion that culture is ordinary—that music is not marginal to daily life, something to be supplied by a chosen few artists, but a necessary part of living.
—Rob Drew, *Karaoke Nights*

Karaoke is a unique musical technology. It does not simply broadcast or disseminate popular music. It actually enables the formation of new pop musical scenes. According to Casey Lum, a karaoke scene arises anytime karaoke singing encourages interaction between individuals who by "being present at the scene are potential performers as well as audience members."[31] In these scenes, Lum observes, karaoke's "programs," or "patterns of behavior," are firmly grounded in its "dramaturgical web" that is further established into a sense of karaoke decorum.[32] Dramaturgical web is a useful analytic for everyday performance, especially since, as ethnomusicologist Deborah Wong declares: "Informal, amateur singing of popular music is common in social gatherings of many Asian cultures. Think of Imelda Marcos crooning into a microphone at countless diplomatic dinners. Chinese wedding banquets often feature singing by the bride, groom, and their family members; I am told that this is common in Java as well. I have been on countless long-distance bus trips with Thai university students and faculty members where nearly everyone got up, one by one, and sang a song into the bus P.A. system to pass the time."[33] In these scenes of karaoke performance, social dramas between strangers, acquaintances, or good friends are mediated through an amateur's performance or rendition of a popular music recording. Karaoke reveals the serious nature of popular recorded music—how it is remembered, honored, and performed—for the average listener. Karaoke's fragile sociality rests on the constant threat or possibility of one's own future performance onstage, and so the Golden Rule applies: do unto others as you would have them do unto you, because your turn to sing may be next. This Golden Rule underlies what some might call karaoke's scenes of subjection—seemingly banal and joyous episodes in which enacted power is enforced through terror and torture.[34] This enforcement of common courtesy goes hand in hand with karaoke's coercive tactics of enforced singing and listening, especially in the more intimate spaces of private karaoke boxes. While one may walk away from or step away during a "bad" or unsuccessful karaoke performance in a bar or club, in the social landscape of karaoke box communities, enduring others' performances and submitting to the group's demands for performance are one's only options.

Throughout Asia, karaoke functions as a social lubricant for a diverse array of business and business-related transactions. In Japan, brochures instruct both male and female businesspeople on the proper etiquette for performing karaoke on the job. In Southeast Asian countries where sexual tourism thrives, soft-core forms of prostitution proliferate in demarcated karaoke boxes or private rooms, where local or imported Asian women serve as GROs (guest relations officers), a rented form of female companionship.[35] Instrumental to certain forms of sociality in Asia, karaoke is also a crucial component of the cultural survival of Asian communities in the diaspora, from Southern California's Vietnamese and Korean enclaves to the urban and suburban Chinatowns of New York and New Jersey. As Lum's book-length study carefully outlines, an ethnically and economically diverse cross-section of Chinese communities (Cantonese opera singers, Taiwanese corporate workers, undocumented restaurant workers from Malaysia) "indigenize" karaoke technology to serve their diverse needs—Cantonese opera singers' rehearsals for public performances; leisurely competition among Taiwanese corporate workers; a therapeutic respite for homesick and undocumented restaurant workers from Malaysia.

In her study of Westminster, California, ethnomusicologist Deborah Wong observes that "economically cut off from their homelands," U.S.-based Vietnamese exiles "have had to create a contemporary sense of self, too, and this has meant creating an immigrant popular culture."[36] Vietnamese immigrants, mainly men, gather in places where either karaoke products are sold (ethnic stores) or karaoke is performed (restaurants). Thus, the lines between public and private are blurred: karaoke products are mainly being sold for home use while restaurants serve "as an extension of the home" for immigrant workers.[37] Or think of Korea-town *noraebangs* as replicas of musical living rooms or bedrooms. In the hands of diasporic and immigrant Asians, the "canned" technology of karaoke actually brings to life places of gathering, commerce, and remembering the homeland through popular music. Karaoke enables songs and artists, from both the United States and Asia, to circulate along different itineraries and resonate in unexpected places. Karaoke embodies and enacts processes of "human interactions and practices whereby certain values, meanings, or social realities are created, main-tained, and transformed as part of culture."[38] This particular part of social life emphasizes different modes of affiliations through popular music and exists in places that trouble not only the divide between public and private but also between the domestic and transnational—translocal scenes such as ethnic restaurants, karaoke/video stores, and even the immigrant home.

While karaoke's popularity for many remains a purely public event ("in spite of every effort by retailers to market it for home use, kara-oke continues to fare best in public") most Filipino Americans first encounter karaoke's magic in the "most mundane and accessible of public contexts"—the house party.[39] It is a customary event that one might fit within a broader repertoire of "immigrant acts," the artistic and everyday practices that complicate popular notions of immigrant life.[40] Often marked by major life events—birthdays, baptisms, home-comings, *despedidas* (bon voyages), even death—these gatherings are multigenerational, multilingual, and multisensorial events that include eating, drinking, dancing, and karaoke singing. These at once public and private events in Filipino America serve as an alternative space of socialization in the face of U.S. racist legal and informal bans to certain public spaces and, therefore, function as self-sustaining sites of infor-mal and cultural citizenship.[41] They both nurture and extend, within U.S. national borders and within the domestic setting, kinship networks established in the Philippines—ones based on biological, geographical, linguistic, and even mere social ties. A blend of familial, regional-based, and even contact associations, these house parties in Filipino America offer models of kinship that challenge the dominance of nuclear family and neighborhood-as-community models in U.S. suburban studies. Scholars such as Rick Bonus, Benito Vergara Jr., and Dawn Mabalon have chronicled the various public spaces created by immigrant Filipinos, from regional/provincial organizations to community-based arts and education centers to commercial establishments, such as grocery and video stores and restaurants.[42]

Yet house parties capture the spirit of these public gatherings in the domestic space of the home and, thus, serve as a particularly salient example of the everyday and intimate nature of Filipino America's "enfolded borders."[43] In the translocal scenes of these house parties, bedrooms breathe the hushed prayers of grandmothers and older women, kitchens cackle with the *tsismis* (gossip) and stories of mothers and aunts, backyard barbecue grills are manned by tank top–wearing fathers and *titos*, and youth often find refuge in the auxiliary spaces of garages and basements. So aptly termed "living rooms," the commonly acknowledged gathering spaces of these domiciles transform into what Alexandra Vazquez has termed "transnational hubs."[44] In these translocal scenes, Filipinos from diverse generational, national, educational, linguistic, gendered, and citizen backgrounds do not simply perform karaoke. Instead, they teach, learn, remember, and invoke particular memories and ways of life through the shared language of pop music.[45]

With a varied repertoire of English, Tagalog, and other Filipino languages, Magic Mics or karaoke players allow both Philippine- and American-born Filipinos another space for learning and rehearsing new languages, phrases, and meanings. Through the lyrics of contemporary pop and traditional songs, the immigrant Filipino or Filipino American can "put on" accents, attempting to approximate linguistic phrases, and feelings not necessarily foreign to their lived experience. Karaoke technology operates as a popular archive and jukebox for listening and performance, aligning with what Allan Isaac has remarked on as a mode of alternative modernity or temporal lag in Filipino America.[46] A cursory glance at Magic Mic's catalogue of more than three hundred songs embedded into the karaoke microphone's chips might lead one to remark on the temporally expansive and often cheesy ballad selections. Songs in English, mostly U.S. pop songs from the past five decades of recorded music, range from World War II torch songs to a song selection more warmly regarded as "AM Gold." They are the songs of yesteryear, the kind most readily accessible and easily associated with childhood road trips traveling through mountainous or rural areas where the only clear sounds coming out of car radio speakers were slow jams of all musical varieties and decades, Engelbert Humperdinck and the Platters, Chicago and Air Supply. While this moniker emphasizes the radio station format most readily identified with these types of songs, its shifting title—from soft rock (1970s) to easy listening (1980s) to, most recently, adult contemporary (1990s)—within the recording industry and popular imaginary also associates it with particular genders (the feminized version of hard rock), generations (adolescent or teeny bopper audiences), and even geographical regions (the California sound of the Beach Boys, the Mamas and the Papas, and Fleetwood Mac).

That these songs are seen as the "weaker" counterparts to a more fully grown and industrialized, often metropolitan, cock-rock alternative is a fact not to be taken lightly. The sentimental often syrupy feelings associated with easy listening songs—longing, heartbreak, and desperation—simultaneously index and, in turn, perpetuate the seeming passiveness of their detractors. Yet the genre's sounds fit right into the performative system of *palabas*, what Patrick Flores cites as an affective mode of externalizing internalized emotions for strategic purposes, as it puts a performer's emotions on display while also smoothing over the crowded difficulties of everyday life—sitting in traffic, standing in packed commuter trains, avoiding life's problems while making *pasyal*, or cruising around air-conditioned malls.[47] A condition of everyday and staged Filipino performance then, this ability to move seamlessly between the past and the present, to allow a soft rock love song's melodies and lyrics to make life that much more bearable, might also fit under the category of "performing the Filipino." A reminder and remainder of U.S. imperial presence in the Philippines, however, these easy listening songs do not necessarily mean easy listening practices as they register the uneven power of the two countries' histories of cultural and musical exchanges.

Whereas the immigrant Vietnamese men of Deborah Wong's study re-create the domestic sphere in the public setting of a restaurant, house parties in Filipino America attempt to re-create the social and familial hierarchies of the Philippines while, at the same time, invoking the intergenerational and intercultural battles and possibilities between Philippine- and U.S.-born Filipinos. And whereas the immigrant and second-generation Chinese Americans, of Casey Lum's study, gather strictly around the musical activity of karaoke singing, in Filipino America, karaoke performances exist alongside other cultural objects and everyday rituals such as eating, gossip, saying prayers, and dancing. Evidencing a certain level of socioeconomic achievement, the karaoke machine (or Magic Mic) finds its place in the Filipino American household alongside other commonplace objects such as rice cookers, carved wooden spoon and fork statues, and religious objects (rosaries, Santo Niño or Virgin Mary statues, and so on). This is not to say that these items appear in every home in Filipino America. Rather, an immigrant or second-generation Filipino in the United States would not be surprised by or question their appearance. Again, tuning into karaoke performance in the domestic spaces of Filipino America does not foreclose the fact that karaoke singing happens in more public and/or commercial spaces (such as bars, restaurants, community gatherings). Instead, it underscores how karaoke technology and singing are deeply embedded in Filipino America's everyday experience of popular music.

This focus on karaoke's place in the domestic sphere allows us to set the scene for one spectacular example of how karaoke might also function as an alternative form of musical training. A backup band that ceases only when the batteries die, karaoke machines provide an affordable domestic training program of rehearsal and performance, another step in developing Filipino cover performers for local or export consumption. Whereas in other contexts karaoke is merely seen as entertainment or diversion, in Filipino America, musical voices regard karaoke as something more serious.

"Because You Loved Me"

On December 19, 2007, sixteen-year-old Filipino singing sensation Charice Pempengco debuted on U.S. daytime television with two jaw-dropping cover performances of ballads by diva songstresses Whitney Houston and Jennifer Hudson. In her preperformance interview with afternoon TV personality Ellen DeGeneres, Charice informed the studio and home audiences, in a strange blend of affected British and Filipino accents, that, yes, this was her first time in the United States and, yes, she did like this country "so very much." "It must be so different than where you're from . . . in the Philippines," pressed DeGeneres to the point that Charice simply replied, "Yes, so very different."

But, aware that she and her audience really came to hear Charice sing, DeGeneres invited the teenager to take her television studio stage.

Handed a microphone, and cued with the song's tonal note played on piano, however, the docile adolescent transformed into a defiant woman. With a powerful and wide-ranging voice that skillfully traveled from the gut-wrenching low notes of the *Dreamgirls* anthem to the sustained high notes of its monstrous ending, Charice's stage presence denoted a mastery of physical comportment usually assigned to professionals. Emanating from a petite adolescent body and innocent visage, her voice bore the emotional sensibility and technical command of a singer at least ten years older. Dedicating the Broadway musical show-stopping number "I Am Telling You" to Ellen's live studio audience of white, middle-aged females, Charice's performance works in the sense that, as Lori Mersh has argued, "The cute *demands* a maternal response and interpellates its viewers/consumers as 'maternal.'"[48]

Able to act "simultaneously innocent in looks and knowing in manner," a quality that Jane O'Connor marks as being "bigger than big and smaller than small," Charice succeeded as a child star.[49] That the song she chose invoked Effie White's (and, in some ways, Jennifer Holiday's and, more so, J-Hud's) story of survival and pronounced an affective command were pop culture details not lost on Ellen's female and queer studio and home audiences. Charice, in turn, played with these details and extended them by changing the lyrics to "you're the best mom I've ever known" (as opposed to "man" in the original). While historical preconditions such as empire, neocolonial dependence, and televisual regimes might have prescribed Charice's emergence, what remains most intriguing are the methodological challenges the pint-size singer's performances and reception present. The star power of a child singer, who narrowly escapes abuses and injustices early in life, is "found" and brought over from a foreign land, displays the mimetic and melismatic talent to successfully render cover performances from a catalog of diva "survival anthems," and moves a particular U.S. audience, in the process. Taking a sad life and making it better through music is a story we love to love and would never admit to hate.

Growing up on the beaches of another Laguna (this one in the central region of the Philippines), Raquel Pempengco raised Charice as a single mother after narrowly escaping death at the hands of her abusive husband. Noticing her daughter's proclivity for singing on the karaoke machine at the tender age of four, Raquel began teaching Charice vocal and performance techniques she herself had learned from fellow entertainers. Raquel Pempengco had also once dreamed of a singer's life. Performing briefly with a local cover band in their provincial home-town, Raquel abandoned this ambition in order to raise her children. As one version of a stage mother, she home-schooled Charice in a singer's corporeal repertoire—with a lexicon of facial gestures (ranging from brightness to excruciating pain) and bodily movements (hands reaching out and bodies pulling away)—skills commonly characterized as "per-forming Filipino." Within the transnational circuit of hotels and tourist bars, as ethnomusicologist Stephanie Ng studies, booking agents and hotel owners assign a certain set of performance traits to Filipino cover band performers: intimate familiarity with U.S. pop songs and ballads, a service-oriented approach to international tourist audiences' affective needs, and quick adaptability to an audience's song requests. Thus, ver-satility and modularity, in the sense that one is able to play any instru-ment in the band, become the condition of economic possibility and survival for the Filipino overseas performing artists (OPA), both in the Philippines and abroad.

Situated within the larger social and migration categories of OCWs (overseas contract workers) and affective laborers, as Ng's work ana-lyzes, these OPAs signal the broader movement and longer cultural history of Filipino performative labor. As Rhacel Parreñas, Robyn Rodriguez, and Catherine Ceniza Choy have argued, the overwhelm-ingly feminized labor force of Filipino migrant/immigrant workers—domestics, caregivers, and nurses—has continually been forced to sub-mit to the demands and desires of both their home countries and host nations.[50] In many ways, the affective labor of caring for the West's chil-dren, families, and elderly speaks to the ways in which even Filipino musical performers entertain and care for the emotional needs of tour-ists and travelers. For the young workforce that remains in the Phil-ippines, in turn, the call center has emerged as one of the most viable economic opportunities in the past decade. Thus, as Allan Isaac's most recent research contends, we should consider the call center worker as performing another type of affective labor—appeasing and sooth-ing angry callers—with their trained voices.[51] Heard but unseen, these workers' everyday performances carry over international airwaves and across various time zones.

As performance practice, *palabas* both highlights and troubles the false binaries between psychic interiority and social exteriority, between staged and everyday performance. It brings into relief the playful and yet premeditated nature of emotional output, its improvisatory and sometimes manipulative manner.[52] *Palabas* finds its musical register in the Filipino cover performer as these singers skillfully manage a crowd's feeling through performance techniques—the breath control to pause singing for dramatic effect, the acting techniques of closing their eyes, swaying their bodies, and gently caressing their microphones, all in a laborious effort to facilitate a sphere of intimacy between music, performer, and audience. Raquel instilled these techniques in a young Charice, who then employed them in the more than eighty singing contests she entered to help her single mother make ends meet. Though she did win some of these local competitions, in 2005 Charice unfortunately did not fare as well with the Filipino television viewing audience of *Little Big Superstar*, placing third in the first season of the children's talent competition. While another nation's television would more effectively disseminate her musical performances a few years later, Charice instead first emerged on the international stage as a YouTube phenomenon. Thanks to the editing work of an avid fan, "False Voice" (aka Dave Dueñas), a nineteen-year-old nursing student and tech genius, who mashed-up Charice's performances with the *America's Got Talent* singing winners in order to show whom *he* thought had more talent, Charice found a broader audience through viral technology, and video of her performance on South Korea's *StarKing* TV show later made it into the inboxes of DeGeneres's producers.[53]

While the Internet's contagious mode of communication helped Charice's performances spread across the globe, daytime television's talk shows tailored her image for a larger U.S. sentimental public sphere. After her initial appearance on DeGeneres's show, Charice was featured twice in six months on *Oprah*—first, as one of fifteen of "The World's Smartest Kids" (first broadcast on May 12, 2008) and then as a featured guest star on "The Most Talented Girl in the World." American audiences watched as the dreams of "the girl with the voice" came true—with not only a webcast visit from her idol and one of Oprah's closest friends, Celine Dion, but also a special invitation from the Canadian diva to join her onstage during her Madison Square Garden (MSG) performance.

On September 9, 2008, television audiences gleefully watched as the daughter of a single mother and abusive father from a faraway land tearfully accepted Dion's gift by way of Winfrey's cajoling. In this moment, a politics of compassion was activated. A "social relation between specta-tors and sufferers," as Lauren Berlant has described, this liberal politics of empathy works through an "emotional complex" in which privileged spectators are faced with the moral and ethical dilemmas of obligation in relationship to sufferers from "over there."[54] It is a brand of affective and ethical relations that Winfrey's particular style of daytime drama propagated through feature stories of celebrities and everyday people that survive "against the odds" in order to connect emotionally with the show's mainly female viewers. "Reporter, catalyst, mediator, teacher, preacher, counselor, confessor, and ombudsperson (in the midst of con-testing views and personalities)" are all roles that Winfrey has crafted over the years and built into a media empire comprising a monthly self-help magazine, cinematic and made-for-TV movie productions on black female abuse and survival, a coterie of professional life coaches and advisers, and her infamous taste-making Book of the Month club.[55] This conglomerate of compassion politics is bolstered by Winfrey's own rags-to-riches narrative of survival and self-made success.

It should be no surprise then that Winfrey's and Dion's introductions consistently referenced Charice's background narrative of survival and motherly love. The physical presence of Charice's mother in the first row of each performance only worked to emphasize this narrative trope. As Dion informed a packed MSG stadium on September 17, 2008:

> This young girl's name is Charice. I'm so excited. She's 16 years old and she's from the Philippines. Let me tell you she has a voice that can literally blow the roof off Madison Square. But the real story is, Charice and her mom escaped a terrifying experience and had to leave Charice's violent father. You know, to start a life on their own, Charice vowed to save her mom from life's desperation. Through prayers and dreams and God-given talent, an incredible voice, Char-ice entered and won every singing contest in her native country and eventually got noticed. By such a fortunate chance people saw the show on Oprah and Oprah wanted to take her under her wing and David Foster joined them . . . But let me tell you one thing, the tal-ent we're not going to talk about because you have that, we're not going to talk about strength because you have that (Celine pointing to Charice's mom Raquel Pempengco) and so the love. And I have to tell you that the family we have to talk about because you have

that too . . . When you go up there you'll be nervous don't be. I will give you an image that you can think about, think about that. All the people you see in front of you are your brothers and sisters. You are singing in your living room and it's your family.[56]

Setting up, yet again, the story line of abuse, survival, and self-made success, Charice's "real story" (as told by Dion) became an uplifting story with her God-given voice and perseverance operating as a vehicle of escape—salvation by way of talent and the benevolence of others along the way.

Against the grain of this repeated trope—where the voice is something that comes from above, untrained and full of lived feeling—the mental picture Dion painted of "singing in her living room" conjures up a form of preparation and home training that for Charice, as well as many other Filipino children, is already familiar.[57] It invokes the tradition of her singing karaoke on Magic Mics, in front of her mother or at a family party, as part of an evening program of entertainment. As mentioned earlier, this domesticated schooling can be thought of as another step in developing Filipino cover performers for local or export consumption, in a global, service-oriented entertainment economy that demands both authenticity and empathy.[58]

With an unstoppable backup band (unless the batteries die), karaoke provides an inexpensive and consistent alternative to live musical accompaniment. With her karaoke machine, an aspiring singer can hone the skills needed for a successful cover performance—to learn a particular musical catalog, mimic the vocal techniques of the original, and rehearse the affected gestures that all express a feeling of the music. For Charice (or any other Filipino, for that matter), the comprehensibility of Dion's command—to imagine "singing in your living room and it's your family"—is nothing extraordinary and can actually be attributed to this alternative form of musical training.

Situating Dion's comment and the figure of Charice as a Filipina child singing sensation within a larger landscape of U.S. compassion politics, however, another audience of brothers and sisters, another type of performance for the family, arises. It is a familial trope best illustrated by turn-of–the-nineteenth-century political cartoons, images that offer us a visual channel of remembering the discursive histories of U.S. war and occupation in the Philippines. Here, the child propagated by cartoonists and imagined by a U.S. reading public was often dark-skinned, primitive, even borderline animalistic—amassing qualities that necessitated an outside presence to sanitize, civilize, even baptize it in the waters of America's benevolent assimilation. Critically hearing Dion's comment within this "genealogy of compassion" for the Filipino marked by a history of imperialist propaganda and neocolonial images, Charice also sings then for a discursive family, making her a "little brown sister" to the U.S. family audience at home.[59]

Is there a particular/receptive market for "foreign acts" that break onto the U.S. pop culture scene at such a young age? Or are they merely fads and one-hit wonders? What can we make of the differences between their reception in the United States versus "back home" in the Philippines? What happens when the child performer outgrows her pint-sized body? How do issues of race and gender intersect and further frame audience reception to their future musical endeavors?

The particular contours and effectiveness of Winfrey's and Dion's style of compassion politics are further accentuated when we compare Charice to another Filipina child singing star who burst onto the U.S. national stage almost twenty years earlier. Josephine "Banig" Roberto, like Charice, began performing and competing in local singing competitions at a young age. In 1989, at the age of ten, she also appeared on U.S. national television, winning the international *Star Search* competition, and then guest starred on another famous talk show hosted by another groundbreaking African American media personality—Arsenio Hall. Unlike his daytime female counterpart, however, Hall "gave audiences a 'high voltage' act that was also a full-fledged representation of African American speech, musical acts, topics and themes . . . showcasing that Black culture and Black entertainment figures could appeal to mainstream White audiences."[60] Trained as a stand-up comic, Arsenio's showcase of controversial talents such as his closest friend Eddie Murphy, director Spike Lee, musical icon Prince, and boxing promoter Don King, as well as political figures such as Spelman College president Johnetta Cole, Nation of Islam figurehead Louis Farrakhan, and a saxophone-playing presidential candidate named Bill Clinton, marked a particular moment in late-night television history.

Lauded for her big voice, a voice that mimicked the vocal prowess of that era's singing divas—Mariah Carey, Whitney Houston, and Patti LaBelle—Banig displayed a different type of black musical feeling and sentiment through the musical catalogue and gestural vocabulary she performed. With a funkier and edgier sound, Banig's vocal artillery of accented grunts invoke a bluesier lineage of Filipino musical performance that includes the likes of R&B singer Sugar Pie de Santo and Latin soul impresario Joe Bataan. With her upbeat renditions of classics by Houston and Teddy Pendergrass, Banig's performances registered with audiences at the level of the body—guts, groins, and even their posteriors, which could not stay in their seats, as the young girl's rousing covers compelled you to get up and shake your moneymaker. After her initial appearance on Arsenio's late-night show, the eleven-year-old signed a contract with Motown Records and recorded her first album, *Can You Feel My Heart?* with Del-Fi Records (the company that produced Ritchie Valens) in 1994. She performed on a national college tour after her album's release, garnering fame among students. Throughout this time, she began and maintained a musical presence in the Philippines, playing solo concerts and recording commercials, as well. In the late 1990s, she made recordings under another U.S. record label (Magnetic Entertainment) that were never released and began writing music for other U.S.-based R&B acts. In the early 2000s, she and her sister Joanna began their own label, Double Play Entertainment, which self-released two albums—*Silent Whispers* (2001) and *Josephine Roberto* (2010), the latter an album of songs all written in Tagalog.

In many ways, these various stops and starts appear to be the result of both Banig's and record labels' attempts to identify both her preferred musical style and, therefore, her target audience(s). While her childhood performances signaled a vocal style and stage presence very much informed by R&B and soul music, her failed attempts to record with U.S. labels signaled Banig's inability either to potentially cross over into mainstream pop music or to find a strong foothold in the genre of R&B music itself. Further, aiming to cater to her fans/audiences in the Philippines and diaspora, her self-produced 2010 album features songs in Tagalog, bearing witness to the ways that foreign acts within a U.S. pop music industry must also always acknowledge and pay homage to their birthplace. These efforts, however, are rarely underwritten or supported by U.S. record labels themselves.[61] I briefly outline Banig's musical career, after her breakthrough television appearances in the mid-1990s, to highlight some of the real-life challenges she has faced trying to stay afloat in the mainstream U.S. industry. In a cautionary rather than absolutely comparative way, they also signal the limits and possibilities of Charice's career since her breakthrough U.S. daytime television appearances.

After her historic duet with Dion, in September 2008, Charice performed at various high profile events: two preinaugural galas (2009), two post–Oscar awards show parties (2009), a Dodger baseball game, and again at a *David Foster and Friends* concert in Las Vegas (2009).

During this time, she also premiered two original songs—"Note to God" and "Fingerprint," each written exclusively for her by famed U.S. pop songwriters Diane Warren and David Foster, respectively. On June 28, 2009, Charice performed her first major concert, *Charice: The Journey Begins*, at the SMX Convention Center in Manila, Philippines. During the concert, Charice revealed that another famed child star, Michael Jackson, had contacted her a few weeks before, about recording a duet after seeing her perform on U.S. television. This dream was thwarted by Jackson's death only days before this particular concert. In 2010, Charice released her first international and self-titled album, *Charice*, which consisted of a mix of dance/club tracks as well as ballads. The marketing of her album faced a setback, however, when Charice's religious mother forbade her to perform in nightclubs with gay and lesbian clientele (and where dance remixes of her songs were being played the most). Soon after, it was announced that she would appear in a recurring role, as foreign exchange student Sunshine Corazon, on the musical/comedy TV series *Glee*. After starring in the season premiere episode on September 7, 2010, however, the character of Sunshine never appeared on the show again.

Since that time, Charice has continued recording songs in the United States (and written by U.S. pop heavyweights, such as Bruno Mars) and has released albums in the Philippines. But she has seemed to garner more media attention for her look—first, in response to her possible plastic surgery (before the age of twenty-one) and then, in response to her short haircut style that preceded news of her coming out as lesbian in 2013. As a light-skinned, Chinese-looking mestiza, Charice's "look" and her affinity with more pop-inflected musical styles fit better within the Philippines' pop culture's preferences, as opposed to Banig's darker skin tone and affinity with R&B and soul music. However, within

U.S. pop culture, Charice has also met the challenges faced by a Filipina singer/performer trying to cross over into either mainstream U.S. pop music or television.

The vocal performances (and repertoire) Charice crafted, at a young age, helped to authenticate her role as the cute girl and child-savior, from that "so very different place," within U.S. daytime television's scenes of compassion politics. The vocal performances (and repertoire) Banig crafted, at a young age, helped to authenticate her within the late 1990s era of African American television and music. Though their futures as U.S.-based pop music artists are still to be seen, their earlier performances do turn our critical ears to the fact that the U.S. pop songs they heard, the stars they idolized back home in the Philippines, were all African American artists, who each battled the racial politics of the crossover at some point in their careers: Whitney Houston, Michael Jackson, Prince. In chapter 3, we listen in on the tropical renditions of another Filipina artist, Jessica Tarahata Hagedorn, in order to hear how U.S. popular musical styles of jazz, early R&B, funk, and soul helped to shape her poetic and performance voice—not only in the recordings and memories she carried from the Philippines to the United States but also in her collaborative performances with other artists of color in the distinct translocal scenes of 1970s San Francisco and 1980s downtown New York.

CHAPTER 3

Jessica Hagedorn's Gangster Routes

Published in 1990, the novel *Dogeaters* propelled its author Jessica Hagedorn onto the national literary stage. Amid the rising tides of U.S. culture wars, the paradox of liberal multiculturalism—whereby unique and distinct racial/ethnic groups safely exist alongside each other despite their separate, ethnocentric political demands—presented itself as an alternative to an America based on and dominated by Eurocentric ideals. According to these multiculturalist mandates, works by writers of color required certain performances of difference and displays of authenticating cultural markers. It was an era transformed as well by postcolonial literary studies. Propagated by these fields and often predicated upon its antiessentializing properties and possibilities, even the idea of cultural hybridity espouses its own set of prescriptive markers. Needless to say, these two critical currents—multiculturalism and postcoloniality— greatly impacted the ways in which critics and scholars figured Hagedorn's authorial voice, especially in her first novel.

Beginning in the 1950s and ending in the mid-1980s, *Dogeaters'* multiple story lines focus on a cast of characters whose lives oftentimes intersect. From the urban poor to the military and celebrity elite, from guerrillas to gay hairdressers, from *balikbayans* and German film directors to local hustlers and nightclub owners, through these various characters Hagedorn's novel renders for its readers various cross-sections of Philippine life. Written in a style often deemed as postmodern pastiche and cinematic in quality, Hagedorn's novel draws from various texts— newspaper headlines and stories, radio shows, historical textbooks, and films. Set in the metropolis of Manila, in the post–World War II years until the martial era, *Dogeaters* has often been characterized as a novel that deals with cities and the urban landscape; the cultural aftermaths of U.S. empire (through Hollywood spectacle, sexual tourism, history, and education); the politics of multiracial societies and mixed-race characters; and the queering of discourses of home and nation.[1] Hagedorn's assembling of such diverse source materials to paint scenes of postcolonial Manila and her own multiracial background therefore have often colluded in authenticating her authorial voice as a clear example of the postcolonial. As further testament to the weight of these discursive trends, although Hagedorn has written three full-length novels since *Dogeaters*, none of them has reveived the level of critical and scholarly attention that has been paid to her 1990 debut.[2]

In more recent years, literary critics have moved away from characterizing Hagedorn's authorial voice—through its hybrid, multicultural, and multilingual elements—as either postmodern (read depoliticized) or postcolonial (read culturally authentic) but never both.

Martin Joseph Ponce's work, for example, has helped turn our ears toward Hagedorn's early poetry and critically overlooked novels in order to emphasize how her "complex poetics" have developed through popular music. By doing so, we tune into the musical and aural qualities of her authorial voice. Drawing our attention to Hagedorn's writing as "staging the interrelation of writing and music as a cross-cultural practice," Ponce argues that her complex poetics are forged "out of the manifold forms invented in the wake of Spanish and U.S. colonization of the Philippines, *as well as* the 'multiculturality' of the United States."[3] Her authorial voice not only serves as evocation or evidence of Filipino cultural hybridity; it also references the limits and demands of liberal multiculturalism's demarcation of cultural hybridity.

In his reading of her 1996 *Gangster of Love*, a novel that tracks a teenage Rocky Rivera's migrations across the Pacific and across the United States against the political and cultural backdrops of 1970s San Francisco and 1980s New York, Ponce argues for it as a "counter-assimilationist immigrant narrative." Listening and working against "the normative trajectory of de-ethnicization, upward mobility, and nuclear familyhood," common tropes of assimilationist immigrant novels, Hagedorn's Rocky instead encounters the characters and places of musical and political subcultures, DIY (do-it-yourself) forms of education, and diverse forms of kinship—single-parent households, open relationships, and other forms of collectivity, such as rock bands. As the author's alter ego, Rocky's writerly voice and "writing (are) enabled by and coincident with her engagements with music."[4] For Ponce, the novel functions as a "portrait of the artist" in that it tracks Rocky's (and, therefore, also Hagedorn's) career and development as a writer, performer, and front woman for a band, The Gangster of Love.

I approach this particular novel as well as Hagedorn's early poetry and performance art, as portraits of the artist as fan, listener, and collaborator. I aim to study how Hagedorn's adoration for and expertise in U.S. popular music has helped shape her poetic and performative voice and grounded her affiliations with other writers and musicians of her milieu. By doing so, the tropical renditions of Hagedorn's poetry and fiction, as well as her collaborative performances with the Gangster Choir and Thought Music, emerge. Listening against literary criticism and liberal multiculturalist tropes of authorial voice as authentic and therefore representative, we are instead able to hear a voice produced by active forms of listening, the kinds demanded by the artistic processes of collaboration and improvisation; by migrations, from one city or nation to another; and by geographical places, especially the music of cities.

This chapter further extends Ponce's work by examining Hagedorn's authorial voice as one not predicated on ideas of cultural authenticity or musical origins but as one that underscores the collaborative production and generative reception of U.S. popular music within and beyond national borders. This approach highlights Hagedorn's authorial voice as one that emphasizes the translocal nature, the "routes versus roots," of U.S. popular music. Ponce's work "explores how Hagedorn's poetics enact what she describes as 'the more positive side of appropriation: you take from many different sources, not to steal, but to pay homage to it, to say these are your influences, to add your own thing.'"[5] In that spirit, this chapter focuses on Hagedorn's poetics as she flips the beat, studying and adopting from others but always adding her "own thing" in poetry and performance.

An artistic form that brings together the musical and literary, poetry, in its written and spoken forms, is another site where we can locate the politics of voice in Filipino America. As Amanda Weidman has defined it, "politics of voice" includes not just "a set of vocal practices" but also a range of ideas "*about* the voice and its significance."[6] Throughout this chapter, equal attention is paid to Jessica Hagedorn's poetic voice, on the page and on the stage. For, as Lesley Wheeler broadly describes, the "voice" signifies the "originality, personality, and the illusion of authorial presence."[7] A focus on Hagedorn's often-overlooked poetic and musical performances—ones developed from and bearing the traces of her artistic collaborations with other writers, musicians, and performers—is important insofar as it unsettles notions of the authorial voice as singular. At the same time, it requires that we keep in mind the impact of changing notions of authenticity—ones based on race, ethnicity, and gender—on the reception of her work.

I begin my study with Hagedorn's "poet's band," the Gangster Choir, a musical group that came alive in two U.S. cities during two distinct historical periods: the Third World literary arts movement of 1970s San Francisco/Bay Area and the early 1980s New York downtown arts scene. The band's evolution followed Hagedorn's own pattern of artistic migration from the West Coast to the East Coast. In each period, the Gangster Choir featured a rotating roster of jazz musicians, such as Julian Priester and Butch Morris; rock and roll vocalists and guitarists, such as Linda Tillery and Vernon Reid; and performance artists, such as Laurie Carlos and Robbie McCauley. While all of these artists went on to become prominent figures in their respective fields, the Gangster Choir's work has been largely overlooked, mainly because of the difficulty of accessing audio and video recordings of their songs and performances. They never recorded an album or received a recording contract. The two demos they did record, in 1975 and 1985 respectively, are now only available to those who visit Hagedorn's archive at UC Berkeley's Bancroft Library. Besides cassette and VHS tapes, most of these performances are found on archaic recording/playback forms.

Yet Hagedorn has written extensively about her band and its history in a few short memoir pieces and interviews. In these pieces, Ponce points out, "Hagedorn not only memorializes the Gangster Choir but also inventories her eclectic musical and poetic influences, including R&B and 1970s funk, early spoken word and Black Arts poetry, French symbolism and surrealism, Filipino kundimans, and a range of African American musicians, from Curtis Mayfield to Martha and the Vandellas."[8] As he further elaborates:

She describes her band The Gangster Choir in terms that further proliferate genres, while evoking its boundary-crossing ambitions: "Pop music, rock music, funkadelic, punkadelic, psychedelic, jazz fusion, acid house, gangsta rap, Bali-ghali, bhangra-jangra, hip-swaying, knee-bending, nitty-gritty, soul music—call it what you will. The Gangster Choir defied categories. The band's surreal name embraced contradiction and ambiguity, a bit of glorification and romantic identification with the rebel/outlaw/outsider." Its half-ironic tone notwithstanding, Hagedorn's description suggests that the type of music she was drawn to, and certainly draws upon, imply a project aimed toward excavating dissident, "outsider" expressive traditions that dwell within the cultures of the former colonizers. These musical practices figure the defiance—the rejection and transgression— of dominant cultural forms organized around nation and race, and Hagedorn seems keen on searching out the underside of the colonizing cultures, those resistant expressive practices that have been marginalized (or appropriated) in the name of national culture.[9]

As referenced in these various manifestations of her authorial voice— her poetry, fiction, and performance writing; personal interviews; and even her own personal record collection—over the years, Hagedorn has been drawn to various "dissident, 'outsider' expressive traditions." According to Ponce, these "marginalized" (or sometimes "appropriated in the name of national culture") popular forms hear the "underside of the colonizing cultures" while they also disobey the rules and norms of "dominant" musical forms.[10] But, armed with a translocal approach to U.S. popular music, I want to fine-tune our understanding that these popular musical forms—jazz, R&B, and rock—do not just dwell underneath U.S. culture. They actually constitute its heart and soul.

In fact, one might say, defiance and disobedience are often intrinsic to those in political and cultural power, as well. As Bay Area poet Nashira Priester reminds us when introducing the Gangster Choir's first performance in 1975: "'Hm,' I know you are all saying. 'Gangsters.' Let it be known that we understand the word 'gangster' in a positive way . . . We understand gangsters as the underdogs . . . and with the irony of the blues. You know, gangsters are everywhere. Nixon's a gangster. And Hoover, and Agnew, and the United States military, and the FBI, and the CIA. Gangsterism is the order of the day."[11] While gangsterism calls up "dissident" and "outsider" figures, ones antithetical to a certain national and political order, it also often characterizes the governmental "order of the day."

Before continuing, I first need to underscore that a study of the Gangster Choir requires a phonographic approach to understand not just its musical sound but also its look. For it was the group's performance as a whole, its eclectic mix of musical genres, its blend of the sonic and literary, and its multiracial lineup of band members that was the basis for audiences' interest as well as its lack of industry success. By drawing from the various forms of performance documentation—archival recordings, memoir, and oral history/personal interviews—that Hagedorn herself provides, I again do not aim to further promote a notion of her voice as solitary. Instead, I use my proximity to these diverse sources, always aware that I can never be closer to these past events or performances. I wield this intertextual method as a salient reminder of the relationship between memory and mediation as well as the fact that Hagedorn's liveness itself, in rendering these past events, is always already mediated. This evidences my earlier claim, in this book's introduction, that tropical renditions direct us toward the burden of liveness for racialized performances. This chapter follows a chronological time line, not to argue a developmental narrative (from live performance to the written word) or additive approach when it comes to genre, but merely to organize a complex artistic career and its migrations, an artistic itinerary that has always already been collaborative and interdisciplinary.

1970s San Francisco/Bay Area and Third World Poetics

In post–World War II San Francisco, art and politics had crystallized into various popular forms. As Stephen Vincent, editor of the independent Momo's Press, recalls, "the division between sacred and populist" within poetry circles was reflected in "how and where poetry was performed" and, in turn, infused the figure of the poet and the event of performing poetry with new meaning.[12] Events, such as the 1963 "Freeway" reading at the Old Longshoremen's Hall in San Francisco's Tenderloin, marked a particular era of West Coast poetry, when writers occupied "both the City and the country" and, according to Vincent, when readings "put the poet back in the position of responding to the City in an *actual* way, letting the poetry move as the City does, responsive to the edges, to the corners, to the voices that flood our City lives." Dubbed by San Francisco Renaissance poet Kenneth Rexroth as "Beats" at a 1955 North Beach gallery reading, a cadre of young writers, including Jack Kerouac, Lawrence Ferlinghetti, Allen Ginsberg, Diane di Prima, and others, became the canonized poets of their time. With their jazz-inflected, Buddhist-inspired, Benzedrine-driven writings, they heralded the city by the Bay as an artistic mecca.

By 1968's "summer of love," a new breed of American youth known as hippies tuned in, turned on, dropped out, and christened the now famous corner of Haight-Ashbury as the psychedelic center, a paraphernalia-filled haven where drug trips—momentary breaks from this reality to explore others—fueled personal transformations. During this time, according to Vincent: "The lone poet as performer and evangelist of personal, social, and political change had been replaced by the rock star and the group. Country Joe and the Fish, the Jefferson Airplane, and the Grateful Dead—let alone Bob Dylan—had clearly taken their impetus from the poets. But more than the loss of an audience to music or to the technologies of sounds and rhythms, the new emphasis was on experiences that were essentially nonverbal."[13]

With a musical style that journalists and record companies labeled the "San Francisco sound," these bands and their audiences shifted countercultural attention away from poetic experimentation toward sensory-heavy communalism. Although more commonly associated with the Haight-Ashbury bands, musical groups from the Mission District—such as Santana and Dakila—also championed this rock style. Heavily influenced by jazz and Latin-based rhythms, these bands emphasized improvisation and freewheeling instrumental solos as a musical antidote to the standard three-minute radio pop ditty.

By the 1970s, however, explosive events that shadowed student strikes for ethnic studies, the Free Speech Movement on campuses, militant nationalist groups' revolutionary politics, and antiwar demonstrations drew attention back to the importance of language, whether in upholding the status quo or in exacting social and cultural change. In an era of FBI covert intelligence operations and Washington scandals such as Watergate, semantics—words and their meanings—played a crucial role in envisioning a political path and future. While a number of self-named "Third World" writers labored to publish their work, such as the landmark *Time to Greez! Incantations from the Third World*, it was mainly through the event of the poetry reading—as with the political rally—that minority artists expressed a sense of urgency and need for unmediated presence through live proclamations and performance.

This new generation of writers—Al Robles, Janice Mirikitani, Ishmael Reed, Kitty Tsui, Thulani Davis, Ntozake Shange, Victor Hernandez Cruz, and many others—carried a new set of poetics and performance styles: bilingual and bicultural poems, declarative or sing-song syncopated delivery, the look and fashion of a new urban bohemia inspired by the sounds of popular and avant-garde musical artists (from Archie Shepp to Sun Ra, John Coltrane to Stevie Wonder) as well as leading political figures such as Angela Davis, Stokely Carmichael, the Black Panthers, and the Young Lords. As writer and critic Thulani Davis remembers, "Poets made conscious efforts to reach people who listened to music more often than they read books," their "sounds, tones, cries, songs even noises" invoking "recent and distant people and events."[14] Along with a concern for the sonic elements of poetry's performance, these Third World poets also paid attention to the fact that "good looks, a certain coolness, and a lot of theater had shaped the appeal of black and brown social movements and their leaders all over the country."[15] In its interanimation of the sonic, literary, visual, and performative, their work both conjures and necessitates a phonographic approach. This Third World literary renaissance took shape not only in San Francisco but in other urban arts centers as well—New York, Los Angeles, and Chicago. This Third World literary renaissance, like its political counterparts, drew from the political struggles and events taking place across Asia, Africa, and Latin America. In Third World literary and political movements there lay the potential for translocal connections. Immigrating to San Francisco in 1961, from a country designated as part of the Third World, a teenage Jessica Tarahata Hagedorn developed her writerly voice amid the politically charged climate of her new home.

Growing up in Manila and in the decade following the 1945 declaration of Philippine independence at the end of World War II, Hagedorn's childhood consisted of "reading the literature of the Western World—Hawthorne, Poe, Cervantes" as well as the expectations of "study(ing) and deconstruct(ing) in loving detail" the Bible's Old and New Testaments and of aping a "mythologized Hollywood universe" that flickered across Manila's movie screens.[16] As she recounts in her introduction to the 1993 collection *Charlie Chan Is Dead: An Anthology of Asian American Literature*, in her grade school classrooms, in both Manila and San Francisco, Hagedorn encountered the same canon of writers. "In my American high school classes, I was again reading Hawthorne, Poe, Melville, Dostoevsky, Dickens, the occasional Emily Dickinson or Bronte sisters." But in neither educational setting did she ever learn about the plight of earlier Asian immigrants such as the *manongs*, Filipino agricultural laborers who largely immigrated in the 1920s and 1930s, were exploited as cheap labor, and "welcomed" to cities along the Western seaboard with race mobs, de jure and de facto segregation, antimiscegenation laws, and signs in public establishments that read: "Positively No Filipinos Allowed." Moving to San Francisco, a city with its increasingly visible Asian and Asian American communities, Hagedorn remembers, "we had easy access to our culture, whether we wanted it or not." Multicultural San Francisco also comprised Chicanos, African Americans, and "an incredible variety of white people of various ethnic origins," something "new and unfamiliar" to the young Filipina immigrant. As she recalls:

> I graduated from high school in 1967, unable to pinpoint the source of my unease. I had been in America exactly four years. There were sit-ins going on downtown on Van Ness Avenue. A strike at San Francisco State University a few blocks from my high school. John F. Kennedy and Malcolm X had been assassinated. The Black Panther Party was born. How did I fit in? Chicanos, African Americans, and even militant Asian Americans were forming alliances. Could Asian Americans, in fact, be "militant"? Were we really a part of the Third World? *The Third World*. Not exactly a term my family would take pride in. Back where I came from, "Third World" lacked glamour. It was synonymous with phones that didn't work, roads that were badly in need of repair, corrupt politicians, and naked children with rickety bones and bellies bloated from hunger. Who was I? [17]

Growing up in late 1960s and early 1970s San Francisco, Hagedorn narrates her "unease," as both an immigrant and a teenager, searching for a sense of identity and affiliation within an ever-changing and volatile social and political landscape. Like many of her contemporaries, Hagedorn grapples with the limited yet popular representation of Asian Americans as model minorities and the political possibility of their militancy. As someone newly immigrated to the United States, in this excerpt, she also questions the force of political terms such as Third World. Emerging from the student-led movements for ethnic studies at San Francisco State University (SFSU) and UC Berkeley, the term *Third World* signified activists' solidarity and affiliation with independence struggles in Africa, Asia, and Latin America. By taking on the designation of Third World, in a similar fashion to the gay and lesbian movement's later claiming of the term *queer*, artists and activists of Asian American, African American, and Latino descent took pride in their oppositional stance to First World culture. Though many were born and raised in the United States, they framed their experiences and struggles as paralleling those of nations designated as Third World, drawing attention to examples of the "Third World in the First World"—"internal colonies" such as ghettos and ethnic enclaves, socioeconomic inequalities, and the U.S. educational system's propagation of Western hegemonic ideals.[18]

By claiming the term *Third World*, these artists and activists did not just acknowledge shared experiences across racial lines. They also organized events, gathered resources, and provided opportunities based on a politics of self-determination. Within San Francisco's literary scene, in the 1970s groups such as Third World Communications and Yardbird Publications worked to promote and foster young and emerging writers of color, as well as those forgotten or previously overlooked, by publishing, organizing readings and performances, and critically evaluating or reviewing their work. Anthologies and collections such as *Time to Greez!*, *The Yardbird Reader*, and *Third World Women* remain, to this day, a testament to the energies of and labor enacted under the banner of San Francisco's Third World literary movement.[19]

Third World worked to signify rebellion from older generations. Noting that it was "not exactly a term [a] family would take pride in," Hagedorn reminds us of the unromantic aspects of Third World life and calls our attention to the diverse positions and experiences of those active within the Third World literary movement.[20] Looking back on anthologies such as *Time to Greez!* and *Third World Women*, it is easy to see how a particular poetics of cultural essentialism was at play in the era's literary circles. As canonical Asian American writer Frank Chin has argued, for example, the metaphor of food often stood in for a "sensual" claim to cultural authenticity. Within these same pages, romantic notions of the "homeland" or "motherland," ones that many U.S.-based cultural nationalists had never visited, prevailed. While these anthologies did the important work of gathering otherwise underrepresented or overlooked writers, they simultaneously propagated certain ideas of what constituted a "Third World literary aesthetic."[21]

First appearing in the 1972 anthology *Third World Women*, Hagedorn's poem "Smokey's Getting Old" was later republished in two other anthologies—*Danger and Beauty*, featuring Hagedorn's writing from the 1970s to the early 2000s, and *Rock She Wrote*, a collection of women's writing focused on rock and roll. The poem opens with an interpellation of sisterhood, seduction, and street-savvy and a question commonly asked of the forever-foreign Asian American—"Hey girl/How long you been here?" But, written in the second person, the narrator provides answers to the questions she asks. What follows, in the poem, signals the narrator's familiarity with the girl's (or "Nellie's," as appeared in earlier versions) experiences. Through a set of questions, Hagedorn's poem assumes and therefore writes from the girl's/Nellie's point of view.

This becomes more evident in Hagedorn's performance of the poem with the Gangster Choir in 1975. Various geographical locations populate the poem: Manila's Quiapo market, central California's Stockton, San Francisco's Mission district, and America's Chinatown. Their naming links an actual place in the Third World with ethnic enclaves more familiar to U.S.-based audiences. "Hey Nellie . . . you remember the barrios and how it's all the same: Manila, the Mission, Chinatown, Harlem, L.A., Kearny Street, the Fillmore."[22] The Third Worldism of internal colonies is made literal through litany.

"Smokey's Getting Old" also works through juxtaposition. It recalls life "back there" (in Manila) through the sensuous memories of girls "who wore their hair loose," "yr grandma chewin' red tobacco," and the smell and taste of "roast pig." Through memories of living in Stockton and having to "talk to old farmers who emigrated in 1941," it renders Nellie's life in the United States a common experience for young Filipinas who married older *manongs*, ones who survived early twentieth-century immigration quotas and antimiscegenation laws. It figures Nellie as similar to other teenage girls living in the Bay Area in the late 1960s through the Narrator's line of questioning: "and did you run away to san francisco / go to poly high / rat your hair / hang around woolworth's / chinatown at three in the morning go to the cow palace and catch SMOKEY ROBINSON cry and scream at his gold jacket **Dance** every friday night in the mission / go steady with ruben? (yr daddy can't stand it cuz he's a spik)."[23]

While rendering common tropes of female teenage rebellion—sneaking out just to stand around, late-night jaunts to "seedy" parts of town, catching your favorite crooner in concert, dating a boy your father would never approve—the poem also evokes a longing for times that have passed. Against the memories of "the sailors you dreamed of in manila with yellow hair" and recollections of when "you and carmen harmonize 'be my baby' by the ronettes," the poem's Narrator paints Nellie in the present day, as a young mother who is "gettin kinda fat" while "smokey robinson's gettin' old."

During its first public appearance in 1975, the Gangster Choir begins its performance of "Smokey's Getting Old" with the Gangsterette vocal trio's a capella treatment of the 1965 Smokey Robinson and the Miracles' hit, "Oooh, Baby Baby." After singing a verse and a chorus, the vocal trio reverts to a doo-wop style of harmonizing that fades into the background and sets the tone for Hagedorn's reading of her original poem. Critically listening to the group's staging of the poem, we can begin to imagine a young female poet's practice of writing while also listening to music on the radio. We will return to these types of scenes later in this chapter. But, for now, we turn back to the beginnings of Hagedorn as a poet and her poet's band The West Coast Gangster Choir.

A few years after Hagedorn's 1961 arrival in San Francisco, a family friend passed along the teenager's poems to Kenneth Rexroth. Impressed by her writing, the Bay Area poet and SFSU creative writing professor arranged to meet the aspiring writer and offered to publish her first poems. In time, Rexroth began to serve as a mentor to the young Hagedorn. As she later remembers: "His flat on Scott Street is the ultimate boho heaven for me. Poetry is respected. Writing is life. I am awed by his library of ten thousand books in all sorts of languages; a kitchen stocked with Japanese goodies. Cubist paintings on the walls; and a living room where you might chance upon James Baldwin, Gary Snyder, or Amiri Baraka (then known as LeRoi Jones)—in town for a hot minute. I am grateful even then for my esoteric and streetwise literary education."[24] For this young poet, Rexroth modeled the ordinariness of writerly life. That is to say, in the everyday place of his apartment living room, Hagedorn witnessed the home library and the gathering of writers as a "life."

Granted, it was not the average struggling writer's life. A major figure in the San Francisco Renaissance and the man often designated as the "Father of the Beats," by the time he began to mentor Hagedorn, Kenneth Rexroth was already a well-regarded poet, essayist, and teacher. Nonetheless, he still chaperoned both Hagedorn and his own teenage daughter on nighttime trips to City Lights Bookstore and local poetry readings.

Coming of age in 1960s San Francisco, live rock concerts also constituted Hagedorn's "esoteric and streetwise" curriculum. Growing up in San Francisco's Lower Haight district, the young writer lived close to venues such as the Fillmore Auditorium and Great American Music Hall. During her high school years, she checked out shows by the day's legendary artists, from rock gods—Hendrix, Led Zeppelin, Pink Floyd, Janis Joplin—to R&B and soul's finest—Muddy Waters, Bo Diddley, Big Mama Thornton, Aretha Franklin, Ray Charles—to rock divas, such as Betty Davis, often neglected by traditional popular music historiographies.[25] Carefully studying each artist's staging and showmanship, Hagedorn would later incorporate her understanding of these elements into her poetry and, later, performances.

By the early 1970s, she had found artistic kinship with contemporaries who brought music and words together in their respective styles of tropicalizations, choreo-poems, and rock 'n' roll poetry.[26] Nuyorican poet Victor Hernandez Cruz, Hagedorn remembers, "could read . . . as if he were the notes of a conga drum." African American playwright Ntozake Shange, in "a particular time in (her) growth as an artist . . . open to trial and errors," began working with musicians and dancers.[27] Hagedorn's particular style of poetry—its rhythm, use of song lyrics, and evocation of musical figures and places—gestured to rock 'n' roll as U.S. cultural export. As the publisher's note on the inside front cover of Hagedorn's first edited collection, *Dangerous Music*, observed, "Her childhood in the Philippines and addiction to rock 'n' roll and black soul music made for the tense lyric beauty in poems about her ambiguous arrival and coming of age in America." But Hagedorn's rock 'n' roll poetry style also cued readers and listeners into the fact that the musical genre's cultural history and presence was indebted to the cultural history and cultural presence of African Americans. Filled with scenes of concert-going and radio listening in cities like Manila, San Francisco, and New York, these early poems, today, serve as a soundtrack for the "counter-assimilationist immigrant narrative" in her work and acknowl-

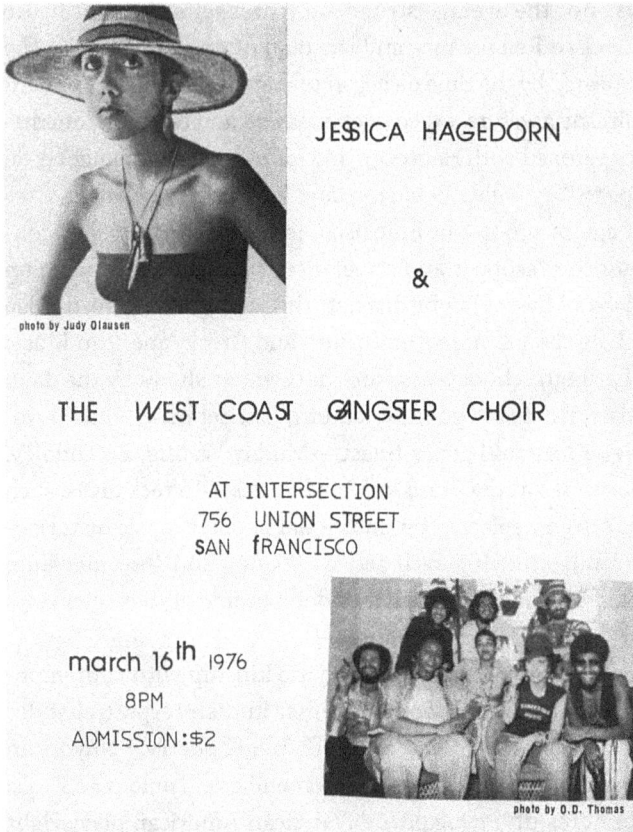

Figure 3.1 "Jessica Hagedorn & the West Coast Gangster Choir" flyer, Intersection for the Arts. BANC PIC 2007/78. Courtesy of the Bancroft Library, University of California, Berkeley.

edges U.S. pop culture and music's influence as beginning in the Philippines.[28] Yet, as elucidated by critic Kathy Mackay's opening statement to her 1976 review of a Gangster Choir performance—"Would you believe Smokey Robinson as the inspiration behind a poem about a teen-aged Filipina?"—to hear such musical traces, one must listen against discourses born from the oft-forgotten historical relationship between the United States and the Philippines.[29]

Both steeped in her makeshift, do-it-yourself, literary and musical education and formally enrolled in the American Conservatory Theatre's (ACT) two-year acting program, Hagedorn began experimenting with poetry performances. At first it was nothing elaborate, she recalls: "it would just be me reciting my poetry and, let's say, a saxophone player or a guitar player . . . or rhythm players, percussionists and such."[30] As time went on, the young poet aimed to move away from more predominant forms of spoken word performance, epitomized in the rhythm-based declarations of performers such as Nikki Giovanni and the Last Poets. Inspired by Sun Ra's staged spectacles and her own collaborations with the Art Ensemble of Chicago, Hagedorn began to imagine "something weird and ambitious," a performance style that might effectively synthesize poetry, music, and theater. As she described in a 1977 autobiographical piece:

> The concept of the Gangster Choir—shades of the old 'Doo-Wop' school, Smokey Robinson, the Flamingoes, some Hector Lavoe chanting, always the tropics lurking in the background, the way we sing, the way we put it out there, the message in the music. The poetics of our lives, this is what I am interested in. It's already been monumentalized in what critics snidely refer to as "pop" music—but very little has been said about poets doing it for themselves. There were those beatniks talking about urban madonnas, but that was an elite and very white cult of people.[31]

Here, Hagedorn's version of rock 'n' roll poetry invokes the everyday translocality of Third World poetics and its link to U.S. popular music. In turn, as she delineates, this version of rock 'n' roll poetry must be distinguished from those of "an elite and very white cult of people." In San Francisco, this would refer to beatniks. In downtown New York, as we shall see in the next section, this took the shape of a white avant-garde and its rock 'n' roll poetic godheads.

In the latter half of 1974, Hagedorn "started putting out feelers" to her amateur and professional musician friends and, over the next few months, gathered an impressive posse. Later conducted by jazz trombonist Julian Priester (formerly of Herbie Hancock's band), the band's personnel during that first 1975 performance included Makoto Horuichi (guitar), Heshima Mark Williams (bass guitar), Duke Santos (congas/percussion), and Augusta Collins (drums).[32] As the West Coast Gangster Choir's vocal trio, the Gangsterettes featured R&B singer Ota Pierce, poet and former KPFA reporter Norman Jayo, and Linda Tillery, former lead vocalist of Bay Area rock/soul jam band the Loading Zone. The process of composing music was mainly a two-way collaboration between Hagedorn and Priester, one that relied on artistic shorthand crafted between a determined poet's musical ear and a composer-musician's ability to interpret the lyrics' necessary "moods."[33] The eclectic band secretly rehearsed in Hagedorn's apartment garage with the goal of recording a demo tape, landing a record deal, and eventually producing a "concept album."[34]

Thanks to the foresight of Poetry Center organizers, that very first Gangster Choir performance in 1975 was captured on VHS and cassette tape. Some of the evening's a capella pieces consisted solely of voices—Hagedorn's lilting intonation in concert with the Gangsterettes' three-part harmonies. Others involved more intricate choral and instrumental arrangements—with the poets' song-speech-acts riding on top of the musicians' funky bass lines, Afro-Caribbean beats, and vamping piano chords, while the trio's polyvocal chorus echoed some of the poem's most striking words and images. Drawn mainly from poems in Hagedorn's first collection, the songs followed two main thematic trajectories—vivid portraits of her former home, the postcolonial city of Manila, and her keen observations on life in her new home, America. In her poetic imagery—one that invokes a particular Third World political and artistic aesthetic—it is a thin line between the past and the present, between "over there" and "right here."

These tensions and commonalities between life in the Philippines ("over there") and life in San Francisco, California ("right here"), are best captured in a call-and-response duet between Tillery and Hagedorn, with acoustic guitar accompaniment. The song begins and ends with Tillery singing "Profits Enslave the World," a poem originally penned by agricultural labor activist Philip Vera Cruz and set to music by Filipino student activist Chris Bautista in 1973.

Sandwiched between the sung choruses, Hagedorn performs her "Song for My Father." The tone of Vera Cruz's poem is polemic compared to Hagedorn's melancholic musings, yet both pieces highlight the ironies of immigrant life in the United States—where "beautiful bright pictures painted / were just half of the story / reflections of great wealth and power / in the land of slavery"—and of her return home to a country now living under martial rule. In each poem, with a certain geographic and temporal distance come stark realizations, forms of per-

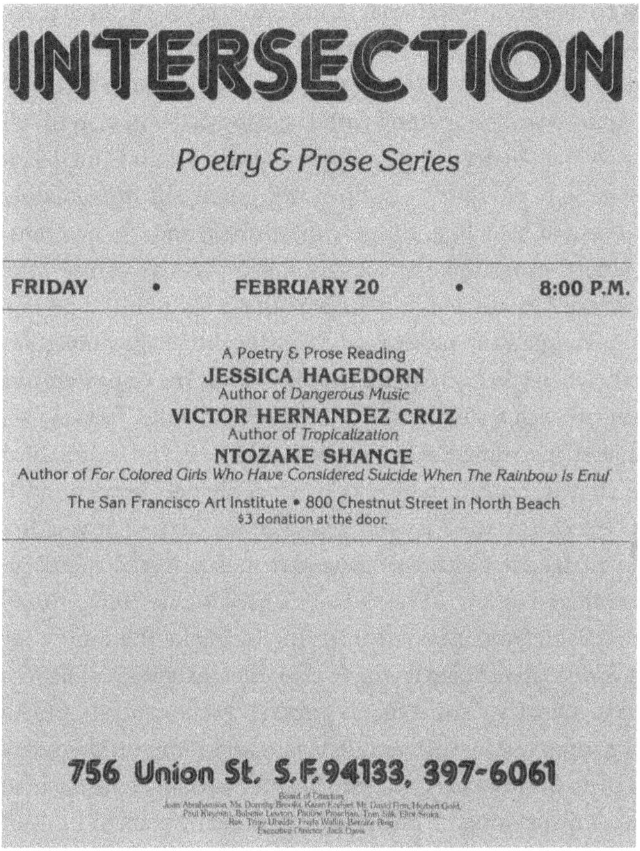

Figure 3.2. "Poetry & Prose Series" flyer, Intersection for the Arts. BANC MSS 2007/160. Courtesy of the Bancroft Library, University of California, Berkeley.

spective that animate each writer's refusal to romanticize life on either side of the Pacific Ocean. Following more traditional forms of poetry performance, whereby a song is sung to complement a spoken word performance, the guitar accompaniment thematically unites the performance's three components: melody, rhythm, and spoken/sung words. For those more familiar with Vera Cruz's work, the two poems/songs constitute a type of intergenerational conversation. For others, Tillery's performance of "Profits . . ." incorporates Hagedorn's own composition so that her poem functions as a more intimate backstory to his poem's own visibly political narrative.

In contrast to this more traditional spoken word style, the final piece ("Trying to Pull a Fast One") of the Gangster Choir's inaugural 1975 performance signals the group's future artistic direction—more of a synthesis of music and words. Opening with Hagedorn's dedication to "all the poets" as well as "everyone who likes to sleaze around the discotheques," the song begins with a simple rock guitar riff immediately followed by layers of bass line, congas, and drums, and, finally, tambourine. Hagedorn proclaims the song's spoken parts as verses: "the search for heritage / grows and grows / but what's the point? / no one really knows nostalgia's the latest rage / for the glitter age knives are more personal / when you try to pull a fast one" while the Gangsterettes respond in unison with a simple chorus—"trying to pull a fast one"—against the layered instrumental tracks. Near the end of the song's third cycle of verse-chorus, Hagedorn offers a reminder to her listeners, both the poets and the con artists: "it's not what you say / it's what you do." Like the double-edged definition of gangsterism that Nashira Priester invokes in her introduction, "Trying to Pull a Fast One" refers to all forms of con artists: from sleazy men trying to "make the moves" at discotheques to deceptive poets trying to trick their listeners/audiences through their semantics ("some man's tricks"). For a majority of the twelve-minute song, the instrumentalists jam and vamp on the notes of the song's melody while both Hagedorn and the Gangsterettes take turns singing and speaking, in the round, previously spoken lines of poetry. But first, and at the very top of the song's outro, Tillery offers an invitation: "We want to ask if the people in the audience would like to get up and dance with us to this music . . . You can get up and it's okay, nobody will say anything . . . you won't get put in jail like Sam and it'll be alright. So come on . . . don't be shy. . . ."[35] Slowly but surely, a few brave souls get up and dance right in front of the band, in turn closing the gap between audience and performers and leading Hagedorn to exclaim happily, "This is like disco-poetry!"

Over the next four years, the Gangster Choir continued performing at poetry festivals and readings, community colleges, theater/performance venues, even North Beach's Keystone Bar. They eventually recorded a demo that industry insiders considered a "hard sell."[36] In 1978, Hagedorn made the cross-country move to New York City along with her "satin sisters," Ntozake Shange and Thulani Davis. With her departure, this version of the group disbanded.

1980s Downtown New York: "A Full Cacophonous Chorus"

Hagedorn's decision to finally make the big move to New York took place after her collaboration with Shange and Davis on the 1977 Public Theater production of *Where the Mississippi Meets the Amazon*. While their style of performing poetry—"poems (set) to music"—remained the same, Hagedorn's writerly and poetic voice had changed. As she recalls in her introduction to the second edition of her collection, *Danger and Beauty*: "I continue writing, well aware that my voice has hardened, become more dissonant and fierce."[37] During these transitional years, Hagedorn also wrote and performed her first one-woman show *Mango Tango* (1978) at the Public Theater. By 1980, she took a break from performing. She began working retail to make ends meet while also writing a novella and book of poetry (which would later become *Pet Food and Other Tropical Apparitions*). It was during this time that William Brown, the last guitarist to play with the West Coast version of the Gangster Choir, moved to New York and, after "constant nudging and badgering," was able to convince Hagedorn to restart the band. Offering to organize the first gig himself, Brown convinced Hagedorn to start simply with "a small thing" of a trio. She replied: "'Oh, a trio . . . well that's new. Keep it really simple' and 'Whoa, maybe I'll write something new. Some new stuff.'"[38] Calling in her friend Eric Turner to play bass, Hagedorn recalls: "It was very avant-garde. Just guitar, bass, and me. Electric guitar. Electric bass. That was really interesting . . . AND it was sort of weirdly successful because it was so weird. The audience was just . . . like I painted my face silver. People were saying I should get gigs down at CBGB's, you know, it was like . . . perfect!"[39]

Having played with another artist the week before, Brown was able to book the trio a gig at the legendary Folk City in Greenwich Village. While the venue was best known for launching Bob Dylan's career, by the early 1980s, bookers opened their doors to unknown bands with the emerging sounds of punk and new wave music. Encountering audiences who were receptive to musical forms other than rock or folk, "the joy of performing" returned for Hagedorn. She began to expand the East Coast edition of the Gangster Choir to include vocalists, percussionists, and other instrumentalists.

The 1980s Downtown New York scene featured an array of artists willing to work across forms and disciplines. Poets collaborated with video and theater artists. Rock musicians brought theatrical aspects to the concert stage. Painters worked hand in hand with graffiti artists and broke down the divide between public and private art spaces. Crossing and blurring the formalistic and disciplinary boundaries of art making, many Downtown New York artists in the 1980s, as historian and archivist Marvin J. Taylor describes, "sought to undermine from within the traditional structures of artistic media and the culture that had grown up around them."[40] Growing up in the age of television, the aftermath of various wars (both "hot" and "cold"), amid various civil rights movements, and now living under the aegis of actor-turned-U.S.-president Ronald Reagan, though the scene itself was diverse and divided, Downtown artists' overarching feeling toward and approaches to the notion of authenticity were ones of disdain, ambivalence, and distrust. They understood themselves as "inhabiting a full-blown society of the spectacle," cultural critic and curator Carlo McCormick argues, where "what was at stake was less a question of reality than the conundrum of how creativity could fabricate something of the 'self' out of, or against, the metonymy of mediation and co-option."[41] With the continuing rise of postmodernism, and in "the age of appropriation without quotation marks, trademarks, or licensing fees," artists questioned previous notions of authorship. Within Downtown discourse, authorship was (more often than not) a collaborative thing or, at the very least, the process of authorship borrowed from familiar documents, artistic and cultural objects, and representations in order to make something new. Here, we can think of hip-hop's form of the remix—taking samples from previously recorded songs and altering them into a new text/narrative—as exemplifying a certain Downtown-centered aesthetic.

Downtown's vernacular consisted of "ironic inversions, proliferate amusements, criminal interventions, material surrogates, improvised impersonations, and immersive experientiality." "Everywhere" in Downtown New York, McCormick writes, "was the authentic fake, the genuine reproduction, and, most pertinently, the regurgitation of our national *pabulum* as an inorganic sugarcoated foodstuff and phosphorescent content-whiz that might take no more from consensus reality than the most absurd terms we could all collectively laugh at."[42] Here, we can think of performance art's use of historical and popular representations (TV shows, minstrel shows, anthropological field studies), as we shall hear later in this chapter when discussing Hagedorn's performance collaborations with Thought Music and their show *Teenytown*'s use of minstrel/late-night talk show forms/formats to comment on certain social and political issues and histories.

Despite the difficulties of defining a Downtown style or aesthetic, what appeared most at stake in its discourse was an oppositional stance against artistic ideas of authenticity, ones steeped in the institutional and hierarchical values of meritocracy and singular authorship. It was less about representing authenticity as that which could be reliable, trustworthy, or fact-checked and more about reframing the falsehoods, ironies, and performances of such authenticity. Thus, though punk rock thrived on certain notions of authenticity, they were not the same as those touted by previous rock traditions and musicians, for example, 1960s and 1970s classic rock, whereby rock authenticity was performed and measured by virtuosic guitar solos. Instead, punk (as well as art rock) authenticity thrived on and propagated notions of minimalism and, sometimes, the amateur. In turn, unlike folk rock, the authentic sounds of punk and new wave depended as much on guitar feedback, electronic sounds, and DJ/producers as they did on the growl of a lead singer's voice or live drumbeats. "A discourse on the nullification of absolutes," 1980s Downtown New York required a "full cacophonous chorus to be heard."[43]

Needless to say, these popular notions of authenticity and authorship resonated and operated differently for nonwhite Downtown artists. Their work was often also informed by and in response to the burden of representation (and authenticating desires) placed on racialized, gendered, and sexualized artists. As a mixed-race African American female artist, Adrian Piper also addressed, while working against, the various ambivalences and demands she encountered as one whose body (and work) could not be read as visibly black (1979–present).[44] Such reading practices, of course, are nothing new and arise out of a longer history of intercultural performance, as underscored by Coco Fusco and Guillermo Gomez-Peña's performance piece "Couple in a Cage" (1992–93). Their endurance performance draws its legibility from, while commenting on, a long-standing Western anthropological discourse of the primitive and racialized Other. The work and public persona of Jean-Michel Basquiat was often required to serve the art world's authenticating desire for low/street art. His work (1979–88) was often framed within a discourse of "primitivist" (read black) art-making practices. In his work and interviews, however, Basquiat not only called out such racialized desires and demands,[45] he also worked within and against the grain of gallery owners, art critics, and fellow artists' presumptions, creating within a mode of disidentificatory practice.[46] Yet, while Basquiat and later performer Grace Jones dis-identified, by working within and against these discourses, their collaborations with more famous white artists such as Andy Warhol and Keith Haring, respectively, underscore the tense and racialized relationships between authorship and collaboration, most especially within Downtown New York's discourse and history.[47]

Against this cultural landscape of artistic values and politics, Hagedorn slowly got back into the process of re-forming a band. Reunited with another West Coast Gangster Choir member, percussionist Bugsy Moore, who took root in New York City after a trip to Africa, Hagedorn began again to take the prospects of a band seriously. "The aim was always to get an album."[48] Thus, the newly christened Gangster Choir set their eyes on booking gigs at venues that "made sense" with this end goal in mind. The band began playing at all the major downtown venues—the Mudd Club, Armageddon (now the Jane Street Hotel), 55 Grand, and, of course, the now-canonical CBGB's—not only to garner subcultural capital but also in hopes of being seen. Understanding the difficulties of standing out and breaking into New York's music scene ("There's like 5,000 bands"), Hagedorn assessed the city's audiences, against her former home of San Francisco, as "tougher." She then realized: "You need to toughen it up and get more musical and . . . muscular. Sharpen our visions."[49]

The vibe of each venue was very much set by seemingly innocuous elements such as band schedule and notoriety. As Hagedorn recalls, at CBGB gigs, all the band members were nervous because "You don't want to fail there. Not only that . . . there were other bands on the bill and they're waiting, they're listening to you. So you want to be as good as, or the best of the four, all that stuff." Having to play two sets in one evening, each band not only needed to keep the attention of ever-changing, always-intoxicated audience members (including other bands' musicians) but also needed to reel in its own band's members, when necessary.

At first, Hagedorn would attempt to book the gigs at noteworthy music venues, such as CBGB's. Yet, after awhile, she relegated the duty to the lead male musicians in the band, finding that club bookers and promoters were more likely to respond favorably to Reid or Morris. This type of selective willingness speaks to rock culture as a male-dominated sphere as well as to the place of female artists of color in such scenes. Even though she did write all the band's song lyrics, since Hagedorn did not play an instrument, she was often relegated to being seen as merely a female vocalist. Hagedorn's onstage vocal performances, however, did not mesh with dominant tropes or ideas of a "female vocalist" or "female lead singer." Because she did not technically "sing," instead performing a type of syncopated speech, Hagedorn did not fall neatly into a certain category of gendered musical authenticity. Unlike CBGB female darlings such as Deborah Harry or even the Talking Heads' Tina Weymouth, Hagedorn's racial ambiguity (and even illegibility) as a Filipina worked to defy the Downtown musical scene and, later, the recording industry's often binaristic notions of race and racial authenticity.

Like the larger Downtown New York scene, CBGB's was also "a state of mind as much as a place," a venue recognizable as "a methodology, an audience, a membership, and a phenomenology of experience."[50] Though it lasted much longer than other Downtown New York venues and is more widely known in mainstream U.S. popular culture, CBGB's was just one of many places within a larger scene. To think of CBGB's, in particular, and Downtown New York, more broadly, as translocal places is to understand them as "processes, always linked by people to other places."[51] The 1980s Downtown New York space was, for its artists, "outside America; even outside New York City."[52] Facing the rising costs of housing, the plummeting rate of social welfare programs, and the increased police state, the artists of Downtown New York envisioned a kinship with Berlin, another urban landscape and arts scene that favored far-out experimentation in the midst of increased social and class divisions.[53] "Rather than divide Downtown [New York in the 1980s] into a succession of movements," McCormick advises, "it is better seen as an ensemble choreography of motion itself best traced in the rise and fall of an infinite list of alternative spaces, storefront galleries, bars, neighborhoods, street corners, and, most important, nightclubs."[54] As Vernon Reid recalls, 1980s Downtown New York was "very tribal." At the same time, "there was [also] the jazz scene crossing over with rock and roll, crossing over with punk, crossing over with funk."[55] The Gangster Choir embodied such crossings. As a band, the Gangster Choir moved between musical genres as well as the experimental music and performance art scenes. A few other Downtown artists gravitated toward interdisciplinary, cross-genre collaborations, while also working to blur the lines between staged and everyday performance. For many, sexual activity and drug use were other quotidian forms of experimentation.

A haven for both free/improvisatory jazz musicians and drug aficionados, the SoHo after-hours venue 55 Grand functioned as a laboratory or playroom. With an audience that "knew what to expect" from the band's regular appearances, as Hagedorn recalls, 55 Grand, when compared to the showcase format of venues like CBGB's, offered a performance experience more akin to an improvised jazz session or jam. With more time for musical exploration in collaboration with fellow musicians as well as the audience, Hagedorn reminisces:

> I loved that place because the crowd would get rowdy and, you know, they got to know us because there got to be regulars coming for us. So you got to experiment . . . while attempting to entertain the crowd because they were supportive and they were having fun and they also welcomed something different. So yes, they want to hear all the usual stuff, you know. 'Make us dance.' But also, 'Oh, weirdness. Ooh, interesting.' So, you want that electricity and I think that it helps when a crowd is drinking and smoking. There is energy coming back at you.[56]

In places such as 55 Grand and, later, The Kitchen, audience expectations as well as the demands for artistic and racial authenticity differed greatly from CBGB's. As experimental arts venues, each one operated with and put forth "a methodology, an audience, a membership, and a phenomenology of experience" that focused much more on listening than on just being seen.[57] Initially centered on presenting video artists (while still located in the actual kitchen of the Mercer Arts Center), over the past forty-two years The Kitchen has become a venue for multimedia, multi- and interdisciplinary artists. In each of its locations and permutations, it has presented the earlier work of various and now-famous No Wave bands, electronic, experimental, and jazz composers, as well as musical acts/bands, choreographers, and performance and visual artists continually pushing the boundaries of musical genre and performance technique.

A multifarious group, the Gangster Choir performed at The Kitchen on a number of occasions, most notably, its final show. By 1985, the group had transformed into something of an orchestra—featuring lead guitar, rhythm guitar, electric bass, saxophone, trumpet, percussion, drums, and piano. Though Hagedorn was the undisputed leader of the band, fellow performance artist Laurie Carlos played an equally important role as covocalist (and, often, cocomposer). A poet, writer, and performer in her own right, Carlos gained notoriety in New York's downtown performance scene by cultivating the role of Lady Blue in the inaugural production of Ntozake Shange's *for colored girls who've considered suicide when the rainbow wasn't enuff* (The Public Theater, 1976–78). In a 1993 interview with Nicky Paraiso, she cites Laura Nyro as a musical influence "in terms of what dramatic line is in a lyric and where music's possibilities can go . . . So much of how I've learned to scream inside of a note has to do with having experienced her music."[58] With the Gangster Choir, Carlos (as well as guest musical artist Paraiso) improvised vocal runs and sounds, virtuosic techniques that served as layered counterpoint to Hagedorn's more direct vocal attack. As Reid remembers, "It was kinda like a downtown B-52s . . . you know? Because they would . . . just do these kinds of tunes . . . do these kinds of . . . hooks in unison. . . . and then they'd go and kinda . . . sing a verse . . . then go and do another chorus."[59] In contrast to musical acts such as the B-52s or Talking Heads, however, the Gangster Choir was also heavily involved in the performance art scene. Thus, their shows functioned less as a musical group performing a set of songs and more as a musical ensemble and performance collective creating a theatricalized soundscape of virtuosically played musical notes, everyday sounds and snippets of conversation, and exotic or strange noises.

While Morris and Reid directed the group's instrumentalists, the thrust of the band's songwriting lay in "lots of notebooks" that Hagedorn and Carlos brought to rehearsal "with all kinds of stuff that they had written." By the time Reid joined the group, rehearsals consisted of "either play[ing] previous recordings of the stuff that they had done" or "a lot of rewriting," but, overall, retaining a type of organic feel and approach.[60] Hagedorn depended on her previous experiences in improvised musical and theater performance to develop a sense of rhythm and timing as well as receptive listening. Within the longer oeuvre of Hagedorn's artistic work, this practice unmistakably drew from her collaborative improvisations, as a poet, with experimental jazz musicians such as the Chicago Art Ensemble, and from everyday dialogues with and storytelling among fellow female poets and performers such as Shange, Davis, and later Thought Music.

Figure 3.3 "The Gangster Choir at 55 Grand (1983)." Left to right: Bugsy Moore (as "Black Jesus," percussion), Tony Bridges (back, bass), Jessica Hagedorn (vocals), Laurie Carlos (vocals), Paul Shapiro (saxophone), Julian Priester (guest artist, trombone), Hiroshi Hirada (back, lead guitar), Steve Bernstein (trumpet). Photo courtesy of Renee Montagne.

Figure 3.4 "The Gangster Choir at 55 Grand (1983)." Left to right: Bugsy Moore (percussion), Vernon Reid (lead guitar), Steve Bernstein (trumpet). Photo courtesy of Renee Montagne.

Thus, the multiracial, multicultural, and multigenre Gangster Choir calls for a phonographic approach, one indebted to Fred Moten's figuration of an "ensemble of the senses" and to Danielle Goldman's study of 1960s improvisational performances that complicate notions of corporeality.[61] In her book chapter on the collaborations between dancer Barbara Dunn and jazz musician Bill Dixon, Goldman argues that the duo's simultaneously artistic and political practices of improvisation not only highlighted what Gavin Bryars has called "the hypervisibility of improvised music" but also challenged commonsense views of corporeality as solely signified through a "*seen* body." In other words, these improvised collaborations between dancers and musicians require our attention to, in Moten's terms, the inter-inanimation between the visual, the sonic, and the gestural. Or, more simply, as Dunn has formulated, that "sound emerges out of gesture—that music exists as a trace, or perhaps extension, of the body's action."[62] Against the presumed whiteness of the late 1960s avant-garde, Dunn and Dixon's collaborative work pushed the envelope of not only sensorial reception but also racial politics: "Presenting audiences with a body that is both seen and heard, they also demanded a sensually complex mode of reception from their audience. Vision alone could not grasp the politics of the ensemble's improvisational work."[63]

Such a "sensually complex mode of reception" is also demanded by the Gangster Choir—as a band that "present[ed] audiences with bod[ies] both seen and heard" and, therefore, challenged certain assumptions of 1980s Downtown New York avant-garde music and performance scenes.[64] As Hagedorn remembers: "Well, we would really make an impression. What a mixture we were . . . it was a very mixed band. You know, there's really nothing like us, in a way. Visually."[65] Against the persistent assumed whiteness of the 1980s downtown/avant-garde/new wave music scene, the group's "corporeal complexity, history, and politics" were memorable but simply disregarded and overlooked.

In turn, Goldman's return to Abbey Lincoln's vocal performance in *We Insist!: The Freedom Now Suite*, a 1961 collaboration with drummer Max Roach and lyricist Oscar Brown, draws our attention again to the gendered expectations and constraints of "song" and "singing." As Goldman describes: "Lincoln exploded expectations regarding 'song' and conventional comportment for the female 'singer,' screaming and wailing rather than merely singing lyrics."[66] Through Lincoln's vocal performance, therefore, we remain attentive to the female singer's body as its own musical instrument and her "screaming and wailing," their own forms of vocal lines that bring together melody and rhythm. The Gangster Choir not only encountered demands for authenticity through the New York Downtown/avant-garde's complex racial politics. They also encountered demands for musical authenticity from the musical recording industry, club bookers, and audiences, ones that were also racialized and gendered matters. While much of the band's personnel changed over the years, jazz conductor Butch Morris and the up-and-coming guitarist named Vernon Reid set the musical backbone for the band's 1980 demo. Though its members were (or became) heavy hitters in their respective musical fields/genres (rock, free jazz/improvisation, funk, and R&B), with its eclectic sound and multiracial "look," the Gangster Choir posed a difficult and nearly impossible marketing task for record executives. Over the course of the Gangster Choir's life, as Hagedorn remembers, "people would get picked up by real bands and get a paycheck." These realities led to the group's disbanding in 1985.

After the "disappointment," "heartache," and "tears" accompanying the Gangster Choir's demise, as well as surviving many years of the gendered divisions in New York's music and nightclub scene, Hagedorn decided: "I'll never do this again." A few years later, however, Laurie Carlos proposed to her: "Why don't we do an a cappella thing? We don't need a band. You don't need all that. Let's do something with just our words and our bodies."[67]

Along with Robbie McCauley, Hagedorn and Carlos formed Thought Music, a performance art trio with the "music inside their heads." With the sponsorship of Franklin Furnace, the performance trio wrote and developed *Teenytown*, a multimedia performance exploring issues of race, gender, and representation in U.S. popular culture. Premiering in February 1988, it was later performed at the Danspace Project (St. Mark's Church) in June 1988. Each performance featured a guest artist. Performance artist Nicky Paraiso performed in the first production while actress/dancer Ching Valdes-Aran and then-emerging actor Samuel "Sam" Jackson appeared in the second. *Teenytown* played upon two infamous popular cultural performance formats—the minstrel show and television talk show (a "modern minstrel show")—both to make "a political statement" and to utilize "the episodic variety structure" as a way of incorporating their individual and cowritten texts together into one show. Named after one of Hagedorn's earlier poems, *Teenytown* also included texts that lent themselves to both Hagedorn's and Carlos's later writings.[68]

Within each of the performance's episodes or segments, the trio culled from and commented on popular cultural references (song titles and lyrics, actors and characters, tropes and themes) from Broadway musicals to vaudeville/minstrel acts, from early Hollywood's racist cartoons to post–World War II U.S. pop music. Drawing on "their shared personal concerns and common interests in music and poetry," including Hagedorn's and Carlos's years with the Gangster Choir and McCauley's training in jazz theater at the New Lafayette Theatre, the performance trio declared: "Our work works together, and we have a kind of music between us. Thought music."[69] As Carlos recounted, through the forms of performance art:

> We were beginning to find our own voices. There were no venues for what it was we wanted to do. None. None in any black world, in any Asian world, there were none in the white world. Performance art was the one place where there were so few definitions. The way that we have conversations, what occurs across time zones, what memory is, what color is, how music affects movement and memory and the texture of breath has nothing whatsoever to do with the Eurocentric playwriting form. The dust comes through the window, the rat cries in the corner, and . . . you start screaming. That's what we're living with. So that is what we're trying to do in our work.[70]

Performing in both experimental theaters and art galleries, as well as onstage and on tour with the dance group Urban Bush Women, Thought Music developed a poetics of performance—both choral and conversational—largely driven by and based in popular music. Their shows featured an ever-changing, oftentimes improvised, soundscape of texts performed as calls and responses—as they created layered echoes of each other's words and lines, for emphasis—and, sometimes, in unison.

A poignant example of Thought Music's performance poetics, its particular style of comedic parody, takes place in the segment titled "The Tonight Show." Riffing on the iconic late-night television talk show, the women appear onstage, as the stage directions note, "all in male drag— McCauley as Ed, Carlos as Doc, Hagedorn as Johnny. White dinner jackets over black tuxedo pants . . . The 'guys' bow and shuffle, preen and guffaw to canned laughter and applause."[71] With their rendering of the late-night entertainer's infamous tropes, the three performance artists draw their audience's attention toward the traces of slapstick comedy and vaudeville techniques apparent throughout the show's opening sequence. After the usual banter with his cohost and bandleader, and before he launches into his requisite opening monologue, Johnny shares a joke with the audience:

JOHNNY: KNOCK KNOCK.
ED AND DOC: Who's there?
JOHNNY: Emmy.
ED AND DOC: Emmy who?
JOHNNY: Emmygrant![72]

Silently laughing at their own jokes, they begin to mime classic comedian gestures in rapid succession before setting up their audience for the second punch line:

ED: Someone once told me, 'If Indians are Native Americans—then what does that make me?'
JOHNNY AND DOC: Immigrant![73]

Here, the joke operates on two levels: the first, as an "accent pun," one that "relies on linguistic ambivalence" and its "double-edged nature" for its success; the second, as a political commentary on who might truly be able to claim an identity as the first (in other words, "real") Americans.[74] The irony of these jokes being told by the normative American pop cultural figures of Johnny (Carson) and Ed (McMahon) was one, most likely, not lost upon Thought Music's audience.

The Place of Music

In a 1994 interview with Hagedorn, Audio Prose Library founder and director Kay Bonetti pointedly asked: "Is there anything that you can identify that you bring from the poetry and from your love of music into the fiction?"[75] Hot off the heels of her then recently published and highly awarded debut novel *Dogeaters*, Hagedorn replied: "Rhythm. And I think the love of language, the sheer wordplay. I love words. The sound of words, and puns. It's very Filipino too. Filipinos love puns and wordplays and they love language, the intonations and the nuances.

They take it seriously. They also play with it."[76] In this quote, Hagedorn depicted for Bonetti (and other readers) her writerly ear—its propensity for puns and wordplay, its love for the musicality of language. Two years later, this depiction took shape in her second novel, *The Gangster of Love*'s lead character, Raquel "Rocky" Rivera. Immigrating to San Francisco, California, from the Philippines as a teenager in the late 1960s, it would not be impossible to imagine the character of Rocky as a literary rendition of or, at the very least, drawn from Hagedorn's own biography—her journey, from San Francisco to New York between the late 1960s and early 1980s, and from being a "closet poet" to the bandleader of the Gangster of Love. As Rocky describes her friend Keiko's Argentinean lover:

> Arnaldo reminded me of my father, with his aura of melancholy charm and his aloof, gallant ways with women. I loved his growl of a voice and the happy accidents with language which occurred whenever we talked. It was like I had audio dysplasia. Instead of seeing double, I heard double, something besides what Arnaldo was actually saying. 'Trouble' when he said 'travel,' 'gender' when he said 'genre,' 'fold' when he said 'fault,' or 'grammatic fever' when he said 'rheumatic fever.' But after laughing and sorting it all out, we'd come to the ironic conclusion that it wasn't a case of miscommunication at all, but understanding.[77]

In this scene of cross-racial/ethnic encounter, homophones (quite literally meaning "same sound") are "happy accidents with language" that mediate a particular shared understanding between two immigrants. They are two words, spelled differently yet sounding the same. Rather than causing misunderstanding or "miscommunication," these words—shuttling between two differently racialized immigrants rather than within a prescribed narrative of assimilation—both mark and constitute a particular sense of double consciousness. It is a sense marked and constituted, not by looking at one's self through another's gaze but, instead, by a type of listening (and hearing) alongside that allows for the proliferation of meaning. As it operates within Hagedorn's "counter-assimilationist immigrant narrative," the homophonic is the condition of possibility, not only for a practice of disobediently listening to narratives of immigrant assimilation (ones that aim to conquer and divide through rhetorics of individuality and exceptionalism) but also, for Rocky and the novel's readers to listen, concurrently and simultaneously, to the divergent and nonstandard. We might think of Rocky's self-diagnosis of audio dysplasia as her recognition, quite literally, of the "abnormal development of an organ or part of [her] body" that is, "of, pertaining to, or employed in the transmission, reception, or reproduction of sound." This abnormal development is not limited to organs or body parts more commonly associated with the auditory (that is, the ears and tongue/mouth) but instead allows for a more expansive approach to the sensations of listening. As the scene suggests, the homophone is the stuff of everyday linguistic exchange.

Throughout the rest of the novel, Hagedorn incorporates other homophonic forms—such as "punny" definitions, jokes, and dream sequences—as interstitial breaks between chapters. *Gangster* opens with a prologue that captures scenes from 1970s Manila and a definition of the "yo yo," at once children's toy weapon, slang term for craziness, and colloquial descriptor for fluctuation or change. Here, we see the trace of previous Thought Music performances and their use and re-citation of accent puns—such as using the words "deduct, defense, defeat, detail" or "devastation" in a sentence. These puns not only serve as "inside jokes" and present-day evidence of "aural be/longing."[78] Instead, like Arnaldo and Rocky's memories of her father, these puns retain an "aura of melancholy charm." They are the souvenirs, contraband, and substitute-objects of particular border crossings and migration patterns.

The Gangster of Love reroutes our attention to a portrait of the artist and fan as a young girl. It renders Rocky's early artistic life, her first years in America, and, in turn, reminds us of the years of practice and rehearsal that precede one's arrival on the page or stage.

The novel's action begins with scenes of Milagros Rivera's break-up with her husband, told from the point of view of her daughter, the novel's narrator Raquel (or Rocky). After a number of failed "revenge-seeking" trips to Tokyo and Hong Kong, Milagros finally decides to leave her husband and immigrate with Rocky and her only son, Voltaire, to America. There, her younger sister Fely greets her. A nurse who immigrated to San Francisco many years earlier, Aunty Fely now works at the city's general hospital, having married a Filipino immigrant widower (Bas), and settled down in the Bay Area Filipino enclave of Daly City. Rather than moving in with her sister, Milagros "roughs" it by choosing to live in a small apartment near Golden Gate Park with her two adolescent children.

Rock 'n' roll infuses the narrative of Hagedorn's novel as Rocky notes in her opening lines: "Jimi Hendrix died the year the ship that brought us from Manila docked in San Francisco." As his idol, Hendrix had inspired Voltaire's style and fashion—his "Filipino Afro" and "royal purple bell-bottoms and gauzy shirts from India"—before he even set sail for the United States. While living in Manila, the young "indigenous Filipino" hippie paid homage to Hendrix with his electric-guitar-playing and the "very public ritual in Luneta Park" whereby he set fire to his guitar. Guilt-ridden with being the one who unearths his father's love affair to his mother, by the time they reach their new home in San Francisco, Voltaire's rebellious streak reaches its peak with the mother-son conflict; as Rocky narrates, it continually "boils down into the same old argument: life in Manila versus life in America."

Whereas Voltaire "was determined to save enough up for airfare back to the Philippines," Rocky remembers: "I was content to hole up in my room, writing and dreaming to the funky music on the radio."[79] Wanting "to be left alone—pretty much all the time these days," Rocky instead retreats into her own world: "I stayed in my bedroom listening to Aretha Franklin and Sly Stone on KSOL, while tapping out minimalist poems on the secondhand Underwood my mother had bought me for my birthday. The poems imitated my male favorites of the moment: Antonin Artaud, Mallarmé, Gil Scott-Heron, and LeRoi Jones."[80] In the sanctuary of her room, Rocky begins to develop her writerly voice through both the acts of listening to the radio and "tapping out minimalist poems." In her listing of Rocky's "male favorites of the moment," Hagedorn highlights a collective of minimalist, avant-garde poets that underscores the novelist's own diverse artistic genealogies. Against the full-bodied and choral sounds of black R&B artists, such as Franklin and Stone, the young poet renders her own songs by way of the pedagogical process of imitation. In a similar style as girls singing along to radio hits, oftentimes replicating dance moves of these songs' music videos, U.S. pop music serves as both soundtrack and inspiration to the identities she forges in the privacy of her bedroom. As she paints for us an everyday scene from a teenage girl's bedroom culture, where the work of musical consumption and artistic production go hand in hand, Hagedorn echoes the calls made by feminist pop music scholars to reconsider female teenagers' bedrooms as productive spaces rather than merely ones of passive consumption.[81]

Radios, and other technological musical devices, play a key role in the everyday life scenes that Hagedorn's *Gangster* presents. In one of her revenge-seeking trips overseas, Milagros is inspired to mambo with one of her many admirers, thanks to the fact that "the radio was on loud, blaring Perez Prado's heated music." In a similar fashion (to this spectacle of their mother's unexpected performance), Voltaire and Rocky, later in the novel, jump up and grab the mic of an archaic karaoke device (known as the Minus One) during an otherwise banal family party, to sing what they can remember of Labelle's "Lady Marmalade." Along with these moments of sociality, for Rocky, radios serve as soundtrack to her processes of world making, not just a bridge to other worlds but, more important, the raw, sonic material by which she makes a new one. Likewise, as detailed in the previous chapter, the actual technological objects of radio and sound systems, for Filipino immigrants in the United States, take on deeper meanings as cultural capital and "luxury" item—in the form of Elvis's "Nakamichi sound system"[82]—and as souvenir or memento—in the form of Rocky's "beat-up transistor radio," the one, she recalls, "I brought all the way from Manila, the radio I left behind when I moved out."[83]

Hagedorn's figuring of Rocky's first (teenage) years in America also complicates the often-simplified trope of the female fan. Though the character of Rocky develops into an artist/performer, as did Hagedorn herself, she never quite escapes the category of fan. That is to say, both Rocky's and Hagedorn's biographies, though fictional and actual, respectively, underscore the blurred lines and slippery divisions between musical artist and fan. While poems by Hagedorn—such as "Motown/ Smokey Robinson"—have been read or categorized as simply a fan's "love letter" to a male pop star, by disobediently listening to these generic and gendered musical codes of conduct, we actually might reimagine a fan's listening practice as integral to helping develop and produce her own writerly style and musical/poetic voice. In turn, as we shall see in the next chapter, the blurred line between performer and fan, producer and consumer, is one of the many characteristics that mark active participation in a musical and/or artistic scene.

The Gangster of Love asks and invites us to revisit and reconsider its author in a time before her first novel. Its renderings of audio dysplasia, girls' bedroom and fan cultures, and music technologies, in turn, offer us a set of concerns and methods for turning back, listening back on her earlier poetry and performances. Hearing double and reimagining musical production and place, *Gangster* offers us new ways of interpreting the tropical sites of Filipino America. Working with and within the musical idioms of jazz, R&B, funk, and, most importantly, rock 'n' roll, Hagedorn's poetic and performative voices direct us in remapping a musical itinerary of Filipino America. To reflect on the role that rock 'n' roll played in her upbringing and how it infiltrated her earlier work, we must remember rock 'n' roll as a U.S. cultural export to the Philippines (and the world) in the mid-twentieth century, as music played and accessible over the radio or experienced live in the seats of Manila's Araneta Coliseum. As an immigrant teenager in the late 1960s to early 1970s, Hagedorn's transition to womanhood and life in America was marked by the era's rebellious sounds, namely those produced in California's Bay Area. Her final stop on her artistic migratory pattern, New York's downtown arts/music scene in the 1980s, exploded the various ideas and genres of rock 'n' roll—punk, new wave, no wave, jazz/rock fusion, to name a few.

Having traversed these various scenes, locales, and historical moments, it seems fitting to end this chapter by meditating on "Souvenirs," a poem from Hagedorn's first single-authored publication, *Dangerous Music*. In it, Hagedorn paints the capital city of Manila as a palimpsest of indigenous, Latin American, and U.S. colonial histories—a tropical metropolis where "life is cheap" and "perez prado / has a number one hit / with 'patricia' / on the radio." Her narrator reminisces:

n tito puente has a hit / n it's latin night
at the coliseum
n you don't know / these musicians
come from someplace / called new york
it's just another major event /
to you /
a ten year old child / twitching her ass
and doing the cha-cha in her seat / at the coliseum.[84]

As the title suggests, musical memories function as "contraband" and "substitute," objects stolen and standing in for places and people. As Susan Stewart has so deftly characterized of the souvenir: it "speaks to a context of origin through a language of longing, for it is not an object arising out of need or use value; it is an object arising out of the necessarily insatiable demands of nostalgia."[85] Published after her first return to the Philippines and Ferdinand Marcos's 1972 declaration of martial law, Hagedorn's poem not only gestures toward a personal longing but, perhaps also, to a society's desire for a time before a political present. Throughout the collection, Hagedorn invokes other Latin jazz and African American musical artists—La Lupe, Eddie Palmieri, Ray Barretto, Jimi Hendrix, to name a few—and other scenes of listening, such as radios in San Francisco, dance floors in Manila, and New York bars. The newly immigrated poet does not (and cannot) easily abandon her memories for the promise of assimilation into her new home, especially when the soundtracks of these two places are parallel. Instead, her poetry and writing are objects that resound the traces of other times and places. In chapter 4, we will listen in on these parallel soundtracks—as played in San Francisco and Manila, specifically—and the ways that songs and other musical events, as contraband and objects standing in for places, help to create and connect two distinct indie rock scenes.

....

CHAPTER 4

Pinoise Rock

It is 1998. Take a walk down San Francisco's Sixth Street and you might just miss the little red door nestled behind a wrought-iron fence before you reach Phil's Liquor Store at the corner of Howard Street. Trying to avoid the South of Market Area's (SOMA) most gritty and unrepentant local residents stumbling in and out of single-room occupancy hotels and liquor stores, you might just pass the little red door on your way to or from the End Up or 1015 Folsom, after-hours nightclubs two blocks southeast on the corner of Sixth and Folsom. On a Friday or Saturday night, in this historically immigrant Filipino neighborhood, young Filipino Americans converse and smoke cigarettes right outside 185 Sixth Street, the address to this little red door.

Slightly ajar, the entryway invites the street's wandering inhabitants to stop by and inquire, "What kind of establishment is this?" In what has become a nightly ritual, one of the young people guarding the door calmly replies: "It's a theater that produces plays, comedy shows, and live music by, for, and about Filipino Americans." Walk through this little red door in 1998 and you have arrived at what comedian and managing director Allan Manalo has designated as the "epicenter of a Filipino American performing arts renaissance"—Bindlestiff Studio.[1] Established in 1991 by a cadre of San Francisco theater artists, Bindlestiff provided an inexpensive rehearsal and performance space for the city's experimental artists, an invaluable resource in a city that would soon undergo the seismic cultural shifts of the first dot-com boom era.

Two brothers and musicians who migrated from the Philippines to South San Francisco in 1989, Jesse and Ogie Gonzales first became involved in the Stiff's productions as background musicians for a Teatro ng Tanan (TnT) production of *Panunuluyan*. In the years before they immigrated to the United States, the same years following the downfall of the Marcos's twenty-one-year martial law regime, the Gonzales brothers were part of a vibrant punk and new wave scene in the Philippines, one that reached from Olongapo to Manila, from broadcast television (*Ito ang Iyong Galing*) to the underground radio airwaves of DXRJ. From 1987 until 1989, they played guitar and drums, respectively, for the Manila-based band Valley of Death (V.O.D.). The band performed at both hardcore and *chong* (punk/new wave) venues, on university tours, and even for an Amnesty International event at the former first lady Imelda Marcos's Coconut Palace. Their name was an ode to their hometown of Marikina where, as Jesse remembers, "they threw all the salvaged bodies, the victims, salvage capital" during the Marcos years.[2] The band was even featured on the legendary Philippine punk label Twisted Red Cross's 1987 compilation *Where Do We Go From Here?*

While they did not officially play music from 1989 until 1995, the brothers did attend major concerts by U.S. heavy metal acts like Metallica and Death Angel, both bands that also happened to feature Filipino musicians. They spent their first years in the United States exploring San Francisco's vibrant indie music scene—hanging out at the Epicenter Zone, a punk meeting place-cum-record and zine shop, and checking out gigs by local bands such as J Church and Jawbreaker.[3] After connecting with San Francisco's Filipino American artists in 1995, through their work with Bindlestiff and TnT, the Gonzales brothers' most formative live music event, in their new home, came in May 1998. Eight months after their appearance at Radio City Music Hall (September 1997) and their win of "MTV Asia Viewers' Choice" award, the revered Philippine indie band the Eraserheads had embarked on their second North American tour and played sold-out shows in New York and Los Angeles, and at the now-defunct Calvin Simmons Theater in Oakland, California.[4] As Ogie remembers, "It was just so cool to see, because it was a bunch of Fil-Ams and immigrants gathered to see this band."[5] Inspired by the throngs of eager fans, the brothers, along with Allan Manalo, then artistic director of Bindlestiff, decided to produce their own music festival. Dedicated to promoting OPAM, "original Pilipino alternatib music," they decided to name it *piNoisepop*, a mash-up of the slang term, *Pinoy*, and the local San Francisco Noise Pop festival.

Until that time, no real venue or event dedicated exclusively to Asian American or Filipino American indie music or bands existed in San Francisco. PiNoisepop's first call for submissions did not limit entrants based on professional status. Entries could be either amateur demos or professional recordings of any musical genre. It did, however, insist on two criteria. The first: each band had to write and perform its own songs (no show or "cover" bands). The second: each band had to have at least one Filipino/Filipino American member. Thus, from its onset, piNoisepop designated itself as a festival focused less on indie Filipino/Asian American music as a "strictly bounded genre" and more on cultivating a scene for OPAM and Asian American indie music.

Distributing their initial call via e-mail to personal contacts and targeted indie, Asian American, and Filipino American listservs and websites, the piNoisepop organizers, including myself, drew from mailed-in submissions, as well as the theater's own house bands and musicians. In 1999, we produced the inaugural piNoisepop music festival, which featured nine bands, mainly San Francisco and Los Angeles–based, over two nights.[6] From the power pop Bandsilog (later renamed the Skyflakes) to the psychedelic jazz combo Bobby Banduria, from the smooth R&B sounds of Daly City's Ethereality to the hard-hitting punk noise of L.A.'s Signal 3, you could catch the diverse musical sounds of Filipino America for an admission fee of only $5. And, though the box office covertly sold bottles of San Miguel beer for $3 a pop, the event remained open to all ages until its last show in 2005.[7]

By listening differently to place-based musical events such as piNoisepop, we begin to uncover the translocal scenes of not only San Francisco but also Manila, where improvised musical exchanges happened in ways both familiar and sometimes unexpected. Translocal scenes, as Sara Cohen defines them, "comprise an informal economy" based upon the "regular circulation and exchange of information, advice, and gossip; instruments, technical support, and additional services; music recordings, journals, and other products."[8] A loose network created by the intimate alliances among its participants—musicians, audiences, and others involved in music-making—these scenes involve both economic transactions and affective relations and, therefore, help index certain material realities as well as structures of feeling.

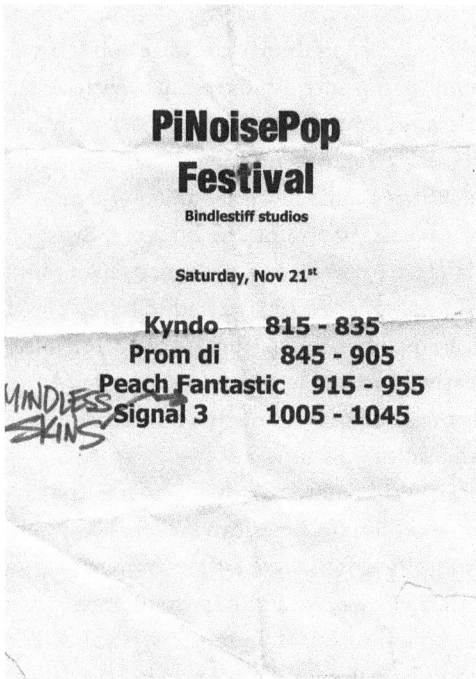

Figure 4.1 piNoisepop #1 set list. Courtesy of Jesse Gonzales.

I open this chapter with this story of piNoisepop's beginnings to signal the intersection of two cultural histories: a late twentieth-century Asian American creative class's energies in producing and distributing popular culture independently; and the mid-1990s resurgence of OPM (original Pilipino music) indie rock as part of a longer Manila history of punk and classic rock. As part of a local and national Asian American indie rock scene, these piNoisepop festivals draw our attention to the relationship between race and musical genre in the United States. In turn, while the authentic "voices" of indie rock are uncritically rendered as always already Western (read American), all other voices (read Third World) are simply suffering under the weight of cultural imperialism. By listening against discourses of musical genre, ones that regard it as simply categorical rather than a performative impetus for making a scene, we are able to hear differently the tropical renditions of Pinoy indie rock. They are not simply derivatives of Western popular music forms. Instead, they are evidence of the routes that U.S. popular music has taken. As tropical renditions, Pinoy indie rock brings these routes to bear on our studies of indie rock scenes in non-U.S. or European contexts.

I begin my study of the translocal scenes of Pinoy indie rock with an overview of field conversations regarding indie rock, race, and authenticity. By doing so, I aim to prove and provide the necessary move from genre, as a mode of aesthetic and stylistic classification, to genre cultures, as a concept that takes into account music's intrinsic role in ways of life. Here, musical genre is the node for translocal affiliations and exchanges, ones that move between localities situated within and beyond national borders. This cultural traffic, these forms of attachment, and these musical characters are what make up a translocal scene. Scene here connotes musical performance as its own event, stage, and geographical location. At the end of this chapter, I map translocal scenes of Pinoy indie rock, from the San Francisco–based piNoisepop music festival to the contemporary Manila indie rock scene, in order to demonstrate how a persistent focus on translocality challenges the demands for authenticity when discussing a Pinoy indie rock sound. I aim to record them with a phonographic approach and in a manner that flips the well-worn tracks of previous scholarly and journalistic writing. That is to say, rather than aiming to define or typify a musical sound, it instead turns to song lyrics, music videos, performance ephemera, and personal narratives and stories to show the various components that go into making a scene.

Listening In on Translocal Scenes

A music scene is a network of relationships, a social ecosystem where every member is necessary despite the overwhelming idea that their purpose emanates from a scene's musicians. A music scene consists of all those involved in the making, distribution, and consumption of music: musicians, songwriters, fans, audience members, journalists/critics, booking agents, promoters and publicists, bar and club owners, roadies, and technicians. Organized around a specific musical genre or within a specific geographical location, all music scenes can boast a shared cultural history of musical personalities, iconic or memorable events, essential recordings, and key venues. Within a music scene, successful presentations of authenticity are key for both musicians and fans, ongoing displays of one's dedication, affiliation, and authority through musical performance and fan knowledge. Scene studies, a broad term encompassing both amateur and professional writing within a music scene, often set the tone for what is considered as insider or outsider status. A shared discourse, scene studies also serve as a cultural resource by cataloging the "music, dress, and deportment appropriate to a scene."

First emerging in 1940s journalistic writings on the "demiworld" of jazz, scene studies have broadened, over the last fifteen years, to include new generations of scholars steeped in documenting the long history and everyday happenings of genre-based as well as geographically bound scenes.[9] The interdisciplinary studies of Andy Bennett, Sara Cohen, Holly Kruse, Barry Shank, and Wendy Fonarow have brought together methods of ethnography, political economy, geography, and pop music studies to account for the complexities of an increasingly global, multinational corporate music industry alongside the continuous and everyday local efforts of musicians, producers, fans, and audiences.[10] Developing alongside the user-generated ethos of the late twentieth century's digital revolution and rising DIY culture, scene studies have required the larger field of pop music studies to rethink how it approaches the political economics of pop music, the impact of scene members on the livelihood of a musical genre, and the ways we determine music's cultural value.

Scene studies' analytics and concerns, in fact, allow us to return to and reimagine popular music's cultural histories.[11] These include more recent examples such as indie music, popularized in the 1990s but with its influences reaching further back to 1970s bands such as the Velvet Underground.[12] A popular music genre with its own set of musical practices and attitudes toward musical production, consumption, and everyday life, indie music shares a set of principles and traditions: the "espousal of simplicity and austerity, a hyper-valuation of childhood and childlike imagery, a nostalgic sensibility, a technophobia, and a fetishization of the guitar."[13] As Wendy Fonarow has argued, this (usually) lo-fi guitar-centered rock or pop style is often accompanied by what many term an "art-school sensibility." In line with this sensibility, indie music and its culture retain strains of Romanticism—"its acclaim for the exceptional man in the guise of the musical genius, its respect for local identities and the working class, and its distaste for middle-class society while being itself middle class."[14] Driven more by melodic and harmonic structures, indie's music highlights, rather than draws attention from, a song's lyrics, ones that often "address the issue of not belonging." Thus, quintessential indie rock songs are characterized as "brooding and contemplative."[15] Indie rock's overarching sounds and sensibilities empha-size *pathos*—emotion, in general, and suffering, in particular—over musicianship and call for self-reliance in the production and circulation of one's own music. Musically and culturally, it celebrates a particular type of authenticity—real (read suffering) feelings, real instrument playing, and real meaning. In this way, indie music and its culture are defined in opposition to mainstream pop music's saccharine-sweet, fab-ricated sounds and the extended guitar solos and heavier sound of other alternative rock formats (nu-metal, grunge, punk). Yet, while the musi-cal genre of indie is still commonly conceived as less masculine than other rock forms, the scenes themselves are still dominated by men.

Despite its alternative or oppositional stances, indie rock also upholds its own conventions and boundaries. Its discourse continues to be based on limited, nation-based definitions of culture. When the term *indie rock* appears in journalistic or scholarly articles, it often already assumes either U.S. or British (read Western) musical culture.[16] In these writings, the relationship between race and indie rock is, at best, evi-dent in its problematic commentary or, at worst, completely absent.[17] If and when the question of race is even broached, nonwhite American and British indie rock artists and audience members must provide an essentialized, cultural explanation for their involvement or fandom (for example, Chicanos/Mexican-Americans' love for Morrissey because it reminds them of *ranchera* music). Or they must constantly narrate ways to understand their seemingly anomalous involvement in a popular music form that is not "easily" racialized (for example, Afro-punk rock-ers). Or they enter as exotic examples of the genre's propensity for hybridity and mixing (for example, Dengue Fever).[18] These discursive limits require us to ask ourselves: What does indie rock have to offer on-going conversations between genre authenticity and racial authenticity? How might our turn to the concept of scenes (both in terms of genre scenes and translocal scenes) help us to broaden the scope of these con-versations?

The discursive hold of authenticity within pop music culture and studies is evidenced by ongoing tendencies toward racial binaries, on the one hand, and liberal categories of the hybrid and syncretic, on the other. They most recently manifest in *New Yorker* critic Sasha Frere-Jones's October 2007 essay, "A Paler Shade of White: How Indie Rock Lost Its Soul," and the backlash his article prompted. Lamenting the lack of "African-American musical styles"—"rhythm," "swing, empty space, palpable bass frequencies"—from the seemingly dull and monotonous soundscape created by today's indie bands, Frere-Jones's critique takes the form of a radical wolf wrapped in liberal sheep's clothing.[19] The lack of "audible blackness" in today's indie rock sound, according to Frere-Jones, is caused by a number of factors: first, white American and British musicians' overwhelming success on rock and roll's charts since the 1950s and, thirty years later, on MTV's music video channel; second, the proliferation of "racial sensitivity" and political correctness in academic circles of the mid to late 1980s; third, the late twentieth-century development of hip-hop music as a site for black cultural visibility; and finally, a "social progress" and democratizing Internet that have now made African American musicians "as visible and as influential as white ones." Unlike the risky "miscegenation practices" of rock and roll's earlier history, such as cultural borrowing, appropriation, border crossing, and intercultural collaboration, today's indie rock is where one finds the growing racial segregation of U.S. popular music culture.

Frere-Jones could and should have taken a few notes from Jessica Pressler, who, in her January 2007 *New York Times* article, "Truly Indie Fans," offers various examples of African American musical artists and fans in punk and indie scenes. Against Frere-Jones's broad claims, Pressler's piece actually does important genealogical work by citing a long lineage of black rock musicians (from early pioneers such as Fats Domino and Chuck Berry to game-changing figures such as Living Colour, Prince, and Lenny Kravitz to more contemporary vanguard acts such as TV on the Radio) as well as their fans, audiences, and documentarians (*Afro-Punk* director James Spooner, Black Rock Coalition president LaRonda Davis, writer-photographer-music blogger Nev Brown, and scholar Daphne Brooks). However, despite today's black rock and "blipster" (black hipster) culture's attempts to disrupt popular assumptions about the relationship between race and indie rock, it often still upholds another set of popular assumptions that "race" only signifies black or African American. Thus, when attempting to move the indie rock conversation beyond the racial binary, U.S. critics often wield terms such as "cross-fertilization" and "hybridity" as ready-made responses.

In her immediate retort to Frere-Jones's *New Yorker* article, former *L.A. Times* music critic Ann Powers hoped to defy Frere-Jones's arguments with a crowd-sourced list, from fellow staff writers, of exceptional examples of racial and musical diversity in today's U.S. popular music landscape. While the list and writers' intentions were well meaning, it is precisely this liberal move toward hybridity as the answer that, as Fabian Holt has warned, "draws attention away from categories."[20] Citing David Hesmondhalgh's statement that "we need to know how boundaries are constituted, not simply that they are fuzzier than various writers have assumed," Holt calls our attention back to the work of genre in popular music. Related to scientific paradigms of classification (most notably, Darwin's evolutionary theories), genres are "discursive modes of thinking about classification and genealogy [that] were adopted and used to legitimize distinctions between 'primitive' and 'modern' societies."[21] Genres do not simply and strictly define categories of musical practice and aesthetics. They also operate, according to Holt, within "a distinctive cultural web of production, circulation, and signification."

The concept of genre is not merely a signifier that issues from the music itself or that is simply found in its aspects. Genre is also produced, maintained, and shared by the members of genre cultures. That is to say, genre is not only "in the music" but also in the minds and bodies of particular groups of people who share certain conventions."[22] In the words of Holt, "Genres are identified not only with music, but also with certain cultural values, rituals, practices, territories, traditions, and groups of people. The music is embedded in all these things, and the culture concept can help us grasp the complex whole because of its capacity to represent a large entity of connections and sharing among many people. Culture also stresses the social and historical dimensions that are ignored when categories are defined only in relation to the music itself."[23] Like the analytic of scene, genre culture moves away from a method of isolating and calcifying music and instead emplaces music within a network of people, practices, and performances. A musical genre cannot be separated from the social and historical dimensions of those who perform, circulate, and listen to its music. Doing so ignores the labor and participation of those active within scenes of a musical genre. It also overlooks the ways that music travels and the force that it carries.[24] "Genre scenes are translocal," Holt also reminds us, "because they share ideas and representations of the same genre with scenes in other cities and often position themselves in relation to each other, with competing localized conceptions or branches of the genre."[25]

While piNoisepop functioned as a central venue within San Francisco's Asian American indie rock scene, it was also one of many hubs within a national Asian American indie culture. Others included the *Ear of Dragon* compilation CD, produced by Chicago's Ben Kim, Sooyoung Park, and William Shin; the indie label Asian Man Records; zines such as New York's *Bamboo Girl*; the Los Angeles–based *Giant Robot* publications and its affiliated stores, to name a few. Drawn together by the genre of Asian American indie rock, these nodes within a larger network helped the scene feel "communal and collaborative rather than fragmented or factional" while also "emphasiz[ing] the dynamic, shifting, and globally interconnected nature of musical activity."[26] Therefore, despite the differences between the Asian American indie rock scene in San Francisco and the ones in Los Angeles, Chicago, or New York, they each remained aware of and supported musicians, venues, and events from each other's scenes, understanding themselves as part of a larger U.S.-based Asian American indie culture.

Genre scenes, as an analytic, also help us listen closely and differently to the affinities established, through popular music forms, between Asian Americans and those musicians and artists from Asian countries. By looking at the increasing numbers of Asian American musical artists currently active in Asian-based music industries such as K-Pop, Canto-Pop, and OPM (original Pilipino music), as the work of Grace Wang and Patricia Ahn directs us, we can begin to reckon with kinship and collaborations rooted in nonfamilial forms.[27] They often signify the various alternatives chosen by various artists in the face of the U.S. pop music industry's limited opportunities. By studying the histories of Korean *rok*, Cambodian psych and surf rock, and Japanoise, as the work of Hyunjoon Shin, Joshua Chambers-Letson, and David Novak illustrates, we are forced to reckon with the musical reverberations of war, occupation, and exchange that also challenge our notions of generic authenticity.[28] Genre scenes, with their focus on the translocal, allow us to tell a cultural history that accounts as much for U.S. war and occupation as it does for the new musical cultures produced locally in its wake.

Genre scenes, with their focus on the translocal, also offer us the chance to undertake the genealogical work of Pinoy indie rock from a non-Western point of view, that is, from a place where the West does not signify a musical origin or end point. According to Wendy Hsu, such an approach also further destabilizes the U.S. racial binary of assimilation, on the one hand, and resistance, on the other.[29] That is, it does not automatically presume Asian or Asian American listening practices and musical preferences as simply attempts to identify with either white or black America. Nor does it turn a deaf ear to the medley of musical affinities formed by Asian Americans in their attachments to pop music from across the Pacific Ocean. Instead, it leaves itself open to the hums and murmurs of musical structures of feeling and to the as yet to be heard and felt politics, alliances, and coalitions they might bring forth.

Before we listen in on two specific translocal scenes of Pinoy indie rock, one in San Francisco and the other in Manila, I want to provide a brief but useful legend to the concept of translocal scenes. Although Pinoy indie rock scenes might simply be rendered as local scenes with links to the national or transnational, I instead want to assert that they formed and continue to develop because of the various encounters and exchanges with people, musical objects, and sensibilities from other geographical locations that happen within a local scene. As Sara Cohen has previously argued, it is often the movement and migration of musical people and objects—songs, tapes, albums, CDs—that have had the most lasting impact on "sounds" often rendered as local. We see this in the historical example of U.S. military men's circulation of American R&B music and its impact upon what became known as the "Liverpool sound."[30] Of course, local music venues and gigs/concerts provide crucial opportunities for face-to-face interaction between musicians, producers, fans, and critics within a specific geographical place, but it is also crucial to consider the impact made by artists, audiences, and musical objects visiting and stopping over, for assorted lengths of time, from other places. For, even in the most local settings—the record store, the radio station, or dive bar—music from elsewhere is undeniably present in and influential on a scene's sounds and sensibilities. I want to reiterate the importance of this approach, especially when one wants to discuss, in a nonessentialist manner, popular music and the scenes it makes outside the United States.

As part of a larger intellectual resolve never to forget the porosity of place and the portability of popular music, "translocal scene" builds on a networked understanding of transitory yet forceful places, people, and political conditions. Various historical predecessors come to mind: the well-established ports of call and centers of trade (port cities); the foreign military bases and the cultures (of performance and consumption) that emerge in their surrounding base towns; the tourist industries and diplomatic (read expatriate) economies that surface in cities as well as smaller towns. We might even stop to consider, as this book's epilogue does, a scene's touring bands, fans, films, journalists, producers, and audiences as constituting and constitutive of their own networks of translocality. While today's Internet technology and its attendant user-generated culture have definitely shifted the speed and geographical reach of popular music, Pinoy indie rock's translocal scenes remind us of the various, sometimes contraband ways that music traveled and inspired new performers, renditions, and musical scenes.

San Francisco

Taking place from 1998 to 2005, piNoisepop occurred in the midst of San Francisco's various cultural shifts and commemorative events. While the late 1990s dot-com industry boomed in the South Bay's Silicon Valley, the city's neighborhoods and districts—most notably the Mission and the South of Market Area (SOMA), where Bindlestiff was located—appeared to change overnight. With the influx of a new creative class (or nouveau riche creatives) came the razing of historic yet long abandoned buildings for sleek and modern lofts and apartment buildings, which would be occupied by this new elite class. Low-income housing and mom and pop–style businesses gave way to the trendy bars, restaurants, clothing stores, and boutiques that specifically catered to those who profited most from the Internet industry's speculative tech rush. The unmistakable sound of shrieking fire truck sirens sonically registered, for native and long-time San Francisco locals, the dot-com industry's slow but steady attack on their urban home.

For Bay Area Filipino Americans, the ominous threat of Y2K not only signaled the drastic and sudden transformations in the look and feel of their hometown, the century's end also echoed the millenarian spirit of political movements from a hundred years back and thousands of miles away. The year 1998 marked the centennial of first president Emilio Aguinaldo's declaration of Philippine independence from Spain as well as the transition to U.S. imperial occupation of the islands and the beginning of the Philippine-American War (1899–1902). This pivotal moment in Philippine history was memorialized through academic conferences, photo exhibitions, performances, publications, and the usual fanfare of community festivals, parades, and similar productions. One of San Francisco's premier fine art institutions, the Asian Art Museum, featured the exhibit "At Home and Abroad: 20 Filipino Artists." In conjunction with the exhibit, the museum programmed a six-week series of performances, panels, films, and festivities, such as the Fiesta Filipina bash that took place in the city's Civic Center. A few months after the "official" celebration of independence (June 12, to be exact), "a consortium of Pilipino American contemporary artists"—including dancer-choreographers Pearl Ubungen, Wilma Consul, and Alleluia Panis; Teatro ng Tanan's (TnT) artistic director Joyce Juan Manalo; creative consultant Sonny Ley, and Bindlestiff's own Allan Manalo—"united to join the international events commemorating the centennial anniversary of the end of Spanish rule in the Philippines," as well as to fulfill the "widespread interest" in contemporary Filipino American art while promoting the "Filipino American post-modern aesthetic."[31] As KulArts' director, Panis spearheaded the event's production, partnering with the SOMA arts institution, Yerba Buena Center for the Arts (YBCA), to present emerging and established performing artists of Filipino descent. Whether celebratory or critical in tone, each of these cultural efforts signaled the period's renewed interest in the highly contested politics of Philippine nationalism and conditions of Filipino belonging in the United States.

Thus, Bindlestiff played a part in the broader flourishing of Filipino American performing arts in San Francisco during this time period. Located only blocks away from YBCA (and its soon-to-be-built neighbor, the Sony Metreon) and in the heart of SOMA's historically immigrant and working-class Filipino communities, Bindlestiff's programming took off that year, earning it the role of "some kind of Mecca for Fil-Am musicians and artists from all over the United States." Its resident experimental theater group Tongue in a Mood mounted not one but two productions: *The Kalat Show* (February 1998), a variety show of sketch comedy hosted by Mr. Kalat (Allan Manalo), featuring the premiere of Bobby Banduria (Kevin Camia); and *Bomba* (June 1998), an evening of scenes and sketches "about sex from the Filipino American perspective" (after spending "400 years in a convent and 50 years in Hollywood"). With the first-ever piNoisepop music festival in November of that same year, the Gonzales brothers established a venue "where lovers of Pinoy rock abroad can witness the prevalent existence of this undying music genre." According to Benjamin Jaime's PhilMusic online review, the piNoisepop festival proved that "Pinoy rock isn't dead here [San Francisco]. And neither is it dead anywhere else in the world." Against claims of Pinoy rock's demise, the fact and success of piNoisepop proved that "it's alive and kicking," making Bindlestiff Studio, the Gonzales brothers, Manalo, and other festival organizers "purveyors of Pinoy rock in a place outside its hometown."[32]

At the same time, piNoisepop was indicative of a mid- to late 1990s energy for producing and distributing Asian American independent music and film. Popular culture scholars Mimi Nguyen and Thuy Linh Tu have marked this enterprise as the rise of an "Asian American creative class"—"a critical mass of young (usually second-generation) Asian Americans," a creative labor force that has "infiltrate[ed] the culture industries in a variety of capacities and fields from advertising, entertainment, and technology to publishing, design, and fashion" while also "gain[ing] greater access to technologies of cultural production, which has enabled them to produce and disseminate their own works with greater ease, efficiency, and independence."[33] With an increased role in the production of culture, this Asian American creative class was also aided by a global marketplace that valued the particular aesthetics of "Asian chic" and corporate America's courting of Asian Americans as a "niche market."[34] This definition of an Asian American creative class underscores the significance of national and transnational shifts on what might otherwise be seen as simply local subcultures. San Francisco events such as the Directions in Sound showcase at the annual National Asian American Telecommunications Association (NAATA; now Center for Asian American Media [CRAM]) film festival and the historic Kearny Street Workshop's APAture showcase, arts collectives like the short-lived Locus Arts in Japantown, music labels like Mike Park's indie rock outfit Asian Man Records and Oliver Wang's hip-hop collective Soulsides Records, and bands featuring Asian American members such as J Church, Versus, Skankin' Pickle, and Skrabbel, to name a few—all these people, organizations, events, and performances contributed to a burgeoning Asian American indie music scene in San Francisco and the Bay Area. Local music venues (such as Bottom of the Hill, Justice League, Great American Music Hall, and Slim's) featured well-known bands with members of Asian or Filipino American descent, yet none actually booked evenings along the lines of "Asian American music." While many of these bands played at local ethnic festivals (Cherry Blossom, Philippine Inde-

Figure 4.2 piNoisepop #8 poster designed by Dino Ignacio. Courtesy of Jesse Gonzales.

Figure 4.3 piNoisepop #9 poster designed by Dino Ignacio. Courtesy of Jesse Gonzales.

pendence, and so on), they were often deemed as merely one-off entertainment acts, relegated to "youth" stages and very rarely building a well-
established network with other local Asian American bands or acts.

Taking place over two to three days and bringing together musical
acts from across the country, piNoisepop existed as part of both the
musical landscape of San Francisco ("the city") and a translocal network of Pinoy indie music scenes. It ran concurrently with its name-
sake—the aforementioned Noise Pop music festival (which continues
to this day). PiNoisepop was one of a number of live music venues across
the city that featured indie rock acts (others include Bottom of the Hill,
Slim's, Kilowatt Club). Alongside Seattle, New York, and Austin, the San
Francisco Bay Area boasts a lively independent arts and music scene,
securing a spot on the nation's list of "Top 10 creative class urban hubs."
This designation is grounded in not only the contemporary but also the
historical, for the city by the Bay and its surrounding areas have housed
and fostered a variety of artistic and musical subcultures. The post–
World War II boom of jazz and blues music in the Fillmore district. The
Beat generation's hold on North Beach's Little Italy. The psychedelic era
of "tune-ins, turn-ons, and drop-outs" that congregated around Haight-
Ashbury and the San Francisco sound of their favorite acts—Jefferson
Airplane, Janis Joplin, and, of course, the Grateful Dead. In the nearby
Mission district, bands like Santana and Dakila incorporated indigenous
instrumentation and Latin/jazz rhythms and percussion into tribal-
sounding, trance-inducing music replete with guitar solos (a minimum
of two minutes long). Also on the scene were the consciousness-raising
sounds of Oakland's underground hip-hop, the consciousness-altered
sounds of the East Bay's recent hyphy movement.

PiNoisepop continued in this tradition by bringing together a generation of Asian American musicians and their audiences through the
event of a music festival. As I discuss at greater length in the epilogue,
festivals are ephemeral yet symbolically enduring events that bring
together otherwise geographically and generically distinct artists and
audiences to perform, network, and informally share music and ideas.
By taking this form and transforming it to serve their own purposes,
piNoisepop staged and made audible certain scenes of Asian American
indie rock at the turn of the twenty-first century. I have explored the
piNoisepop music festival in the contexts of Filipino American centennial celebrations and the rise of an Asian American creative class

in order to emplace it within two cultural histories: Asian American indie rock and diasporic Pinoy indie rock. By doing so, I aim not only to extend discussions regarding U.S. indie rock music and racialization but also to focus on other ways we might listen to Filipino America's relationship to this genre.

The next section begins with a trip to the city of Manila, as figured by the traveling writer Spalding Gray. Armed with the nuanced concepts of genre scenes and translocality, I listen against a Western discourse of noise and categorizing desires for a "Manila sound." Instead, I listen for the musical cultures that rumble underneath and clamor beyond the cacophony of a city's pursuit of modernity and progress. Here, the music, the words, the venues, and broadcasts of Manila-based Pinoy indie and punk rock musicians, their songs and histories, guide my disobedient listening practices while leading me toward a different set of translocal places.

Manila

Upon return, you are reminded that Manila is a city of noise. Cranes moan before the morning rush hours, working to build the latest highrise apartments. Cars honk to signal a multitude of messages: "Hey, I'm cutting into your lane," "Hey, you're cutting into my lane," or "Hey, I'm still here." From above, the loud rumble of LRT/MRT train tracks drown out the tiny voices and large open palms of beggars on the ground. These urban sounds become that much clearer after reading Jean-Luc Nancy's *Listening*. He instructs us to listen not only with ears turned outward but also with the requisite "turning inward" so that sounds may resonate.[35] This active, bimodal form of listening—tuning in or tuning out, when necessary—proves the best way for you to survive Manila.

For many first-time visitors, Manila's noise—produced by "the clash of various ways of life and modes of production"—is hellish and traumatic.[36] Recounting storyteller Spalding Gray's *Conde Nast Traveler* narration of his first encounter with the tropical metropolis, Neferti Tadiar writes:

> One interference after another interrupts his quest, not to mention his narrative: gridlock, "pollution . . . so foul you had to roll up the windows," "horns constantly honking," a woman who keeps singing

Tracy Chapman songs outside of his inexpensive hotel—he cannot sleep, and after the woman with her insistent singing drives him to desperation and a change of room, a bulldozer that roars all night long. It becomes clear that what encapsulates Manila's chaos and confusion is its incessant blare of discordant sounds. Gray wouldn't have been able to take in the sights even if he wanted to: in Manila, there is so much noise that it gets in the way of seeing.[37]

In spite of continued efforts to modernize the capital city—by removing the eyesores of squatter homes and covering up squalor with beautification projects, such as those administered by former First Lady and Metro Manila mayor Imelda Marcos in the 1980s—the excess of Manila's "flotsam and jetsam" persists sonically despite the façade of development. While the smooth sounds of soft rock—not "The Talking Heads or Clash or even Twisted Sister" as Pico Iyer had remarked—cushion one from the grueling noises that seem to signal progress as well as the harshness of tropical heat and the shock and smog of urban life, they also signal the city's sonic throwback tendencies. As department store and taxicab radio playlists easily slide between contemporary Top Ten love songs and yesteryears' soft rock hits, they do more than just invoke an archipelagic propensity for sentimentality. Their temporal lag is musical evidence of the Philippines' alternative modernity, the palimpsest of cultural influences present in contemporary Philippine culture.

Five years before Gray, Pico Iyer found shelter in the Manila district of Ermita. Originally built by the Spanish in the sixteenth century (its name taken from "La Hermita" or the Hermitage since it originally housed an image of the Roman Catholic Virgin Mary), Ermita was home to U.S. colonial government buildings and hotels as well as a number of Philippine universities during the same colonial period. During World War II, it was the site of various massacres and bombings by the Japanese. Along with the neighboring district of Malate, Ermita renders the urban aftermath of the country's multiple colonial occupations. These days, it serves as an inexpensive alternative to Makati's commercial business district. For tourists on a budget and tourists on a sexual mission, Ermita and Malate provide a plethora of "hospitality services" to make first-time visitors to Manila feel at home.

But, for some of Manila's residents, the streets of Ermita signal something different than the simulacrum experienced by Iyer.

Kamukha mo si Paraluman
Nung tayo ay bata pa
At ang galing galing mong sumayaw

Mapa boogie man o cha cha
Ngunit ang paborito
Ay ang pagsayaw mo ng El Bimbo
Nakakaindak, nakakaaliw
Nakakatindig balahibo
Pagkaggaling sa eskwela
Ay dideretso na sa inyo
At buong maghapon ay tinuturuan mo ako
Magkahawak ang ating kamay
At walang kamalaymalay
Na tinuruan mo ang puso ko
Na umibig ng tunay

At lumipas ang maraming taon
Hindi na tayo nagkita
Balita ko'y may anak ka na
Ngunit walang asawa
Tagahugas ka raw ng pinggan sa may Ermita
At isang gabi'y nasagasaan sa isang madilim na eskenita
Lahat ng pangarap ko'y bigla lang natunaw
Sa panaginip na lang pala kita maisasayaw

[You looked like Paraluman
Back when we were still young
And you danced very, very well
Whether boogie or cha-cha
But my favorite
Was when you danced El Bimbo
It made me groove,
it made me crazy,
it gave me goosebumps
After coming home from school
I'd go straight to your place
And every afternoon, you would teach me
Our hands could hold each other

And no one would care
You taught my heart
How to love genuinely

Many years had passed
And we hadn't seen each other
I heard that you already had a child
But did not have a husband
They say that you were a dishwasher in Ermita
And one night, you were run over on a dark street corner
All of my aspirations suddenly melted
Only in my dreams can I dance with you]

In their 1997 "Ang Huling El Bimbo," Pinoy indie rock band the Eraserheads tells the story of first love, a childhood romance explored in afterschool sessions of dancing the tango-esque El Bimbo. The slow but driving ballad's narrator looks back upon these scenes as an irreplaceable first lesson in "learning how to love, truly." Infused with nostalgia, he idealizes his first love in the iconic image of classic Philippine screen star Paraluman when, in actuality, word on the street is that she has become a single mother and dishwasher in Ermita. Accidentally killed one night while standing on a neighborhood street corner, his first love—the song's narrator realizes—can now only be encountered sa panaginip (in his dreams), transforming Ermita from a site of daily drudgery to one riddled with a hazy and melancholic past. With a music video directed by then-emerging film director Aureus Solito, "Ang Huling El Bimbo" has served as an anthem for Filipinos coming of age in the years after martial law, at the end of the twentieth century. With its historic win at the 1997 MTV Music Video awards ceremony (as the first Philippine band to win an MTV Asia Viewers' Choice award), the song, its video, and the band figure importantly in a translocal OPM/Pinoy indie musical imaginary.

The Eraserheads were a Pinoy indie rock band responsible for the resurgence of the band phenomenon in the mid-1990s. Formed by the members of two failed bands in 1989, its lead singer-guitarist Ely Buendia, guitarist Marcus Adoro, bassist Buddy Zabala, and drummer Raimund Marasigan met while students at the University of the Philippines Diliman and dorm mates in its Kalayaan Residence Hall. Taking its name from famed auteur David Lynch's 1977 film, the quartet formed a band to pique the interest of girls. Thanks to the campus's regularly scheduled events and concert series, they slowly developed a cult following. As members in the era's underground music scene, they played regularly at Club Dredd but failed at the audition for the venue's house band. The Eraserheads were unable to play covers (customary for most Pinoy combos, at the time) because, according to Zabala, "Hindi kami ganoon kagaling tumugtog ng music ng iba" [We weren't good enough to play other people's music].[38] The Eraserheads instead cultivated a multigenre rock sound—drawing from the styles of reggae, folk, and alternative rock.[39] But, with the syrupy ballads and synth-pop stylings of Manila Sound artists still dominating the airwaves, the band faced rejection from record label executives for not being "pop enough." As a rebuttal, they titled their 1991 demo "Pop U!" Professionally recorded by producer and UP graduate student Robin Rivera, the demo caught the ear of BMG Records' A&R director Vic Valenciano, thanks to Buendia's job as student copywriter at the label. Valenciano took a chance and signed the band to a three-record deal.

With simple, catchy melodies and lyrics that spoke about real, everyday people and situations, the Eraserheads' unconventional and unpredictable rock sound appealed to their fellow college-aged and postcollege fans (or "E-heads"), as did their frequent use of local references and *kolehiyala* slang. In 1993, the group released "Electromagneticpop!," its first album, which took its name from a Voltes V character. The album featured the band's then underground hit and now iconic tune, "Pare Ko." Staged as a dialogue between friends, the narrator of "Pare Ko" tells his all-too-familiar adolescent tale of unrequited love— expressing romantic feelings for a female classmate only to be spurned. The term *pare* refers to the compadrazgo system that permeates the island nation's sociality—from the "bossism" of government politics all the way down to the everyday favors one must ask of a stranger. And, while the song's chords remain simple (transitioning between G and C with an occasional move to the minor key of E), the lyrics appealed to the E-heads' audience through the use of contemporary, middle- to upper-middle class slang (*dehins*, "TL," *letseng pa-ibig 'to*) and, most notably, the phrase *'tang ina* [fuck]—an obscenity that the Philippine Association of the Record Industry (PARI) attempted (but failed) to censor and gained the Eraserheads that much more popularity. In 1994, they were awarded Album of the Year in the alternative-rock station NU107's rock award ceremony. Hailed as OPM's version of the Fab

Four, the band were coined "the Beatles of the Philippines"—clean-cut enough for parents yet defiant enough to be marked as cool.

Officially disbanded in 2002, the band's individual members have continued in their musical endeavors—forming their own bands, producing other bands' albums, and even hosting local television shows that promote indie music and its production. Their songs provided a soundtrack to a generation of musicians, film directors, writers, and DJs, both in the Philippines and abroad. Their legacy as a band, however, lies not only in their music but also in their ability to manifest an audience for Pinoy indie rock and, in turn, pave the way for future indie bands and musical acts.

When looking for a distinct Manila, or Filipino, indie musical sound, one might be surprised, even dismayed, to find that many of today's bands resonate with and alongside what might be called global indie rock sounds. Here, "global" does not merely stand in for indie rock music made by Westerners, or Americans, though, of course, their influence cannot be denied. Global, as will be further explored in this book's epilogue, signals the various musical forms and artists that circulate among various cultural circuits, not simply "East meets West" but also trans-Pacific, inter-Asia, global South-South, Philippines–Filipino American, and so on.

Though designated by the generic label of OPM (original Pilipino music), today's Pinoy indie musical acts do not display a shared set of musical styles or attributes, anything that one might label as a "Manila Sound." Manila Sound, in fact, already references a musical generation of artists, who worked in various genres and garnered popularity throughout the 1970s and early 1980s. Manila Sound encompassed a wide swath of musical acts: the disco-inflected VST and Company, the folk-rock female vocals of Sampaguita, the novelty act Hotdog, and then-teen pop idol Sharon Cuneta. With its catchy and melodic tunes, smooth and lightly orchestrated sound of recordings, Manila Sound is often considered as the musical accompaniment to the Martial Law era of Philippine history. As writer Albert Ascona recalls in a 2008 *Rogue* article on the unofficial history of Pinoy punk: "As a pre-history to the Pinoy punk era, the mainstream musical landscape could have most certainly been personified by the likes of Starland Vocal Band's timeless morsel of sugary pop; it was too nice, it was too happy, it was too sweet; it was much too unreal, like the 'New Society'—the yellow and red-clad 'Metro Aide' and the 'Love Bus' phenomenon, Masagana 99 and the Green Revolution."[40] Thus, like the San Francisco Sound, the generic designation of Manila Sound indicates a particular place at a particular time. Though an important part of the city's evolving musical history, there is no way in which the label could encompass the Pinoy punk generation that grew in opposition to it, let alone the contemporary OPM/Pinoy indie rock scene that, in the early 1980s, was still to come.

It is 2008. You take a walk down De la Rosa Avenue from your apartel (apartment hotel) in the expat Legazpi Village. It is Friday night, way after the harsh tropical sun has set and equally oppressive afternoon commute has ended. Like Los Angeles, California, Manila is a city not designed for walking. As Tadiar beautifully articulates, the city's flyovers provide automobile commuters and tourists with an "aerial sight" of the city, one that saves them from the shocks of encounter experienced by those traveling on foot. "Of course," Tadiar reminds us, "this transcendent perspective is not legitimately available to the lower classes who, as pedestrians and public transportation commuters, are routed through crowded ground-level streets."[41] But, tonight, you decide that this side street, one that parallels the main strip of Ayala Avenue now bustling, at this hour, with call center workers about to begin their nocturnal shifts, will serve your purposes best. Much easier than getting into a cab and explaining to the driver all the one-way directions that will get you to the small and quiet residential street where you will surprisingly find one of the most iconic venues in today's Manila indie rock scene.

Saguijo Bar is literally on Guijo (*sa Guijo*) Street in San Antonio Village, a bohemian outpost on the edges of Makati's central business district. Thanks to multiple trips and your trusty Manila street map book, you know just where to go. The venue, which has hosted gigs featuring various indie acts of all genres and after-parties for larger concerts (such as the 2009 Eraserheads reunion performance) since 2005, is so unexpected that even your Manila-born and raised companions, on their first visit to Saguijo, cannot imagine where you might be taking them.

Walking down Guijo Street, you begin to join the other pairs and groups of young hipsters ambling toward the faint sounds of bass and guitars. You are greeted by a Team Manila–designed mural of José Rizal and an outdoor smoking area filled with plastic white tables and chairs covered by just enough tarp to keep away the occasional summer evening downpour. You might also surprisingly run into a famous Pinoy indie rock musician, depending on which bands are playing that evening.

You pay the standard Ph150 gate fee, which usually also gets you one free beer to start. Past another outdoor patio area, this one populated by wooden benches and tables, the building's glass windows allow you to peer in from stage right of the venue's small performance area. Open the door to the right of those windows and you find yourself having to navigate in the tight, almost nonexistent, spaces between that evening's performers and their audience. Good luck finding somewhere to stand or on making your way to the simple, almost makeshift, bar area. No fancy cocktails here, only beer and shots of local rum. What Saguijo lacks in frills, it makes up in heart, and you begin to imagine that this is exactly what draws big-name acts back to this dive club. To shrink the divide between musician and fan, to feel a crowd's energy in all its intense immediacy, to get back to why one plays live music in the first place.

Since the mid-1990s emergence of the local band phenomenon, bars and clubs such as Saguijo, Route 196, Mayric's, 70s Bistro, Mag:net café, and B-Side at the Collective, to name a few, have taken up the mantle of presenting local indie talent and, at the same time, serving as incubators for emerging musical acts. And though some of these venues—especially Route 196, which is located along Katipunan Avenue, the main artery along which Ateneo University and the University of the Philippines campuses run—maintain the usual indie scene connection to university towns, others find themselves in both commercial and residential areas, on the outskirts of tourist and business districts. Following Sara Cohen's and Fabian Holt's lead, we need to think and talk about these places and the people that make the music—genre cultures instead of simply genre categories.

First hitting the airwaves in 1987, NU107 radio station quickly became known as another important institution for developing and strengthening the local Pinoy indie rock scene. Bought by banker Atom Henares, the radio station's arrival coincided with an executive order by then President Corazon Aquino requiring all radio stations to play at least three original Pilipino musical compositions an hour. With its tagline "Home of New Rock," throughout the 1990s, NU107 featured both American grunge and alternative bands such as Pearl Jam, Soundgarden, and Nirvana, as well as local and then-emerging Pinoy indie rock bands such as the Eraserheads, Wolfgang, the Youth, Rivermaya, and others. Its regular weekly show, "In the Raw," featured demos and DIY recordings by local and unsigned bands, helping to develop the burgeoning Manila indie rock scene. Its annual NU107 Rock Awards celebrated Pinoy rock legends and honored each year's best rock talents, creating a sense of legacy among and excitement about all forms of Pinoy rock—from punk to classic to indie.

Having completed an undergraduate degree in mass communications at UP in the years leading up to the 1990s, Myrene Academia decided to join the latest radio station as a newscaster. Taking advantage of the eagerness of free labor and young DJs-in-training to work graveyard shifts, NU107 and its affiliated services offered Academia access to the latest modern rock music from across the globe. With NU107's paid subscription to "Century 21," a service that compiled the newest singles and top hits for each musical format/genre onto CDs delivered directly to radio stations, Academia and other emerging radio DJs of the time were able to hear the latest music from overseas at a faster rate than if it had been accessed via major record labels' local Philippine affiliates. Armed with these paid subscription service CDs and her own self-made expertise in alternative and new wave music, in 1993, Academia began hosting her own show, "Not Radio," on Saturday nights at 9 p.m.

The show's title came from the fact that it did not focus on one musical genre, that Academia was allowed to play almost any music not featured on other shows or radio stations, and by the fact that she began not so adept at radio plugs. As she remembers:

> So, I got my show . . . and then, the station manager . . . his name was Chris . . . goes, "Oh yeah, I'll go ahead and give you Saturday night at 9 [pm]." And he didn't have any block timers yet or any regularly scheduled shows, at that time. It was music all the way. So, Saturday night at 9 . . . it was pretty free, so he gave me that. So I really did not get my plug together . . . and my first few CDs were like, "Uh uhuh . . . Nine Inch Nails' first album." And then I got Ministry . . . it was like a mix talaga. And that's why I named it "Not Radio" din . . . kasi it was *parang na wala* . . . I wouldn't be forced to just play one sort of thing. I'd just have to play stuff that wasn't on the regular playlist. Or that wasn't being played on other stations. Basically, I was allowed to play more things as long as it was newer stuff . . . or stuff you didn't hear otherwise . . . [*Parang* stuff you couldn't hear.] *Parang*, if I were a kid now, at that time . . . if I were a kid and I didn't have any friends from the States, I couldn't afford to buy the music magazines . . . *Oo*, or the CDs . . . what chance would I have of listening to new stuff? So

'yan . . . yun lang yan . . . this is what I wanted to do, sorta, "This is what's out there." To give the kids a choice lang . . . *kasi* you might be more inclined or . . . "Oh, I'd rather listen to this *pala*" or . . .[42]

Like many Manila youth who grew up in the years near the end of martial law and advent of Internet technologies, Academia depended on analog forms of media technologies for her own schooling in new wave and rock music. In high school, she first heard Echo and the Bunnymen's "The Killing Moon" through a friend's mixtape, one most likely concocted from the record store A to Z's contraband recording system. She read and learned about U.S. and European bands through back issues of *Rolling Stone*, *Spin*, and *Sassy* magazines, about Filipino bands and Western pop song structure through *Jingle* magazine. By 1993, she found herself at the helm of what was to be the most adored radio show of the Manila indie rock scene that emerged in the 1990s. And what made it so popular among that generation's listeners and burgeoning indie musicians was precisely the fact that "Not Radio" became associated with each person's first time hearing of what would soon become their favorite U.S. and Philippine indie rock acts.

Along with analog forms of media, such as venues, radio stations, music magazines, and record stores, prevalent among previous Pinoy rock scenes in the 1980s and early 1990s, today's Pinoy indie rock scene is also networked together by more recent online platforms such as the social networking sites (SNS) of Facebook, YouTube, Twitter, and Tumblr. The transition between these media eras has not been cut and dry. Instead, as aptly captured by Henry Jenkins's term *convergence culture*, old analog forms and their new digital counterparts collide in today's participatory culture.[43] But, before we travel along these bold, new itineraries, we must further explore how translocality has resounded throughout the history of Manila's popular music scenes. Bearing in mind popular music's performative labor, its ability to *do* something, I now turn to a song that tracks a genealogy of Pinoy musical culture, telling the history of a place through lyrics.

Wala pa nung Myx
Wala pa nung MTV
Wala pa nung Internet
Wala pa nung Ipod at mp3
Wala pa nung cable

Wala pa nung cellphone
Wala pa ring CD or DVD
Meron lang Betamax
Sa Jingle magazine
Natutong mag-gitara
Sinifra ang mga kanta
Sa cassette at plaka ah

[Back when there was no Myx
Back when there was no MTV
Back when there was no Internet
Back when there was no iPod or MP3
Back when there was no cable
Back when there was no cellphone
Back when there was no CD or DVD
There was only Betamax
From Jingle magazine
You learned how to play guitar
You deciphered the song lyrics
From cassettes and albums]

In the chorus of the 2008 hit song "Betamax," Sandwich front man and former Eraserheads' drummer Raimund Marasigan sings about the days before the turn-of-the-twenty-first-century barrage of digital technologies, returning listeners to a time when aspiring musicians earned their musical training through the guitar chords of print publications like *Jingle* magazine or by deciphering (*sinifra*) lyrics by repeatedly listening to songs on borrowed LPs and dubbed cassettes. Marasigan's lyrics resonate with the stories of many contemporary OPM indie rock musicians that I have interviewed—the pedagogical importance of predigital forms such as radio shows and personalities, song hit magazines, record stores, and, of course, one-on-one interactions with other aspiring musicians and fans.[44] The song's lyrics sound out a litany of OPM idols: from classic rock legends Pepe Smith and Mike Hanopol to Manila Sound pop stars such as Rey Valera, VST, and Sharon Cuneta, with a nod to underground punk bands such as Dead Ends, Betrayed, and Identity Crisis, and musical outlets such as NU107 radio and Club Dredd. On one level, "Betamax" sells a nostalgic vision of OPM, one that encompasses various forms and genres as well as appears unsullied by outside musical and cultural influences. Performed as a directive, however, the song reminds its audiences of OPM's musical lineage, a history that disrupts a narrative of translocality as "new" and that challenges those who lament the lack of an "original" Filipino musical culture.[45]

In the history of Pinoy rock, more broadly, there have existed various hubs and places, both familiar and unexpected, where musicians and fans have gathered to make, hear, and share music. In the 1980s, A to Z record store, in Quezon City's Project 2 subdivision, served as one of those musical centers. Owned by music writer Tony Maghiram, the store was mainly known for its community board—where bands would list want ads for new members as well as post flyers for upcoming gigs—and its lending library–style system. For a small fee, something along the lines of ten pesos or today's equivalent of fifty cents, the store's owners would make bootleg cassette copies of various Philippine and U.S. rock and pop acts for their customers. As Sandwich guitarist Diego Castillo remembers, "You would buy your own little cassette, you'd tell them what you wanted, and they would tape it for you."[46] Here, young aspiring musicians, including the Gonzales brothers of piNoise-pop fame, were allowed access to album liner notes. As Jesse Gonzales recalls: "Yeah, sometimes we'd go to A to Z records to copy the lyrics. . . . from the actual [liner notes]. Sometimes, we'd want to play a cover of a song by the Descendents but then, we couldn't figure out the lyrics. We'd be like, "Alright, let's go to A to Z." And then we'd be like, "Boss, *paki-hiram nang* lyrics" ["Sir, can we borrow the lyrics?"], and we'd copy it."[47] Figuring out the lyrics to indecipherable American rock songs, they would add these hits to their band's playlist of cover songs.

This type of alternative pedagogy was also offered in the pages of *Jingle*, a magazine with national distribution that offered both the lyrics and guitar tablatures of the latest hits as well as reviews of local bands' shows and recordings. As Castillo recalls, the bimonthly publication featured a section reviewing local underground shows, gigs that for a fourteen-year-old were:

> The ones you couldn't go to! So all the kids at school were like, "*Chong, nabasa mo yung ano . . . si Teddy Diaz ang galing . . .*" (Dude, did you read that one . . . man, Teddy Diaz is so good!) And, you'd never see pictures . . . so you had, *iba ibang nang iksura* (a different sense of what things were like) so like, "*Wow ang galing*" (Wow, how

cool!). We'd know some of the bands from their covers . . . like, "Oh the showstopper . . . blah blah blah . . . Private Stock they, they closed the show with The Clash's 'Tommy Gun.'" *Parang*, "Wow, someone played 'Tommy Gun'!" *Eh parang ganoon kayo* . . . (It was like, "Wow, someone played 'Tommy Gun'!" That's how you were . . .)[48]

For these teenage fans and musicians, many of them too young to venture out to gigs and without enough expendable cash to buy the latest tapes (or even their own tape-to-tape machine to dub copies), the resources offered by places like A to Z or publications like *Jingle* magazine were invaluable.

During the Cold War years of the 1970s, when the neocolonial relationship between the United States and the Philippines strengthened, U.S. military bases also served as unlikely cultural hubs for the growth of Pinoy (classic) rock. At the height of the Vietnam War, and under Ferdinand Marcos's regime, Subic Naval Base and Clark Air Force Base were premiere R&R stops for servicemen on their way to and from fighting the "hot wars" in Southeast Asia. Many Pinoy classic rockers either began their musical careers playing in cover bands in the bars and clubs of towns surrounding the bases or maintained some formal or informal ties to these musicians. In the case of the Juan de la Cruz Band's lead singer Pepe Smith, some were even the actual offspring of U.S. or foreign military officers and local women. As Philippine music journalist Eric Caruncho recalls: "During Olongapo's glory days (which the rest of the world remembers as the Vietnam War), there was scarcely a night club that didn't have its own band. Hordes of GIs, fresh from the killing fields, poured into the clubs, demanded beer, poontang, and rock & roll music. Musicians used to hang out in the Olongapo public market. A bandleader could go there and literally pick up, say, a bass player and a lead guitarist for the night's gig, the way you'd pick up a kilo of beef."[49] Within a translocal economy of performative labor that included GROs ("guest relations officers"), dancers, and other types of sex work and hospitality services, Filipino rock musicians labored within the tradition of fellow cover performers and overseas performing artists (OPAs). U.S. soldiers, often requesting songs unfamiliar to these Filipino musicians, dubbed copies of the latest albums (by bands such as The Clash, Sex Pistols, AC/DC) sent to them from back home. Repeatedly listening to these recordings, musicians playing in these cover bands not only perfected guitar licks and solos to perform for their GI patrons, they also studied song structure and rock vocal prowess, learning skills that laid the musical foundation for Pinoy punk/rock scenes to come. These accounts remind us of the ways in which artists and institutions in the capital city of Manila operate beside and in collaboration with artists and institutions in other Philippine cities such as Baguio, Cebu, or Olongapo. As with the Excursion Tours of contemporary Manila-based bands, discussed in this book's epilogue, this history broadens our definition of translocality to include networks of places within a single nation.

During this same time, Manila-based bars and disco clubs also served as alternative sites for musical training and education. To properly entertain the expatriates and visiting diplomats who frequented these venues, the musical labor force of club DJs had to familiarize themselves with the latest sounds from the United States and Europe—punk and new wave. One of the premiere dance music venues in the early 1980s, Club ON stood on the corner of Buendia Avenue and Roxas Boulevard. Owned by Sonny Tanchangco, whose father was the head of Marcos's food ministry, Club ON and its DJs were able to entertain their audiences' requests, thanks to informal systems of acquiring pop music from overseas. As musician Buddy Trinidad recalled:

> *Noong 1979–1980 nagpupunta na 'ko ng Club On.* There was also another ON DJ. His name was Larry. *Kaibigan ko 'yun kaya nagkakaroon ng pagkikita dun. Dati ang raket ng plaka, dapat may kilala kang* flight attendant, stewardess. You'd give her a list of records you heard about. She'd leave on a Monday. *Eh puta,* Friday she'd be back, eh. So it was easy to get the records you wanted. My tito was a pilot. He used to get records for me. Then I also befriended Sonny. *Si Sonny din ang daming mga plaka.* He also had flight attendants as contacts. [Back around 1979–1980, I would go to Club ON. There was also another ON DJ. His name was Larry. He was my friend and was how I heard about the place. Back then, in order to scam albums/LPs, you needed to know a flight stewardess. You'd give her a list of records you heard about. She'd leave on Monday. Then, fuck, Friday she'd be back. So it was easy to get the records you wanted. My uncle was a pilot. He used to get records for me. Then I also befriended Sonny. Sonny also had a lot of records/albums. He also had flight attendants as contacts.][50]

In these translocal scenes of performative labor, Filipino cover band musicians and DJs created informal networks of musical education by circulating and sharing pop music introduced and carried over by U.S. soldiers, expats, and Filipina airline stewardesses. While these contraband LPs and dubbed cassette tapes helped these musicians stay ahead in their professions, they also provided an alternative, makeshift form of musical education that animated later Pinoy indie scenes.

As Arnold Morales of 1980s punk group Betrayed (and, later, 1990s band Put3ska) remembered:

> *Ang unang encounter ko sa* punk, *may* kabarkada akong *Fil-Am* na taga- Pampanga, taga-*U.S. base. Classic rocker,* naka-*moptop,* kamuka ni *Peter Frampton. Ang dala niyang plaka,* Sex Pistols. God Save the Queen *yata. Eh kasagsagan ng* Pinoy Rock. *May mga* magazines *din sya, kasi nga* rocker *siya. Pintugtugan niya ako ng* Pistols *sa* phonograph. *Malapit din lang kami sa* DZRJ. *Tambayan talaga namin 'yun. Pati 'yung* band scene *noon, alam ko na kasi pag- agpa-* party *sa amin, may mga banda na talaga. Dumating yung* punk rock *through* Howlin' Dave *kasi nagpapatugtog sya sa* ere *ng* Pistols. *Kasabay noon, may mga* Joe Jackson *at* The Police *na din. Meron ding* XTC. [My first encounters with punk, I had a Filipino-American friend who was from Pampanga, from the U.S. base. (He was a) classic rocker, had a mop-top, looked like Peter Frampton. The record/album he brought: Sex Pistols. God Save the Queen, I think. This was at the height of Pinoy rock. He also had magazines, because he was, in fact, a rocker. He played the Sex Pistols for me on the phonograph. We also lived close to DZRJ (radio station). That was totally our hangout. Even the band scene back then, I knew about it already because when there were parties in our neighborhood, the bands would definitely play. Punk rock arrived through Howlin' Dave because he played the (Sex) Pistols on the air. Back then, he also played Joe Jackson and the Police. There was also XTC.][51]

Morales's account parallels Raimund Marasigan's own memories of discovering new wave bands, like The Cure and Echo & the Bunnymen, in the mid-1980s through tapes provided by friends and relatives visiting from the United States.[52] Alongside these more individual examples of obtaining and hearing new music from Europe and the United States, through means both within and outside Philippine national borders, there was DJ Howlin' Dave, the first Philippine radio disc jockey to broadcast the latest new wave and punk sounds.

For those not privy to their personal copy of the latest American or British rock hit, punk rock's sounds first came over the Philippine airwaves in 1978. Former Club ON DJ Howlin' Dave (aka Dante David) is credited as the first to play the explosive sounds of U.S. and British punk music on the air. Through his radio show "New Wave Nights," broadcast on weekday evenings on DZRJ-AM, Howlin' Dave brought to many budding Filipino musicians and rockers the latest sounds from across two ponds. At the same time, Howlin' Dave also utilized his access to radio airwaves to cultivate emerging local talent. Here, we can think of Dave as a historical predecessor to someone like Myrene Academia. Sounding the call in the early 1980s, Dave announced: *"Baka may* recordings *kayo diyan . . . dalhin ninyo dito, I-e-ere naming kung puwede . . ."* [Maybe you guys out there have recordings. . . . bring them here to the station and we'll try to play them, if we can . . .] and spurred many new and still-forming local acts into action by promising them a potential means of distributing their recorded songs. Almost a decade after, NU107's owner Atom Henares also sounded the call for new and emerging OPM bands to submit professional and amateur demo recordings and broadcast the best of them on his program, "In the Raw." These accounts of analog media forms, and the ways in which they helped original Pilipino musical (OPM) forms such as classic, punk, and indie rock flourish, fly in the face of the cultural imperialist view that non-Western cultures passively consume U.S. and European popular music. Instead, these stories show how Filipino rock musicians have flipped the beat on Western pop musical objects and media in the service of developing local scenes and sounds.

While this chapter focuses on the translocal qualities of scenes in two different cities, the epilogue attempts to further map the translocal by focusing on the circulation of Pinoy indie rock musical performers and feature films in the Philippines, the United States, and beyond. Listening against the popular discourses surrounding the Internet's impact on musical distribution and reception, I instead argue for the crucial duties that interpersonal relationships and live performances continue to serve. This, of course, is not to fetishize the live as the real or authentic experience. Nor is it a means to disregard the central role that media and its technologies play. It instead hopes to further highlight the ongoing practices and performances of musical doing, renditions constituted by and constitutive of Filipino America's musical life, required to maintain translocal musical scenes.

Epilogue

Rakenrol Itineraries

Gibson Bonifacio has lost his voice. He has chosen to remain mute and silent since witnessing the death of his twin brother. A feature film in 2012 by Philippine director Marie Jamora, *Ang Nawawala* [What Isn't There] opens with college-age Gibson's (Dominic Roco) first return to Manila. After three years away studying abroad, Gibson arrives in time to celebrate Christmas and New Year, a holiday season when the inner workings and dysfunctions of families bubble just below the surface. In its opening sequence, *Ang Nawawala* captures two recognizable scenes for Manila homecomings—an airport baggage claim's moving conveyor belt filled with brightly marked luggage and *balikbayan* cardboard boxes, and the brightly lit ads that litter the city's main thoroughfare, Epifanio de los Santos Avenue (EDSA). Once inside the Bonifacios' upper-middle-class home, with its own highly stylized mise-en-scène, the viewer is saturated with a sense of melancholy and lament. *Ang Nawawala* portrays the subtle and everyday coping mechanisms of each family member in the decades-long wake of an unspeakable, yet palpable, family event. Their father Wesley (Boboy Garrovillo) continually attempts to feign a cheery disposition, one that is echoed in the carefree innocence of the youngest sibling, Promise (Sabrina Man), who was not yet born when Gibson's twin Jamie (Felix Roco) died. Their eldest sister, Ate Corey (Jenny Jamora), works just as hard as her father to maintain family coherence. In many ways, she is the sage, omniscient observer of the family's dynamics, except that she continually dotes on her dopey boyfriend, Michael (Marc Abaya). A deeply tragic figure, their mother

Esme (Dawn Zulueta) numbs any possible pain with her bottles of pre-scription pills. Over dinner, all family members, except for her, are eager to ask questions about Gibson's life in the United States and to update him on the life he has missed in Manila. Despite the verbal onslaught, this everyday scene is also permeated with its share of awkward glances and extended periods of silence. Gibson's abstention from speaking is not the only muteness that fills their home. As the film progresses, however, we learn that Gibson does, in fact, speak—to the ghost of his deceased twin brother as well as through the moving images he captures with his video camera.

After this initial dinner scene, Gibson's childhood friend Teddy (Alchris Galura) arrives and whisks him away from his family's emo-tionally fraught life. He brings Gibs to an art gallery opening where he has plans to meet his friend Simone (Mercedes Cabral) and to show him one of the city's newest hot spots. On the small second-floor landing of Finale Art File gallery, Jamora's camera does a slow 360-degree panning shot that opens with a cameo performance by electronica/live drum duo Tarsius (featuring Pedicab frontman Diego Mapa and Radioactive Sago Project drummer Jay Gapasin) and that ends by settling in on Teddy and Gibson surveying the room. Here is where Gibs literally bumps into the hip and sexy music nerd Enid (Annicka Dolonius). After their chance meeting, the duo, along with Teddy, Simone, and her boyfriend Mac (Kelvin Yu of the local band the Itchyworms) end up at a local eatery (Shift, an actual restaurant located across from the real-life Saguijo bar). Hearing the opening chords of the Eraserheads' "Minsan," they launch into an impromptu sing-along performance, complete with air drum solos, while Gibs head bops along with the group. The other three remi-nisce about how important the song was during their college years.

Rakenrol (2011), like Jamora's film, is another coming-of-age feature, more comedic than melancholic, set in the Manila indie rock scene. Directed by Quark Henares and cowritten by Sandwich guitarist Diego Castillo, *Rakenrol* is an unrequited love story that centers on Odie and Irene (Glaiza de Castro) in their journey to form a band. They first meet in high school, sharing their love and admiration for local OPM/Pinoy indie rock bands. When they enter college, Irene learns of Odie's song-writing and musical skills and convinces him to start a band. Initially assigning herself the role of band manager, Irene inadvertently ends up the band's lead singer. Along the way, they meet Mo (Ketchup Eusebio), a former guitarist with the punk band Titik O, now a barista; Jun-four (Alwyn Uytingco), a novice drummer with limited musical skills but much heart; and former child star turned band manager Matet de Leon. Whereas the lead characters of *Ang Nawawala* occupy Makati dive venues (such as Saguijo and B-Side) and Quezon City bars (such as Route 196) mainly as audience members, *Rakenrol*'s leads navigate the city's indie music scene as a fledgling band—the Hapipaks—that encounters a cast of heart-warming as well as unsavory characters. Pinoy pop celebrities, including male model Diether Ocampo (as Jacci Rocha, the lead singer of a "*pogi* boy rock band" and Irene's "super-crush") and Pinoy indie rock's unofficial poet laureate and the Eraserheads' lead singer, Ely Buendia, also make cameos. Popular actors Jun Sabayton and Ramon Bautista, as Mo's "art for art's sake" roommate Francis (aka Yagit) and as avant-garde music video director Flame Tigerbluden, respectively, bring their brand of uproariously bizarre humor to the film.

Described as their "love letter" to the scene in which they grew up and currently belong, Henares and Castillo's film opens with Odie's voice-over narrating his personal history and love for OPM/Pinoy rock music—from witnessing, as a child, his father's love for Pinoy rock to his cousin's flagrant punk rock performances during their adolescent years to the formative event of watching the Eraserheads live in concert. From there, the film launches into a sequence of iconic Pinoy rock images that are set to Pinoy punk band Urban Bandits' rendition of "Manila Girl," as the film's credits appear. Within the span of three minutes, this opening sequence provides, through a montage of photographic images, a brief thumbnail sketch of Pinoy indie rock's musical predecessors—namely, Pinoy punk and classic rock—and the scene's current stars.

As tropical renditions, both films also disobediently listen to nationalist and global tropes regarding Philippine indie cinema. Against contemporary Philippine indie cinema's propensity for stories of the working class and the urban poor, Jamora actively chose to focus *Ang Nawawala*'s story line on a Manila-based middle-class family. As Henares has asserted, *Rakenrol* should be considered as one of the first Philippine cinematic examples of the "band movie" genre. Both based their first feature films on familiar experiences and hope that their storytelling choices embolden other indie Philippine filmmakers to diversify their representations and story lines beyond norms set by Philippine nationalist and global cinema industries.

While their films do not easily fit within the paradigms of authenticity set for Filipino indie cinema, Jamora's and Henares's Pinoy indie rock authenticity has aided them in the production and distribution of their films. Because of their direct involvement in this musical scene, both Henares and Jamora were allowed a different level of access to musical artists and places. While centered on fictional narratives, both films were set in actual Manila-based venues, featured performances by real Pinoy indie bands and musical acts, and spotlighted classic OPM and contemporary Pinoy indie rock songs. In these ways, both directors' indie rock authenticity is made evident. Both films also inadvertently serve as archival documents of the Manila indie rock scene. Many places and institutions featured in *Rakenrol* and *Ang Nawawala*, such as Mag:Net High Street, Mayric's, and radio station NU107, no longer exist.

In the context of indie cinema, be it U.S.- or Philippines-based, authenticity is also marked by the persistent (to the point of now becoming "commonsensical") and valorized notion of grassroots, ground-level, DIY production and distribution as one without the stain of assistance from corporations or other industry entities. In other words, to be truly indie is to struggle financially. While Jamora's film was cofinanced predominantly by her own personal savings and by the NCCA (National Commission for Culture and the Arts), as well as financiers, producers, and crowd-funding platform Artiste Connect, Henares's film received much of its financial backing from its executive producer Vicki Belo, a beauty and fitness mogul who also happens to be Henares's mother. Listening and working against the authenticating tropes of indie cinema, both filmmakers have worked in the mainstream industry (for Regal Films and other commercial television and film endeavors) as well as on indie projects. When it comes to economics and production, the clear lines that indie narratives of authenticity attempt to draw are often blurred.

Issues of class and economics plague not only matters of production but also filmic content, as evidenced by critical attention to *Ang Nawawala*. In his review "Burgis na Juvenilia," University of the Philippines film professor Rolando Tolentino takes *Ang Nawawala* to task for the fact that "there is no self-reflexive gesture or insight presented about the upper class."[1] *Ang Nawawala* seemed "unapologetic by nature" about its characters' class position and, according to Cinemalaya judge

Figure E.I *Ang Nawawala* official film poster. Courtesy of Marie Jamora.

Figure E.2 *Rakenrol* official film poster designed by Inksurge. Courtesy of Quark Henares and Diego Castillo.

and well-known cultural critic Bienvenido Lumbera, part of a trend, evident at the 2012 festival, of films centered on middle-class and upper-class themes. When viewed alongside a "standard" set by many other Cinemalaya films, a majority of which focused on "the marginalized and disadvantaged," Tolentino contends that Jamora's film's characters and plot "just aren't compelling." Instead, *Ang Nawawala* "underscores how trivial the concerns of the privileged class are compared to the perpetual struggles of those in abject poverty" and "reaffirms popular capitalist and consumerist media and culture." "Extremely bored by the MTV (music video) moments," Tolentino concludes that these scenes have "mainly to do with the merchandising of the CD (album) version itself" since "nothing much happens during these moments apart from the characters nodding their heads to the music and dancing."

Tolentino's review is useful for the ways in which it reveals a few underlying concerns and inclinations as well as expectations leveled by the study of Philippine independent/indie film. Philippine independent cinema is commonly defined as working within the filmic genre of social realism. As UP film scholar Patrick F. Campos points out, "references to 'Philippine cinema,' whether local or international, popular or academic, almost always refer to the so-called golden age of Philippine cinema (1975–84) as a central trope by which to understand and discursively define the current indie phenomenon."[2] Taking place at the height of Ferdinand Marcos's martial rule, this Golden Age of Philippine cinema was characterized by the narratives and filmic techniques of directors such as Lino Brocka and Ismael Bernal. According to Campos: "The thematic preoccupations of the key films of the period were the necessity and/or tragedy of mobility and anonymity, the systematic oppression of individuals and regulation of bodies, and the search for identity; their imagery was based on 'creative' visualizations of poverty; their preferred mode of narration was 'realism'; and the setting of arguably the most defining films was the city."[3]

Veering toward social realist narratives of the urban poor, iconic films, such as *Maynila sa Kuko ng Liwanag* (Manila in the Claws of Light) and *Manila City by Night*, made their mark both locally and internationally. In a martial law society, where media was highly regulated and censored, for these filmmakers to decide to make realist films was, in itself, "a political statement." In the film criticism circles of the 1970s and 1980s, ones "not limited to but indelibly defined by, the writings of the members of the only critics group in the Philippines at the time, the *Manunuri ng Pelikulang Pilipino* (MPP)," these films' "brand of urban realism" matched the local group's own artistic preferences. As MPP member Lumbera proclaimed in 1984, Filipino filmmakers should aim for "social change, nationalism, and social consciousness," "expunge the scars of colonial past," contribute to the attainment of "progress and stability," help "secure for the people freedom from foreign domination and raise the level of their consciousness regarding rights and obligations."[4]

With such critical backing, these Golden Age films set stylistic and political norms for Philippine cinema. Not only expected but applauded by global film industries, urban realism sets a local standard within the Philippines where, as Campos writes, "Every other major mainstream director, in the last four decades, has made a 'poverty film,' at times considered the crowning glory of their careers."[5] As will be further explored in my discussion of the *Word of the Lourd* series, within the Philippine indie cinema lexicon, a poverty film often translates to a festival film, that is, a particular genre (largely not musicals or comedies) described as "dark, serious, challenging and linked to classic or emergent auteurs."[6] The added fact that Tolentino's review was written in formal Tagalog underscores the fact that the standards under which Philippine indie cinema is measured continue to be those of a particular nationalist bent. Ironically, what nationalist Philippine film critics expect from local indie films corresponds, more often than not, with what the global film festival circuit desires.

Tolentino's review prompted further discussions among Manila-based online critics regarding the place of class and class dynamics in Philippine film and filmmaking. In her December 2012 online review, Mara Coson places Jamora's film alongside two other contemporary Philippine indie films (Marty Syjugco's documentary *Give Up Tomorrow* and Gino M. Santos's "bling ring" send-off, *The Animals*) in order to mark the possibility of more than "just a passing trend" of films "made by and for the privileged." In regard to *Ang Nawawala*'s failed commercial success, Coson writes:

> While it was extremely popular among pockets of the local music scene, its commercial release failed to produce the numbers it had hoped for, and the film was nearly pulled out before its run had

ended. There were many things that may have been lost in translation for a mainstream audience: the stylistic influences of Wes Anderson, the portrayal of "young love" in the context of an opaque "scene," and the role of music as a character in the film. But in a sense, the confused reception was expected. *Ang Nawawala* is a film written for music and for music itself; it is the director's homage to her experience, and for this reason the film's near mainstream failure hints at its success.[7]

While Coson's piece makes sweeping assumptions regarding a Philippine "mainstream audience," what it does adequately point out are certain standards under which *Ang Nawawala* might be regarded as an independent film. It maintains its "art cred" and indie authenticity precisely through its failure to become a box office success, its being set within a seemingly obscure or, at least, nonmainstream "scene," and its artistic nod to other indie film styles and makers (not just Anderson but, I might add, Hong Kong director Wong Kar-Wai, as well). This last point gestures to one type of global indie style, one marked by highly stylized art production, strong emphasis on its soundtrack (for storytelling purposes), and an overall emphasis on mood. Therefore, the category of "indie film" cannot be simply defined by filmic content or the economics of its production and reception but by its shared artistic sensibilities, as well.

A few months after Coson's article appeared online, critic Alice Sarmiento responded, on the same *Manila Review* website, to previous critical writings. In regard to Tolentino's review, which mainly seemed to question whether Jamora is speaking "for" her audience or "to" her audience, Sarmiento strongly countered that Jamora's film worked from the autobiographical, a genre less preferred than the hagiographical in Philippine film. Sarmiento opens the essay by taking Jamora's film to task for its "deterritorialized aspects—from the language to the production design—which incited a number of conflicting and conflicted reactions since the film was released, in mid-2012." But then, perplexingly, she moves on and applauds Jamora's use of specificity to tell a larger story:

By setting *Ang Nawawala* in the middle of Metro Manila's independent music scene (with a little cameo from the art world), Jamora manages to erase the specifics of time and space, manipulating a universal medium to speak to a broad audience about a very particular subject. This is where she is most successful: by taking the bricolage of her own life—formed by literary nerdiness, bands with small audiences, and pockets of the city that were never very popular to begin with—she manages to weave a web of references that can safely cradle anyone's experience, whether actual or aspirational.[8]

In describing Jamora's filmmaking ability "to weave a web of references that can safely cradle anyone's experience, whether actual or aspirational," Sarmiento's review makes universal a particular middle-class experience and rehearses precisely what Tolentino, Lumbera, and other Philippine critics warn against. However, Jamora herself has underscored how the film has reflected her particular upbringing and interests—in telling a solidly middle-class family narrative, featuring both contemporary and historical OPM music, and pivoting her story around twins and the withholding of one's voice.[9] With its real-life settings and contemporary musical performances, Jamora's film is actually marked by "the specifics of time and space." By criticizing Ang Nawawala for its "deterritorialized aspects," despite the film being shot in actual locations, Sarmiento's review rehashes Philippine indie film criticism's beat on how and which places in Manila can and should be figured through film.

I want to listen against these calls to continue viewing Ang Nawawala from simply a class-based standpoint and instead also consider the film as a coming-of-age love story set in a music scene. In line with the ethnographic disposition of many Philippine new realist films and in the style of musical movie genres, this particular indie music scene is not just a setting but also an important character in both Jamora's and Henares's films. When we shift our understanding of these films' "MTV moments" from one of mere commercialized backdrop to one where the music emplaces the viewer and tells its own story, we not only call attention and challenge prescriptive notions of Philippine independent filmmaking. We also leave ourselves open to Pinoy indie rock's ability to figure other places, people, and shared feelings, in film and music, in live and recorded performances.

But first, we must pause and consider the popular tropes of Philippine indie cinema that Ang Nawawala and Rakenrol listen against. Commonly known but nowhere officially outlined, these tropes were the

Figure E.3 *Word of the Lourd* cast. Left to right: Ramon Bautista, Lourd de Veyra, Angel Rivero, RA Rivera (director), Arvin "Tado" Jimenez, Jun Sabayton. Courtesy of RA Rivera.

satirical fodder of a 2011 *Word of the Lourd* (WOTL) series titled, "Make Your Own Indie Film." Interstitial videos played during Akyson TV5's evening news program, WOTL starred indie-crossover broadcast journalist, poet-novelist, political satirist, and Radioactive Sago Project bandleader Lourd de Veyra. Directed by filmmaker and Pedicab band member RA Rivera, this series also starred Rivera's regular collaborators—actor-comedian Jun Sabayton, actress-TV host Angel "Erning" Rivero, TV-radio personality Arvin "Tado" Jimenez, and actor-comedian and UP Film Studies professor Ramon Bautista.

The show opens with de Veyra, Jimenez, and Bautista standing in front of the UP Film Institute marquee and announcing, in a matter of fact tone, the reason for the series. "Like skateboarding, surfing, and doing cocaine, indie film has become ever popular." Proclaiming the maxims "anyone can become a film director" and "indie is art," the series takes on a mode of how-to/instructional videos starring Sabayton as the director-in-training and with cultural metacommentary from de Veyra. Over the course of three short videos, "Make Your Own Indie Film" tackles common tropes associated with indie film production practices and styles, all the things necessary so that, as Sabayton repeatedly barks at his all-in-one cameraman-director of photography-production assistant sidekick, "We can make it into Cannes!" The series pokes fun at the notion of art for art's sake. The lofty ideals expressed in one scene, in which Bautista declares "a film director needs to be able to think deeply because art is deep," are juxtaposed with the economic realities portrayed in the next, in which director-producer Sabayton calls his potential financial backers—Mom, Mama Charing, and Kuya Willie—from a *sari-sari* store's landline. It parodies common camera techniques for signaling realist aesthetics—from "moving cameras" to real-time filmmaking, from bad lighting to *kahirapan* [squatter area] location settings, from fuzzy sound to the recurrent musical trope of flutes (to mark the indigenous and the local)—as well as familiar characters—the prostitute, the "gay element," the call boy, and the *taong grasa*.

Literally translating to "greasy people," *taong grasa* typically define homeless people, beggars, and vagrants, often with mental health issues. As both film and TV characters, they symbolize the most extreme cases of Philippine abject poverty while their condition signifies the moral compass of Philippine society. In their series, de Veyra, Sabayton, and crew lay bare the artfulness of *becoming* taong grasa. Going to speak to one of the "maestros" of Philippine indie film, acclaimed actor Ronnie Lazaro, Sabayton earnestly asks: "How do you become a *taong grasa*?" Lazaro immediately laughs but then answers, in all seriousness, with a laundry list—dirty nails, carbon paper and oil on the skin, and a matted and unkempt hairstyle (ironically, one that Sabayton already sports in *WOTL* and as Yagit in *Rakenrol*). When Sabayton tries to enlist both Lazaro and Joel Torre, another well-known indie and commercial actor, for his low- to no-budget film project, however, his "artsy-fartsy" indie ideals are crushed. Sensing that he has no film budget, both Lazaro and Torre directly confront Sabayton with every working actor's question: "Can you pay my talent fee, *direk*?"

By turning to these segments of *Word of the Lourd*'s "How to Make an Indie Film," I demonstrate that Pinoy indie media makers are well aware of certain common filmic tropes. These are not just examples of Filipinos' self-deprecating humor. They are parodies by those in the business of indie media. By respectfully poking fun at them, a different generation flips the beat, making something their own and in their own way. Knowledgeable of Philippine indie cinema's long history, their humor works precisely because of their ability to identify recognizable characteristics and still pay homage to Philippine indie film's traditions and artists.

This epilogue listens against familiar critical and curatorial tropes of what has been deemed Philippine indie film as Jamora's and Henares's films do against its assumed narratives, techniques, and styles. It continues by examining the U.S.-based film festivals where both films have screened. Here, even when films are grouped and marketed within familiar filmic genres, they still rely on national designation. In contrast, this chapter moves toward nonfilm festival screenings and events to make evident the translocal audiences of Pinoy indie rock culture. By also listening in on the unofficial shows of Philippines-based bands (Ciudad, Sandwich, Taken by Cars) in the United States, of U.S.-based bands (Versus, +/-) in the Philippines, and of Manila-based bands in other Philippine cities, it begins to reckon with different strains of artist collaborations and the building of new audiences. These events offer us alternative channels through which to hear Pinoy indie rock's translocality. In this epilogue, I examine translocal scenes of Pinoy indie rock in the postdigital/post-Internet age of the early twenty-first century. I am interested in how translocality operates in these scenes and how these instances add to and challenge our approaches to the study of music, media, globalization, and migration.

This final chapter disobediently listens to simple notions of cultural imperialism and musical authenticity by listening in on the tropical renditions of indie Filipino films; performances by Philippine-based indie rock bands in prominent U.S. music festivals and showcases; artist-initiated/DIY tours of U.S.-based indie bands in the Philippines; and U.S.-based productions/tours featuring Philippine-based indie rock bands. By examining the alternative, sometimes extranational, circuits that Pinoy indie rock constructs and circulates along, I end this book with an expansive reflection on the ever-growing and ever-changing contours of Filipino America. By closely viewing and listening to scenes in *Ang Nawawala*, at the very end of this epilogue, I want to finish by considering what is at stake in moving music and sound away from mere backdrop and toward its place as atmosphere, event, and even a character in film. A Sandwich show at B-Side. An Eraserheads' song transformed into a group sing-along. Listening to old records in one's bedroom. Hearing new songs at the local record store. In this process, a phonographic approach not only helps us take into account the multisensorial scenes of Pinoy indie culture. It also returns us to the liveliness and possibility of listening to and reckoning with silence.

Festivals

Along with their shared focus on Manila's indie rock scene, both *Rakenrol* and *Ang Nawawala* have benefited from screening at a diverse set of film festivals—Manila's Cinemalaya Film Festival, vc's (Visual Communications) Los Angeles Asian Pacific Film Festival (LAAPAFF), and the New Filipino Cinema events at San Francisco's Yerba Buena Center for the Arts (YBCA).[10] Started in 2005, Cinemalaya is a film competition and festival that takes place every July at the Cultural Center of the Philippines (CCP). *Ang Nawawala* premiered at Cinemalaya 2012 as one of the ten New Breed Category feature films—projects awarded a seed grant for production—and won both the Audience Award and Best Original Musical Score. The year before, *Rakenrol* made its Philippine premiere as the festival's closing night film. But since the film received no funding from the Cinemalaya Foundation, its screening was deemed a special exhibition that even featured a postscreening concert on the CCP grounds (right outside the theater building). Whereas Jamora's film followed a common trajectory whereby Cinemalaya helped launch the film's distribution overseas, the 2011 Cinemalaya screening of *Rakenrol*—which had already premiered in Los Angeles and New York earlier that same year—served as a homecoming for the film.

With sold-out screenings at Visual Communications' LAAPFF (in 2011 and 2013, respectively) and YBCA's New Filipino Cinema events, the success of the films speaks to their appeal for audiences both in Manila and the United States. Circulating within a translocal network of Asian American and Filipino film festivals, in cities such as Los Angeles, San Francisco, and New York, the presentation and reception of these films underscore the politics and importance of festivals, more broadly, as events centered around arts and culture.[11] Since the 1990s, Asian American film festivals have turned their programming attention away from *solely* U.S.-based Asian American productions and more toward including independent films produced in Asian countries.[12] By following a genre-driven curatorial style, events such as YBCA's New Filipino Cinema work to define (or, at the very least, set certain parameters around) the category of "Filipino indie cinema."

As tropical renditions, both *Ang Nawawala* and *Rakenrol* do the social, cultural, and affective work of dramatizing, and inadvertently archiving, the contemporary Manila indie rock scene. They draw upon Jamora's and Henares's connections to this translocal scene and the ways each director works within familiar filmic genres (the coming of age love story, the "making of a rock band" film). As tropical renditions, these films are shaped by colonial pasts. The fact that Manila has one of the longest histories of filmmaking in Southeast Asia is due, in large part, to the Philippines' long history of U.S. colonialism.[13] Through the mobile form of cinema, these films have reached out to and found audiences in other node cities within the network of Pinoy indie rock's translocal scenes. As tropical renditions, these films circulate within the context of film festivals, online/social media networks, and DIY/artist-initiated screenings, all sites where certain logics of authenticity dominate. In the context of film festival curation, authenticity exhibits itself through both audience members and festival screening committees' desire to experience cinematically the supposed realities of a place or people and the ways in which these demands are met by certain types of narratives, characters, and locations (such as those of "poverty porn" described above).

Festivals are components of broader translocal scenes (such as Pinoy indie rock). They simultaneously exist on the levels of the "local, translocal, and virtual."[14] Temporally bound and often geographically situated, festivals are ephemeral events that operate at a level of "intensity" while also performing a certain amount of "boundary-work" and curatorial labor. Film and music festivals often promise a representative sampling of artists and styles. Such programming allows audiences, perhaps initially drawn to the event by one of their old-time favorites, the opportunity to stumble on a new band or musician. Coming together from geographically dispersed locations and drawn away from "the expectations of everyday life," festival participants immerse themselves in a culture while they can also "experiment with different identities."

As events closely linked to a particular city or town, festivals draw our attention to place. They hold much value, be it positive or negative, in terms of tourism and relations between local and nonlocal artists, community members, and inhabitants. Certain places and, in particular, cities appear conducive to particular types of festivals—for example, piNoisepop and San Francisco (with its large Asian American arts scene and cultural history); Noise Pop and San Francisco (with the city's notoriety in relationship to indie culture); CMJ music marathon and New York (with the city viewing itself as the media capital of the world). At the same time, places have been made famous by festivals such as Cannes, Sundance, South by Southwest (SXSW) and, in many of these cases, locals are often left to debate about these events' lasting impact before and after the "circus" rolls in and out of their city or town. The connections between festivals and the larger political economies of cities and film and music industries are made clear whether a festival feeds into those industries or takes a stance in defiance of them.

Festivals demand a certain level of commitment (specifically, time and money) from artists and audience alike. At the same time, they offer a performative promise—to craft a space where "public displays" of identity and culture, ones otherwise denied or looked down on in the mainstream public sphere, can take place. As individuals seeking such moments and places, receptive audiences and performing musicians stand to benefit from the profoundly transformative effects of an arts- and culture-centered festival. As one Michigan Womyn's festival attendee noted, "[It] becomes a place I can immerse myself in this amazing creation we rebuild each year, and return to my daily life knowing that the way I wish the world could be is possible and actual."[15] Similar festivals also contain such a kernel of world-making potential as they allow artists, audiences, and fans to craft an intimate public organized around their strong dedication to and passion for particular artistic objects, performers, values, and tastes. In other words, these festivals allow us to imagine a world where a different set of principles and values is what drives everyday life. Harkening to their religious origins, festivals are transformative events that also mark a particular place and time.

Against the popular discourse of festivals as "time out of time" rituals, however, I instead side with scholars, such as Monica Sassatelli, who approach them as "social phenomena to be contextualized in the particularities of modern society," in turn, arguing for their "sociability."[16] In this sense, we can recognize the South by Southwest (SXSW) festival and the CMJ Music Marathon as events that occur within a transnational indie musical culture as they impact and are impacted by larger cultural and industry-driven "social distinctions or tastes," and thereby "offer a source of legitimacy to artists within [its] genre."[17] Attuned to the histories of both festivals, we can immediately track how *indie* has persistently functioned as a marketing category and set of cultural values. While its authenticity discourse might be based upon anticorporatism, indie musical culture has persistently functioned alongside and (sometimes) within the corporate music industry. Gathering and showcasing artists whom they deem to be the newest and biggest talents (at least, as drawn from the submission pool of applicants), these festivals broadly hold cultural capital and a particular promise for bands: to be heard by music industry insiders on their stages in the hopes of being dubbed the "next big thing." This opportunity is offered to bands from across the United States as well as the globe. With the large number of bands participating in each of these festivals, programming and schedules emphasize showcasing acts rather than the development of further artistic collaborations.

In early 2011, *Time* magazine (Asia edition) named the Manila-based Taken by Cars as "one of the five new bands to watch for" that year. Invited to perform at the 2011 SXSW festival, the band initially declined because they were in the middle of recording their second album, *Dualist*. But, more important, they were also not financially prepared to cover the costs of travel. They made it a goal, however, to be prepared to raise the necessary funds in order to say "yes" when they were invited again the following year. With an original plan of raising 500,00PhP (a little over $11,000) to cover travel/airfare and lodging costs for the band's five members and their manager, the group was only able to raise 67,500PhP ($1,500) on the crowd-sourced fundraising website Artiste Connect, a Philippine-based version of America's own Kickstarter. However, thanks to a fundraising concert performance, just days before they left for the United States, the band was able to raise the remaining funds.

Taken by Cars began in 1998, when three of its members (Bryce Zialcita, Derek "Siopao" Chua, and Bryan Kong) were high school sophomores. Back then, their only wish was to play gigs at Saguijo in Makati. Over the next eight years, the group struggled to find a sound to settle into. After taking a hiatus from playing gigs and instead focusing their attention on songwriting and recording, by early 2007 they had agreed upon a band name and a lead singer, Sarah Marco. They also began to garner a following via their Myspace band page. In February 2007, they submitted a demo copy of their single "A Weeknight Memoir (In High Definition)" to "In the Raw," NU107's radio show that featured local and emerging Philippines-based indie talent. Signed to a distribution deal with Warner Music Philippines, the following year the band released their debut album, *Endings of a New Kind*. In his review of the album, musician Diego Mapa noted that although listeners "can hear Bloc Party, css and New Young Pony Club in their music, Taken by Cars are doing something that sounds different and refreshing. The drums party like a drum machine, the riffs are shimmering, the bass is distorted like an analog keyboard, and Sarah Marco's vocals are gonna rip all the men's boxer shorts to shreds."[18]

With an electro-rock sound that is familiar to indie music fans/listeners worldwide, Taken by Cars' sound has particular appeal for young female fans and all Pinoy indie rock listeners who yearn for a strong female vocalist and front woman as well as non-Tagalog-speaking fans/listeners. Save for their physical appearance and visual style, Taken by Cars challenge certain expectations of the OPM genre of Pinoy indie rock. All their song lyrics are in English and, therefore, the band's music does not distance listeners who do not speak or understand the archipelago's national language. At the same time, for those seeking an authentic Manila indie rock experience through the presence of Tagalog words, slang, or popular street phrases, Taken by Cars does not quite deliver. They lean more toward Pinoy indie rock musical sounds and images that are much more in line with, and therefore more capable of crossing over to, a global indie culture. Much of the journalistic coverage surrounding Taken by Cars' appearance at the 2012 SXSW festival focused on the fact that they were the first Filipino band to perform on this internationally recognized stage. While the band members themselves recognized it as an honor to be able to "represent" on behalf of the Philippines and play alongside 1,500 other bands from around the world, Philippine news media outlets also emphasized the star-making power and crossover potential of an SXSW performance (for example, listing a number of U.S.-based artists who "got their break" performing at the annual festival such as John Mayer or The White Stripes).

In many ways, especially because of the SXSW festival, Austin, Texas, itself has become a translocal site of indie music and culture. While the city boasts a vibrant, local music scene, it is the annual festival, now in its twenty-eighth year, that has placed it on the global map of pop music and culture. Featuring evening showcases as well as daytime conference panels, workshops, and discussions, SXSW has expanded its generic reach to include film, interactive media/technology, and education. Constituting a large portion of the city's tourist economy and landscape, it also boasts that it is "one of the biggest global music market places in the world" where "deals get done while parties are had."[19]

The case of Taken by Cars' appearance at the 2012 SXSW festival therefore reveals the paradox for non-Western musical acts within global indie culture—to carry the burden of representing their nation while, at the same time, presenting an accessible musical style and sound. Lauded by Filipino and Filipino American media outlets as the first Filipino band to be accepted and to play the international festival, when asked "What is your main goal in playing SXSW?," Taken by Cars' lead singer Sarah Marco followed suit with this sentiment of musical nationalism: "We'd just really want to get the music out there and represent ourselves, our country, our music in the best way possible. It would be great if there [is] a positive response, but the fact that we're playing SXSW and are going to be [in] the same stage and venue with some of our most admired bands is a huge accomplishment."[20]

Yet, these nationalist sentiments are still tinged with an eye and ear toward the business of making and marketing non-U.S.-based music. Whereas a number of fan and media blogs noted the importance of SXSW in helping catapult previously indie musicians into mainstream success, for insiders such as TbC's manager, Mike Shih, "recognition" of international acts no longer translates to merely success and "making it" in U.S. markets. Instead, he hoped "the recognition . . . that we are a band from the Philippines and we know how to make good music too" (with the help of the Internet and social media) will lead to "people from the outside" "looking in" on Philippine-based musicians, in a way "similar to the success model of Bollywood and K-Pop."[21] However, what Shih and other like-minded proponents of Pinoy indie rock/music might have failed to consider is the ways that governments and private business sectors (in the case of Bollywood and K-Pop) have created infrastructures for the production, distribution, and marketing of their national cultural exports.[22] The same, unfortunately, cannot be said for OPM or Pinoy indie rock music.

Playing at the CMJ Music Marathon in 2009, the lo-fi trio of Ciudad made less of a splash than their Pinoy indie rock colleagues. Their first trip, as a band, to the United States received less Philippine media attention and fanfare than TbC's performance at SXSW three years later. Like Taken by Cars, Ciudad was also formed while its members were in high school (in 1994, to be exact). Since its inception, the band has featured Mikey Amistoso (lead vocals/guitar), Justin Sunico (drums), Mitch Singson (bass guitar), and Jeff Cabal (rhythm guitar). After playing at historic Manila indie venues, Club Dredd and Mayric's, in the late 1990s, they gathered a loyal following and caught the attention of BMG Records, which, in 2000, released their debut album (*Hello! How Are You, Mico the Happy Bear?*). Making their way onto local music critics' "album of the year" lists, the band independently released their next two albums—*Is That Ciudad, Yes Son It's Me* and *It's Like a Magic* (a collection of previously written yet unrecorded songs)—in 2002 and 2005, respectively. With a melancholic and wistful sound, reminiscent of U.S. indie acts such as Death Cab for Cutie, Elliott Smith, and +/-, the group's song writing style, according to critic Erwin Romulo, produces "gorgeous, effortless pop from even the most mundane of subjects."[23] And, like Taken by Cars, all of Ciudad's song lyrics are in English. Released in 2008, their fourth album *Bring Your Friends* was the most critically acclaimed, heralded by all three daily newspapers in Manila (the *Philippine Star*, the *Philippine Daily Inquirer*, and the *Manila Bulletin*) as one of the five best albums of the year.

Ciudad's members also paid for their stateside trip to play CMJ with their own money. But, unlike their compatriots, they did not attempt an online campaign via a fundraising website such as Artiste Connect. Instead, the trio drew on their personal resources—of friends, colleagues, and fans based in the tristate area—to find couches to crash on and additional gigs to play. Having met and befriended the members of +/- (plus/minus) the previous year, during the band's impromptu Manila tour, Ciudad rehearsed for their CMJ performance at the Brooklyn-based band's studio. Recordings of that rehearsal, aptly titled "The Brooklyn Sessions," are featured on Ciudad's Bandcamp page.[24] While the CMJ music industry showcase was the main reason for the band's travels to the United States (and, most likely, the reason given on their passport and visa applications), they also managed to create their own minitour—consisting of a few local New York City–based gigs organized along with local bands featuring Filipino American musicians. As musician and journalist Ted Reyes noted in his review of the Manila trio's gig at Fontana's Bar, an underground music venue located at the crossroads of the city's Lower East Side and Chinatown: "To a community used to sky-high ticket prices to see Filipino artists, Ciudad's New York tour is not only a refreshing idea, but a sign of things to come."[25] Reyes and similarly minded fans hoped that this DIY approach marked the beginning of a new business approach for touring Pinoy indie music acts.

Trip Lang: Musical Excursions

A distinction must be made here, then, between how Manila-based indie bands function as part of a showcase at a major music festival as opposed to headlining smaller gigs produced by local U.S.-based Filipino/Filipino American musicians. In the case of Taken by Cars at SXSW and Ciudad at CMJ, each performed as one of the handful of bands—often back to back and without any generic or thematic connection—on a festival evening's roster. Though such a mode of presentation does allow for more musical surprises than the average gig, it also fosters the sense that bands have been given the "privilege" to play SXSW and/or CMJ Music Marathon. Here, the market-driven festival serves as the unifying force, taking precedence over the disparate groups. In the case of the DIY/artist-organized gigs, however, traveling Pinoy indie rock bands encounter warmer audiences—that is, fans more familiar with and casual listeners more open to these bands' sounds.

For Ciudad, Taken by Cars, and, as discussed below, Sandwich, though their appearances on musical showcases' main stages anchored their visits to the United States, smaller gigs—organized by both Filipino American musician friends as well as immigrant Filipino events production companies—provided occasions for them to reconnect with U.S.-based fans, friends, and family members as well as potentially reach new listeners. These smaller gigs often featured local bands as opening acts, both to draw different audiences to the event and to share the sounds of U.S.-based talents with their Philippine-based counterparts. These smaller gigs functioned in a similar fashion to niche events such as Asian American and contemporary U.S.-based Philippine film festivals, reaching out to distinct audiences already invested, at some level, in these particular cultural forms. Yet, whereas subcultural capital in the film festival settings exists at the level of "Asian American cool" (especially palpable and valuable in Los Angeles and San Francisco, two West Coast cities with large Asian/Asian American populations) and "global/international cineaste," these smaller gigs featuring OPM/Pinoy indie rock bands register subcultural value in two distinct ways—cultural nostalgia and global indie culture.[26]

Organizing and producing shows in the United States featuring Pinoy indie rock bands is no small feat. Along with the legal challenges of obtaining artist/performer visas for each band member come the economic challenges for U.S.-based producers, mainly immigrant Filipinos, to raise enough funds to cover the cost of airfare, lodging, and artists' fees. Without major corporate sponsorship, these costs, more often than not, get passed along to concertgoers with show ticket prices averaging $50–$70 each. Though the value of live performance is on the rise, especially as a response to this era of digital downloads and sharp decreases in album/CD sales, these average ticket prices can turn off the casual listener—someone unfamiliar with or without strong emotional ties to these bands and their music. As a result, many of these shows and concerts instead function as "nostalgia tours," that is, as events that help certain audience members and fans recall or relive their youth, their life in the Philippines, through the music that most likely accompanied it.[27] To emphasize further the quality of nostalgia that these shows and concerts invoke, they are generally more successful when featuring bands that have been officially "broken up" for a number of years, thus adding to the sense that one is musically traveling back in time, both in a personal and broader pop cultural way.

One particularly salient example of a nostalgia tour performance was the 2012 North American tour of the Eraserheads. Stopping in cities such as San Francisco, Los Angeles, Toronto, and Jersey City, the tour's concerts were organized by different local (and often first-time) concert promoters. Despite the uneven production value between each venue and gig, what remained consistent were the sold-out audiences each night. By selecting tour stops in cities where large numbers of Filipinos lived, the band was guaranteed to draw local audiences. However, with ticket prices averaging $70–$100 each, they sold to audiences not only familiar with but also longing for the rare experience of hearing the band perform live. A rare experience not only because it took place in the United States but also because the band has performed only twice in Manila itself (in 2008 and 2009, respectively) since officially breaking up in 2002.

Without the nostalgia effect of a band such as the Eraserheads, current and emergent acts such as Taken by Cars and Ciudad cannot summon ticket sales at such exorbitant prices. As part of an effort to increase interest in and exposure to Pinoy indie rock music and its bands, many U.S.-based promoters, including myself, have benefited from organizing gigs that feature a number of local bands and charging a more accessible price of $10–$20 per ticket.[28] Charging such low prices can never cover the full amount of Manila-based bands' travel and lodging costs. However, the sale of band merchandise (T-shirts, CDs, stickers)—otherwise available only in the Philippines—can make up a large part of the band's revenue while on tour.

With these examples, I want to think about the different means by which Pinoy indie rock bands make their way onto U.S. stages. As promoted on their 2012 Los Angeles tour, a mainly "Noypi" (a riff on "Pinoy," a slang term referring to immigrant Filipinos) style promoter had booked Sandwich along with another popular indie rocker (Glenn Jacinto) and other local bands at Filipino restaurants in suburban cities (Cerritos and Panorama City) that are overwhelmingly Pinoy-populated. Booking them at these Pinoy-owned establishments in Filipino enclaves did not expand their audience base beyond these communities and demographics. The assumption here might have been that they would *only* attract an immigrant Pinoy audience already familiar with their music. At the same time, it set these touring Filipino and Filipino American indie bands/musicians apart from the larger global indie rock soundscape in which they regularly participate, as musicians and fans. It is interesting that events promoters often think that what draws immigrant Filipinos to these establishments—perhaps a nostalgia or longing for goods, services, and food from "back home"—is what will attract touring musicians when, in fact, what these musicians want to experience are the quintessentially "American" goods, services, and food items they cannot readily get "back home."

This Noypi-promoted Sandwich tour was organized in conjunction with the band's performance at the 2012 "Take Me to the Philippines" concert—an evening of Filipino music curated by Apl de Ap (aka Allan Pineda) of the chart-topping U.S. hip-hop act the Black Eyed Peas—that took place at the Hollywood Bowl. Again, due to the larger, corporate-sponsored event, the costs of Sandwich's travel and lodging were covered. Curated in a mode of musical nationalism, the showcase format of "Take Me to the Philippines" racially and culturally tied the band to the other musical acts while generically distancing them as the only indie/

indie rock act of the evening.[29] Although the event appeared under the sponsored banner of KCRW's World Music Series, a majority of the acts were U.S.-based, further illustrating Filipino musical life as "foreign in a domestic sense." Through their use of Tagalog lyrics and cultural references, Sandwich was marked as Philippines-based. Yet, with their unquestionably rock musical sound, they also illustrated something besides traditional/folk or an older generation's "Filipino music." From a curatorial standpoint, the band's place in the evening's line-up underscored the specific challenges faced by Pinoy indie rock music in the United States.

A comment I overheard while exiting the show proved very telling of the audience's reaction that evening and clues us into how musical acts might be marketed to a diverse audience of Filipino Americans and U.S.-based Filipinos. As one audience member noted, the show's first half was relegated to "traditional" folk musical acts (for example, the rondalla and the "Harana Kings" and the OPM pop and jazz songsters Gary Valenciano and Ogie Alcasid) while the second half appealed to the younger American-based generation—through mainly R&B and hip-hop performances, such as the singing group Legaci, Culture Shock dance troupe, and the Black Eyed Peas. Smack in the middle of both sets, Sandwich performed as the requisite rock band. On first hearing, Sandwich's sound registered as raucous and noisy to that evening's mainly older, first-generation audience, exemplifying a "rock is rebellious" discourse. What is interesting about this particular audience reaction is the fact that Sandwich is actually more "pop-oriented," as far as the Manila indie rock scene goes. Namely, there are heavier elements such as the Pinoy punk, hardcore, and metal bands that exist in the scene. What both music festival showcases as well as U.S.-based nostalgia tours bring into relief are the challenges of organizing and curating along the discourses of community, where *community* suggests a type of lowest common denominator aim toward consensus versus genre cultures and scenes, where *scene* suggests an approach based on musical genre preferences and lifestyle choices. Turning our ears back toward the Philippines, we uncover examples of this scene-based approach to musical events organizing.

As fans of indie music from around the globe, directors Marie Jamora and Quark Henares have worked hard to convince U.S.- and European-based indie bands to tour the Philippines. In 2008, they focused their energies on organizing a few major shows for +/- and Versus, two legendary indie rock bands with Filipino American members. Already scheduled to visit Japan and Taiwan on their own "Authentic Asian Food and Beverage Tour," both U.S.-based bands were convinced by Jamora and Henares to visit and make their performance debuts in Manila. An influential band in the early 1990s scene, over the past twenty-five years, Versus has featured at least one, and up to three, of the Baluyut brothers—Richard (guitar/vocals), James (guitar/keyboard), and Edward (guitar/drums)—each of whom, at one point or another, split from the group and went on to form/perform with other bands: +/- (plus-minus), Whysall Lane, and the Pacific Ocean. Within Manila's translocal scene of Pinoy indie rock music, all three brothers and their various band offshoots are admired not just for being Filipino American but also for being some of the most revered and well-recognized musicians in the U.S.-based indie rock scene.[30]

In 2008, Henares and Jamora, with the help of another devoted +/- fan, worked to bring the band to Manila. After incessantly e-mailing the group through Facebook, the devoted fan contacted Henares—who, at the time, owned Mag:net Café—about helping to arrange for the band's first visit to the Philippines. As Jamora remembers: "They were already on tour . . . so basically, they were going to pass by Japan, and all we needed to pay for was their trip from Manila to Japan. And then, we would work it out . . . instead of paying for the Manila to the States (flight), which is more expensive . . . so it all worked out."[31] Paying for much of the self-made tour with their own funds, Henares and Jamora organized two concerts for both +/- and Versus: the first night, at Warehouse 135 in Makati, featured local opening acts Ciudad, Taken by Cars, and Ang Bandang Shirley; the second night, at Henares's own Mag:net Café at The Fort, featured local opening acts Us-2, Evil-o (Henares's own band), and the reunion of Jamora's band, Boldstar. Booking shows in this way served two purposes: first, to ensure the attendance of local audience members by including familiar local acts; second, to make the visiting bands aware of local talents, which in turn might lead to future collaborations between U.S.- and Philippines-based bands.

By taking this DIY approach in organizing a minitour for visiting indie rock bands, Henares and Jamora, in many ways, mirrored the efforts of U.S.-based events production companies that host visiting Philippine rock, pop, and indie rock acts. Yet their efforts were strikingly different in that: (1) as major players within the Manila indie music and pop culture scenes, Jamora and Henares had close ties to a large media and publicity infrastructure (including radio station NU107, TV station MYX Philippines, as well as local bars and venues); and (2) their shows played not only on local audiences' nostalgia and curiosity for Versus and +/-'s music but also spoke to the duo's long-term intentions to build friendships and future collaborations with them as fellow artists.

With this successful minitour under his belt, the following year, Henares established the Manila-based production company, Intercept. Its mission: to bring internationally recognized indie acts to Manila and organize intimate yet successful gigs for them at the city's most well known indie venues. The first major musical event Intercept produced was the 2009 Versus and +/- concert in Manila. The concert took place on December 18 at Encore Fly Superclub (formerly known as the ultra hip/swanky nightclub Embassy). Admission was 850Php—though six times more than the average price for a local show in Manila, the gate fee did include two free Jim Beam drinks and the more nationally recognized group, Sandwich, as the opening act. Having met and heard local bands and musicians the previous year, the U.S.-based bands' 2009 concert set featured Manila friends, including members of Ciudad, Ang Bandang Shirley, Boldstar, and Itchyworms. Having just played the CMJ Music Marathon and two additional gigs while in New York, Ciudad members, especially lead singer-songwriter Mikey Amistoso, had developed a closer friendship with +/- members, in particular James Baluyut, who helped organize and appeared onstage with the Manila band at their October 2009 gig at Fontana's Bar.

These kinds of musical events and collaborations take place alongside and below the institutional radar of the traditional music industry. Rather than simply market-driven or nostalgia-based, the impetus for producing such events is steeped in shared affinities of genre culture—as musical performers, listeners, and fans. Mostly paid for out-of-pocket, these events are organized and occur in a punk/DIY fashion with local musicians securing not only venues but also musical instruments, organizing not only gigs but also pre- and post-show hangs and dinners, music and record store shopping trips, and recording studio sessions, for their visiting counterparts. Through the production of these local minitours, various types of personal and professional exchanges take place, animated mostly by the collaborative spirit of Pinoy indie rock and its translocal scenes. As tropical renditions, these gigs and excursion tour performances, from Manila to Los Angeles to New York to Baguio and beyond, not only bring Filipino America—postcolonial places and alternative modernities across the globe constituted by the history of U.S.-Philippine relations—into relief. They also help us imagine how to create scenes beyond dominant models of musical nationalism.

During a research trip to the Philippines in September 2011, I had the honor of joining a group of Manila-based indie bands and DJs on their first ever Excursion Tour to Baguio. The invitation came directly from Pedicab frontman Diego Mapa, who had organized the show in collaboration with a local Baguio musician, Jethro Sandico. As Mapa announced at the end of the September 17 show, about three months earlier he woke up one morning and realized that he wanted to play a gig in Baguio.[32] The realization was immediately followed by the sobering thought that he would need to find sponsorship to cover the costs. Instead of following down that train of thought, Mapa instead reconsidered, "How about if we just played with friends?" As part of a circle of musicians within the Manila indie rock scene, Mapa called on and invited his band friends to participate in the Excursion Tour, constantly reminding them, "Okay, *wala etong pera, wala etong pera,* ha?" [Okay, there's no money in this, there's no money in this, alright?] Agreeing simply to split the gateshare (earnings at the door) and pay for their own travel and housing expenses during the weekend, Manila-based bands, including Bagetsafonik, Taken by Cars, Pedicab, Gaijin, and DJ Mon (of apparel/design company Team Manila), and their family and friends made the six-hour trip "up the mountain" to the City of Pines, also known as the summer capital of the Philippines. Since that time, Mapa and friends have replicated the excursion tour model in two other Philippine cities, Davao and Cebu. Each time, they have collaborated with local musicians both to benefit from their local knowledge as well as to feature local bands as opening acts for Manila-based ones.

These Excursion Tours and other artist-initiated DIY minitours inspire me to think differently about Pinoy indie rock and Pinoy indie culture, more broadly. In their willingness to shift location and focus from the metropolis of Manila to other Philippine cities, through their organizing efforts and musical performances, these excursion tours disrupt unitary narratives of Philippine musical nationalism and insist upon an "archipelagic perspective." This perspective, as defined by UP professors Merlin Magallona and Jay Batongbacal in their collection *Archipelagic Studies: Charting New Waters*, takes into account the geographical realities of the Philippines as a nation "fragmented into more than 7,000 islands. Separated and surrounded by about 2.2 million square kilometers of waters, the islands are rounded by coastlines 17,640 kilometers long." Such realities are continually overlooked by the "Procrustean framework of an externally sourced paradigm," namely that of continent-based notions of nationalism as well as transnationalism.[33]

Rather than subsuming indie musicians and venues under the banner of the national, a banner under which it is often placed for export to international film and music festivals, excursion tours operate with a translocal understanding of the Philippines. In other words, by organizing events and tours that operate underneath the radar of corporate sponsorship and in collaboration with musicians from other Philippine cities, Diego Mapa and his Manila-based crew recognize that Philippine indie music and culture does not only take place in the capital. Manila instead operates as an important but not singular node within a larger network of Pinoy indie rock scenes.

As we saw in the previous chapter, this translocal network between the capital and other Philippine cities (namely, the military base town of Olongapo) was also evident during the era of Pinoy classic and punk rock, when the exchange of musical objects and styles took place within a network of Olongapo-based musicians, U.S. military servicemen, Manila-based DJs, airline stewardesses, and visiting expats and Filipino Americans. While the excursion tours similarly remind us of the archipelagic perspective of Pinoy indie culture—as a vibrant culture taking place in various sites across the Philippines—I also want to connect them to other DIY musical tours and events featuring Pinoy indie bands that have taken place in U.S. cities such as San Francisco, Los Angeles, and New York. By doing so, I mean to extend the archipelagic perspective to "a planet-spanning, temporally shifting set of islands . . . affiliated with and indeed constitutive of" Filipino America. Here, "islands" refers less to a geographical designation (though one could argue for the island of Manhattan, let's say) than to a geocultural formulation of freestanding or independent musical events—independent in that they do not solely depend upon a national or international industry entity (à la South by Southwest, Tanduay Rum, and so on) but instead operate on a local and/or regional level as well as within a larger translocal network.

While the Internet has definitely shifted the nature and business models of global and domestic music industries in the last twenty-five years, with social networking sites (Facebook, YouTube, Tumblr) and blogs creating a participatory culture that has shifted industry's ability as gatekeepers or tastemakers, Pinoy indie rock artists and their fans still thrive on the intimate and improvised connections cultivated through live events and in person. While musical recording and distribution technologies undoubtedly play important roles, one cannot underestimate the power of people—namely, musicians and their fans—in animating and keeping alive these circuits of popular music. After all, these Facebook pages, YouTube videos, and Tumblr sites would be nothing if it were not for the shared love of *rakenrol*.

One for the Road

With a character like Gibson who does not speak, *Ang Nawawala* tunes into popular music, gestures, video, and album art as forms of communication alternative to speech. In turn, throughout Jamora's film, technological devices such as headphones, cell phones, and record players bring listeners together while the narrative tunes us into the important roles that pop songs play—delivering messages often difficult to speak, capturing shared moments and memories among friends. Alongside gigs and performances, film screenings, and locales such as record stores, these technologies facilitate encounters that happen in the flesh, in a particular place and time. As a translocal subject—a Filipino student studying abroad and returning home for the first time—Gibson himself embodies one of the most important yet overlooked ways that popular music travels and circulates.

Throughout the movie, we witness Gibson's deep love for classic OPM songs. The day immediately following their "Minsan" sing-along, described at the beginning of this chapter, Gibson and Teddy visit a small secondhand record store, an actual shop called Vinyl Dump, located in Quezon City and where Jamora dug for and found many of the *haranas* (love songs) that appear on the film's soundtrack. Teddy sits near the exit while Gibson eagerly digs through the store's crates. Indicative of the digital generation, Teddy sarcastically reminds his friend that there is a "thing" called the Internet where one can download songs; somewhere, as he describes it, "away from the dust and the dirt of the past" that the record store epitomizes. His soliloquy is interrupted when a woman places a vinyl LP on the store's record player. Close-up as she lightly sprays, then brushes the record and sets the needle on it. As the shot pans away from the spinning record, we hear its prefatory crackle. "There. You see that crackling sound?" Teddy exclaims. "It's like an AM radio station. *Ang dumi* [it's dirty] . . . it's awful." Just then, Enid unexpectedly enters, having just received a text informing her that the store was having a sale. "Hey! I have this record," she exclaims. "Hipsters," Teddy replies, with judgment, under his breath. Sifting through the albums, Gibson and Enid "speak" to each other through album covers, the titles functioning as their own dialogue—Quiet Life (as Enid remarks, "Dude, it's you"). Do You Really Want to Hurt Me? (Gibson retorts). Paranoid. Are We Not Men? Virgins and Philistines.[34] Defeated, Gibson backs down, his ego only saved by a new track, an OPM love song played on the store's record player. He props himself in front of the store's listening station and, seated in the middle of the store with his eyes closed and head tilted back, he deeply listens in a manner just like his mother, Esme. Sensing Enid's hand next to his, as she has positioned herself closer to him, he opens his eyes and smiles. As we witness at various points in the film, Gibson's world is filled with the sounds and sights of Filipino pop music. They do not merely serve as backdrop, or background noise, to his long-awaited return home or to his budding romance. Instead, OPM and Pinoy indie rock/pop songs, albums, and bands, as well as Manila's indie venues and gigs, function as their own cast of characters.

Such scenes of deep and shared listening occur repeatedly throughout Jamora's film, so that we get a sense for how music and sound envelop—in other words, resonate with—Gibson. Driving home after attending their first gig together, checking out recent indie fave The Strangeness at Saguio, Enid parks her car in front of Gibson's family's home. As they sit and discuss their respective holiday party costumes, she interrupts their conversation:

"Hey, I have a song I want to play for you."

She gently places her Hello Kitty headphones over his ears, while he pulls out his own 1960s retro-styled headphones to place over hers. As they both press play, the viewing audience hears acoustic guitars strumming a rollicking [2–2] tempo. Ciudad's Mikey Amistoso's recognizable falsetto enters, in a register akin to indie legend Elliot Smith.

Figure E.4 Still from *Ang Nawawala*. Courtesy of Marie Jamora.

An original composition performed under Amistoso's solo project entitled Hannah & Gabi, "Fin Legs" plays. Listening to the dream-like ditty, Gibs lights up a joint, takes a puff, and turns to blow the smoke "shotgun-style" into Enid's mouth, as a set-up for a kiss. The camera spins to Gibs's side of the car presumably to take on his point of view. As it spins back toward Enid's side of the car again, "Fin Legs" gives way to "'Wag Na Sana 'kong Gumising Mag-Isa" [Hopefully, I Won't Wake Up Alone], another original song written by Itchyworms' Jazz Nicholas, featuring vocals by Uela Basco, and meant to pay homage to 1970s OPM band Cinderella.[35] As the first song cross fades into the next and the new ballad swells into its chorus, the background area (outside the car) becomes brightly lit, giving the audience that otherworldly feeling of falling in love, a feeling that pop songs express best. In the next scene, we find Enid and Gibson making out on a squeaky couch inside his childhood bedroom, their kissing only interrupted by her astonishment at his adept tongue.

"For a guy who doesn't speak, you're a really good kisser."

Of course, the audience knows that Gibson actually *does* speak but only to his deceased twin brother, Jamie. Throughout the film, whenever Gibson retreats to his bedroom, after tense interactions with family members or awkward first moments with Enid, Jamie is there. Whether he is appearing as an apparition or as an imagined conversation in Gibson's mind is up to the audience to decide. What is known [and what *is* there] is that these brothers converse with each other, as siblings do after many years of sharing secrets and a childhood bedroom. They tease each other and laugh at their family members' idiosyncrasies. They share smokes and reminisce on their family's past from their own points of view. But, as Gibson's romance with Enid develops, Jamie begins to sense his brother's increasing detachment.

During the Bonifacio twins' final conversation, one that takes place beside his tombstone, Jamie reminds Gibson that he is still the one lucky enough to remain alive. "Do you blame me?" Gibson asks. With a blank stare and no verbal response, Jamie shakes his head no. At this point, we realize that, as much as Gibson desires to be viewed independent of his brother, so much of his identity is wrapped up in being the twin that remains. A witness to the traumatic event of his brother's death, it is after this event that he refuses to speak.

Jamie lifts up a lit joint and asks, "One for the road?" The remainder of this climactic scene takes place in silence, each brother taking turns smoking and passing the shared joint, looking at each other with tears quietly falling from their eyes. Despite the absence of words and even sound, we still hear the echoes of grief, mourning, and resolution in each brother's facial expressions. By the end of the scene, Gibson releases his codependent relationship to his brother, and in doing so, he is also freed of his need to withhold speech. This freedom is not utopic in its form of liberation. Instead, for Gibson, it is a letting go of prior ways of thinking, an annihilation of his previous notions of self. A form of "self" destruction and surrender, so that he can return to his past, his family, his friends, in a different manner.

By listening against Gibson's refusal to speak, as Jamora's film requires, we hear echoes of QBert and the Invisibl Skratch Piklz's refusal to subscribe their work merely to their Filipino identities. By deeply listening to the ways Gibson does speak, we return to everyday scenes of karaoke, as well as the poetry/performances of Jessica Hagedorn's Gangster Choir, reminded that a voice is produced, in different ways, and of the affective politics these productions engender. Throughout this book, voice has taken on various meanings and purposes—authenticating, prescribing, and often limiting identities. But equally as important have been the practices of listening, against and beyond, in order to hear even the silences and gaps as forms of expression.

When something isn't there, what do we allow to persist in its place?

Perhaps it was always there, we just didn't know how to listen? If no longer apprehended as lost or missing, then, how do we make it resound (or sound again) but with a difference?

By writing this book, I have aimed to release Filipino America's popular music, its writing and study, from a dependence on tropes of the merely mimetic or derivative, on the one hand, and the necessarily authenticating, on the other. Instead, by paying close and persistent attention to the processes and politics of these tropical renditions, I have committed myself to an ongoing practice of surrendering myself to the music. Like Jamora's Gibson, and the many musical artists within this book, we too should leave ourselves open to listen, imagine, and voice differently—in ways alien, experimental, archipelagic, and moving; in ways that flip the beat, a continual making that is all our own.

Flip the Beat: An Introduction

1 Thanks to Sonjia Hyon for helping me to fine-tune this idea.

2 Such as those taken by white American female photographers Jessie Tarbox Beals and the Gerhard sisters (Mamie and Emme).

3 Marlon Fuentes, "Extracts from an Imaginary Interview: Questions and Answers about *Bontoc Eulogy*," in *F Is for Phony*.

4 Kirshenblatt-Gimblett, "Objects of Ethnography," 389, as quoted in Fuentes, "Extracts from an Imaginary Interview," 121.

5 Fuentes, "Extracts from an Imaginary Interview," 118.

6 Fuentes, "Extracts from an Imaginary Interview," 119.

7 Lisa Gitelman, *Always Already New*, 71.

8 A phonographic quality remarked on by the modernist era's greatest writers. For more on this, see Friedrich Kittler's *Gramophone Film Typewriter*; and Bennett Hogg, "The Cultural Imagination of the Phonographic Voice, 1877–1940."

9 I am borrowing this theoretical image of a "phonographic mise-en-scène" from Fred Moten's definition of it as a "primary scene of (phonographic) audition," one particularly painted in Adorno's seminal essays, "Curves of the Needle" and "The Form of the Phonograph Record." Fred Moten, "The Phonographic *Mise-en-scène*," *Cambridge Opera Journal*, 269–81. See Michael Taussig, "The Talking Machine," 193–211.

10 Fuentes, "Extracts from an Imaginary Interview," 124.

11 Fuentes, "Extracts from an Imaginary Interview," 124.

12 See Oscar Campomanes, "Filipinos in the United States and Their Literature of Exile"; Elizabeth Pisares's chapter, "Do You (Mis)Recognize Me: Filipina Americans in Popular Music and the Problem of Invisibility"; and Sar-

ita See's *The Decolonized Eye: Filipino American Art and Performance*, among others.

13   E. San Juan Jr. as quoted in Martin Manalansan, *Global Divas: Filipino Gay Men in the Diaspora*, 11.

14   Frances Aparicio and Susana Chavez-Silverman, eds., *Tropicalizations: Transcultural Representations of Latinidad*.

15   Isaac, *American Tropics*. For other writings on the tropics, especially in regard to its geophysical and geocultural dimensions, see Hayden V. White, *Tropics of Discourse*; Edouard Glissant, *Caribbean Discourse*; and Jonathan Pugh, "Island Movements," 9–24.

16   Philippine military marching bands at the 1904 World's Fair; diasporic and U.S.-based Filipino jazz bands/ensembles that emerged during the American period of occupation and evolved into the 1980s Manila smooth jazz sound of Marcos's martial rule; the post–World War II U.S. pop musical sensations of R&B/soul vocalist Sugar Pie de Santo and the "King of Latin Soul" Joe Bataan; diasporic and U.S.-based Filipino hip-hop MCs, producers, and musical groups; the Pinoy folk rock musicians prevalent in the United States and the Philippines during the late 1970s and 1980s; and the classically trained Filipino nationalist composers covered in Christi-Anne Castro's book-length study, to name a few.

17   Sara Cohen, "Mapping the Sound," 117–34.

18   Deirdre McKay, "Everyday Places," 2.

19   While scholars such as Christi-Anne Castro choose to focus on the everpowerful (and always salient) category of the nation and national (in studying music and the Philippines), the increasingly complicated movements and migrations of today's Filipino musicians (and their musics) require the more flexible framework that *translocal/translocality* offers. See Castro's *Musical Renderings of the Philippine Nation*.

20   Moten, *In the Break*, 229.

21   For more on contemporary artists' reimagining of this historical formation, see the Galleon Trade Arts Exchange, an ongoing exhibition and cultural exchange between artists based in Manila, San Francisco, and Mexico and organized by visual artist Jenifer Wofford; www.galleontrade.org, accessed October 15, 2015.

22   Antonio C. Hila, *Musika*, 114.

23   D. R. M. Irving, *Colonial Counterpoint*, 2.

24   Irving, *Colonial Counterpoint*, 2.

25   Irving, *Colonial Counterpoint*, 2.

26   See Mary Talusan's "Music, Race, and Imperialism," 499–526; and Clairborne T. Richardson's "The Filipino-American Phenomenon," 3–28.

27   For more on this early history, see the following books and complete essays: Doreen Fernandez, *Palabas*; Nick Joaquin, *Manila, My Manila*; and

José S. Buenconsejo, "Parodies of Traditional Comedia and Hollywoodish Spectacle."

28 Renato Constantino, "Miseducation," 178.

29 Constantino, "Miseducation," 185.

30 Castro, *Musical Renderings of the Philippine Nation*.

31 Kandice Chuh, "It's Not about Anything."

32 See See, *The Decolonized Eye*, xxxiii.

33 Oscar Campomanes, "Filipinos in the United States and Their Literature of Exile," 53.

34 As Antonio Tiongson explains, "Like Enriquez, Pisares argues Filipino American youth respond to their 'perceptual absence' by either identifying as Asian American, constructing 'a racial discourse around the notion of brownness,' or fetishizing 'ethnic markers.'" "Filipino Youth Cultural Politics," 144.

35 Vicente L. Rafael, *White Love and Other Events in Filipino History*, 77–78.

36 See Benito Vergara Jr., *Displaying Filipinos*.

37 Frank D. Millet, *The Expedition to the Philippines*, 1–2, as quoted in Vergara's *Displaying Filipinos*, 1.

38 As Fred Moten writes, "Whereas Ferdinand de Saussure claims that the value of the sign as 'not reducible to but rather only discernible in the reduction of phonic substance' . . . it is impossible that sound, as a material element, should in itself be part of the language. Sound is merely something ancillary, a material the language uses [13], Edouard Glissant details the Creole—'forged as a medium of communication between slave and master'—and his composition of a language where 'noise is essential to speech' and 'din is discourse.' Living and operating under systems of rule whereby (certain) 'speech was forbidden,' Glissant writes, 'slaves camouflaged the word under the provocative intensity of the scream. It was taken to be nothing but the call of a wild animal.' This is how the dispossessed man organized his speech by weaving it into the apparently meaningless texture of extreme noise" (Moten, *In the Break*, 7).

39 Alexander G. Weheliye, *Phonographies*, 2.

40 Josh Kun, *Audiotopia*.

41 Moten, "b jenkins," in *B Jenkins*, 95. For more on Moten's formulation of what he terms a "photophonographic," see "Black Mo'nin."

42 This performance studies approach of inter-inanimation is very much informed by Rebecca Schneider's work on reenactment theories that work against naively seeking to unhinge live performance from mechanical reproduction, precisely by fetishizing the live and liveness.

43 "The refusal to neutralize the phonic substance of the photograph rewrites the time of the photograph, the time of the photograph of the dead. The time of the sound of the photograph of the dead is no longer irreversible,

no longer vulgar, and, moreover, is indexed not only to rhythmic compli- cation but to the extreme and subtle harmonics of various shrieks, hums, hollers, shouts, and moans" (Moten, "Black Mo'nin,'" 66).

44 See Jonathan Sterne, "Hello!" in *The Audible Past*, 1–30.

45 As Stewart writes, "This souvenir (the picture postcard) domesticates the grotesque on the level of content, subsuming the sexual facts to the cul- tural code. But the souvenir also domesticates on the level of its operation: external experience is internalized; the beast is taken home." Susan Stew- art, *On Longing*, 134.

46 For more on the importance of reading practices in approaching the colo- nial archive, see Mark Rice, "His Name Was Don Francisco Muro," 49–76.

47 Vicente Rafael, *White Love and Other Events in Filipino History*, 83.

48 Constantino, *Miseducation*.

49 Charles Bernstein, introduction to his edited collection *Close Listening*, 3–28.

50 In his 1981 essay "Notes on Deconstructing the 'Popular,'" Stuart Hall grapples with the paradox of approaching the "popular" as either "resist- ance," on the one hand, or "containment," on the other. Instead, by recog- nizing the double movement between these two poles, Hall sees a third option: "popular culture" as the battleground upon which shifting struggles, constant transformations, and mutual constitutions of meaning take place. Thus, he reminds us that within popular culture (and the term *popular*, more broadly): "There are points of resistance; there are also moments of supersession. This is the dialectic of cultural struggle. In our times, it goes on continuously, in the complex lines of resistance and acceptance, refusal and capitulation, which make the field of culture a sort of constant battle- field. A battlefield where no once-for-all victories are obtained but where there are always strategic positions to be won and lost" (460).

Chapter 1: Sonic Fictions

1 DJ Babu (Chris Oroc), "Interview with Christo Macias," May 1996, accessed July 31, 2010, http://www.bombhiphop.com/newbomb/bombpages /articles/DJ/Turntablism%20Mailing%20List%20FAQ.htm.

2 As Juliana Snapper has written, "In the last decade, turntablism has bur- geoned into a vital international subculture organized around a seemingly obsolete technology, rooted in musical virtuosity, and fueled by sonic inno- vations." See Snapper's "Scratching the Surface," 10.

3 See John Carluccio, Ethan Imboden, and Raymond Pirtle's *Turntablist Transcription Methodology* handbook, accessed October 15, 2015, http://ttm -dj.com.

4 Oliver Wang, "Spinning Identities."

5 For a more detailed overview of this historical shift, see Antonio Tiongson Jr.'s dissertation "Filipino Youth Cultural Politics."

6 *Scratch: The Movie*, directed by Douglas Pray, DVD.

7 Kimberly Chun, "'Scratch' and Sniff with DJ QBert."

8 For another example of a literal "word scratcher," see Josh Kun's lucid examination of pop artist Jean-Michel Basquiat's work and its relationship to phonography in "Basquiat's Ear, Rahsaan's Eye," in *Audiotopia*, 113–42.

9 Many thanks to Alexandra Vazquez for the intellectually productive term *turntablist methodology*.

10 I borrow this concept from Martin Manalansan to connote the "alternative modernity" and "imaginary topographies that construct the United States and the Philippines as physically contiguous," immigrant Filipino and Filipino American times and spaces created by over a century of direct colonial and neocolonial relations between the two nations. Martin Manalansan, "Introduction: Points of Departure," in *Global Divas*, 1–20.

11 *Scratch: The Movie*, interviews with DJ QBert and Mixmaster Mike.

12 See Benito Vergara Jr.'s essay, "Betrayal, Class Fantasies, and the Filipino Nation in Daly City," 139–58. In 2001, Daly City ranked fifth in the nation for the highest percentage of foreign-born population, with Filipinos comprising one-fourth of Daly City's numbers, making it the most densely Filipino-populated locale outside of the Philippines.

13 Other members of the Invisibl Skratch Piklz (ISP) included Yogafrog, Shortkut, and D-Styles. This configuration of turntablist-DJs composed the ISP team from 1997 to 2000 but other DJs affiliated with the ISP crew before and after that time period included DJ Apollo, Disk, Flare, and A-Trak.

14 From *Scratch: The Movie*.

15 Dave Tompkins, "Science Friction," 45–47, 45.

16 McKay, "Everyday Places," 2.

17 Excerpt taken from "DJ QBert (The Book)," http://www.djqbert.com/news/?news_id=8, accessed January 2011.

18 One need only look as far as *Scratch: The Movie* to witness the ways in which the space of turntablist production is primarily the domestic space: from Mixmaster Mike's bedroom to DJ QBert's kitchen to the X-ecutioners' basement.

19 From Vazquez's unpublished dissertation chapter on freestyle artists titled "Instrumental Migrations."

20 For more, see Marko Cristal's undergraduate thesis, "The Evolution of Dance Crews in Southern California and Its Influence on the Filipino-American Experience," Departments of History and Asian American Studies, UC Irvine, June 2012.

21 Garages stand as an architectural and sociological challenge. Post–World War II suburbia's focus on the automobile requires a rethinking of the internal structures of two-story homes to include the space of the garage.

Garages in suburbia are supposed to serve the purpose of storage of tools of technology (i.e., lawnmowers, autos, power tools) while the aesthetics of the everyday shifts from building facades in the urban outward to the manicured lawns of front and backyards in the suburban, where aesthetics privilege the visual as environmental and a nature that is tamed. What are left out of such dialogues, however, are the aesthetics of the aural and bodily that are developed in the performances that occur within the suburban home's liminal space.

22 In a poetic sense, this metaphor of the garage and parent and child marks the space of Filipino American identity formation, where the history of the Filipino through America's eyes is the configuration of an unwieldy "little brown brother," benevolently assimilated by U.S. imperialism's structures of education, language, and mass media. Filipino American cultural productions in ancillary spaces such as the garage are a continual gesture toward these forgotten histories through an excess of sounds, bodies, and technology in performance, and have their own system of logic.

23 Caleb Kelly, *Cracked Media*.

24 Kodwo Eshun in *Modulations*, 100.

25 Mark Katz, *Capturing Sound*.

26 *Scratch* magazine, 68.

27 Alondra Nelson, "Introduction: Future Texts," 10.

28 Jeffrey A. Weinstock, "Freaks in Space," 327–37.

29 Stephen Hong Sohn, "Introduction: Alien/Asian," 6.

30 This generation of science fiction–inspired artists, precisely through genre-specific practices, remarks on the alienating processes of immigration and colonization, the globalizing effects of biotechnology and posthuman labor, and hybrid forms of Asian American bodies (through adoption and multiraciality) and their racialized future. See Sohn, "Introduction: Alien/Asian," 8.

31 As quoted in Snapper's "Scratching the Surface," 18; Geert Lovink, "Everything Was to Be Done."

32 Snapper, "Scratching the Surface," 17–18.

33 Snapper, "Scratching the Surface," 17.

34 See Karen Shimakawa's *National Abjection*.

35 Sarita See, introduction to *The Decolonized Eye*.

36 William Friar, "QBert (aka Richard Quitevis)."

37 Snapper, "Scratching the Surface."

38 As Rodriguez writes, "The overarching argument of this book is that the production of the 'Filipino American' is defined—essentially and fundamentally—by a complex, largely disavowed, and almost entirely undertheorized relation to a nexus of profound racial and white supremacist violence" (11). This nexus, in his formulation, centers upon the "historical encounter" between the United States and the Philippines at the turn of

the twentieth century, one comprising war and empire, "white supremacist colonization and genocidal conquest." Though I do share Rodriguez's
concern about any politics that attempts to forgo or forget this history,
I would contend that there exist a number of decidedly "Filipino American"
artists, staged and everyday practices, and events whose work might
require an extension, or even reworking, of his formulation. See Dylan
Rodriguez, *Suspended Apocalypse*, 89–90.

39 As quoted in Josh Kun, "Unexpected Harmony."

40 William Friar, "QBert (aka Richard Quitevis)."

41 Thanks to Shane Vogel for pointing out this affective distinction in DJ
QBert's quote.

42 Snapper, "Scratching the Surface," 12.

43 In the case of freestyle vocalist Jocelyn Enriquez, a simple scan of album
covers over a four-year period (1993–97) illustrates the problem and promise of what Elizabeth Pisares terms the Filipino's "perceptual absence"
in U.S. popular imaginary. It is this absence that, at once, allowed and
demanded Enriquez's visage shift along a spectrum of racial ambiguity—
possibly Latina, possibly black, and then finally, quintessentially Filipina—
while her unquestionably freestyle/dance music sound remained. The
power of this dependence on a language of visibility for Filipino American
musical artists is only doubled by the difficult task of defining Filipino music or a Filipino American sound. See Elizabeth Pisares, "Do You
Mis(recognize) Me," 172–98.

44 Pisares, "Do You Mis(recognize) Me," 192.

45 From Vicente Rafael's introductory essay, "Episodic Histories," in *White
Love and Other Events in Filipino History*, 4.

46 Sarita See, *The Decolonized Eye*, 128.

47 See, *The Decolonized Eye*, 128.

48 See, *The Decolonized Eye*, 140.

49 Kandice Chuh, *Imagine Otherwise*.

50 Here, Flash is referring to the distinction between analog and "fake" digital
samples of scratching. David Toop, "Hip Hop," 99.

51 Brian Massumi, *Parables for the Virtual*, 3.

52 Snapper, "Scratching the Surface," 13.

53 Toop, "Hip Hop," 92.

54 I first encountered this magazine cover as the opening image of Oliver
Wang's seminal study, "Spinning Identities." I thank him for his continued
support and the critical groundwork he has laid in studying generations of
Filipino American mobile DJs and identifying what he calls "Filipino futurism." This writing appears in his book *Legions of Boom*.

55 Dave Tompkins, James Tai, and Brian "B+" Cross, "Science Friction," 45–47.
As Sarah Jackson notes in her essay, "The reference to Area 51, a top-secret
military zone in the Nevada desert around which thousands of rumors of

UFO contact have revolved, in addition to the 'secret government' comment, place the tone of this article fully within the conspiracy theory camp." Sarah Jackson, "Bay Area 51."

56 Thanks to Oliver Wang for suggesting the provocative term (and political possibilities) of "Filipino futurism."

57 Here, I am indebted to the collection *E.T. Culture: Anthropology in Outerspaces*, edited by Debbora Battaglia, for the interdisciplinary possibilities of bringing together diverse notions of alien and home societies, visitations and encounters.

58 As Mark Katz writes, "In fact, the machinery on stage was never intended to produce music, but to reproduce it: the musicians perform using turntables, records, and a mixer. But instead of merely letting the machines play, these DJs—also known as turntablists—bend the equipment to their will, altering existing sounds and producing a wide range of wholly new ones." See Katz's *Capturing Sound*, 115.

59 Moten, *In the Break*, 33–34.

60 Moten, *In the Break*, 33–34.

61 See Debbora Battaglia's "Insiders' Voices in Outerspaces," in *E.T. Culture*, 10–11.

Chapter 2: The Serious Work of Karaoke

1 Norimitsu Onishi, "Sinatra Song Often Strikes Deadly Chord," *New York Times* (Asia Edition), February 7, 2010.

2 Pico Iyer, *Video Night*, 5.

3 Iyer, *Video Night*, 164.

4 Iyer, *Video Night*, 2–3.

5 Jean Mallat, *The Philippines*, 458.

6 Mallat, *The Philippines*, 458, as quoted in Burns, *Puro Arte*, 11.

7 Lucy Burns, *Puro Arte*, 11.

8 Lee Watkins, "Minstrelsy and Mimesis," 72–99.

9 Elizabeth L. Enriquez, *Appropriation of Colonial Broadcasting*, 12.

10 Watkins, "Minstrelsy and Mimesis," 80.

11 Burns, *Puro Arte*, 126.

12 Jackson Gan, as quoted in John Bowe's "How Did House Bands Become a Filipino Export?," *New York Times Magazine*, May 29, 2005.

13 Neferti Tadiar, *Fantasy Production*, 3.

14 Tadiar, *Fantasy Production*, 3–6.

15 Stephanie Ng, "Performing the 'Filipino' at the Crossroads," 280.

16 Ng, "Performing the 'Filipino' at the Crossroads," 283–84.

17 Iyer, *Video Night*, 62. By "cover performance" I mean not only the performance practice of rendering songs but, also, the sociality cultivated by cover technology (karaoke, CPDRC) and the consumer culture that "fran-

chises the familiar"—amateur singing contests, cover bands, OPM song-books, and live karaoke nights, to name a few.

18 Burns, *Puro Arte*, 119.

19 See visual artist Phil Collins's transnational karaoke art project as documented in Suzanne Weaver, *Phil Collins*.

20 George Plasketes, "Re-flections on the Cover Age," 137–61; Deborah Wong, *Speak It Louder*; and Christine R. Yano, *Tears of Longing*.

21 Alice Sarmiento, "This House Is Open but You'll Have to See It My Way," http://alicesarmiento.wordpress.com/2012/04/13/this-house-is-open-but -youll-have-to-see-it-my-way/, accessed October 15, 2015.

22 Walter Ong, *Orality and Literacy*.

23 See http://www.ovguide.com/mail-order-brides-m-o-b-9202a8c04000641 f80000001b61a77a, accessed October 14, 2014.

24 Rob Drew, *Karaoke Nights*, 7.

25 Drew, *Karaoke Nights*, 41.

26 Casey M. K. Lum, *In Search of a Voice*, 11.

27 Drew, *Karaoke Nights*, 49.

28 Deena Weinstein, 'The History of Rock's Pasts," as quoted in Drew, *Karaoke Nights*, 18.

29 Drew, *Karaoke Nights*, 25.

30 See Tia DeNora's *Music in Everyday Life*.

31 Lum, *In Search of a Voice*, 11–12.

32 As Lum writes: "Because there is a customary expectation that audience members will take a turn singing sooner or later during the course of the event, no karaoke participant risks denigrating the performance of others, at least not in the public view or in the front region" (13).

33 See the chapter, "Karaoke, Mass Mediation, and Agency in Vietnamese American Popular Music," in Deborah Wong's *Speak It Louder*, 77.

34 See Sadiya Hartman, *Scenes of Subjection*.

35 See Francesca Tarocco and Xun Zhou, *Karaoke: the Global Phenomenon*.

36 Wong, *Speak It Louder*, 77.

37 Wong, *Speak It Louder*, 74–75.

38 Lum, *In Search of a Voice*, 7.

39 Here Rob Drew is describing the scene of karaoke bars but it also seems fitting in describing the quotidian quality of house parties (Drew, *Karaoke Nights*, 11).

40 See "Immigration, Citizenship, Racialization: Asian American Critique," in Lisa Lowe's *Immigrant Acts*.

41 I imagine these house parties in Filipino America serving a similar function as house parties popular among African American gays and lesbians in the 1940s. See E. Patrick Johnson's chapter, "Mother Knows Best: Blackness and Transgressive Domestic Space," in *Appropriating Blackness*, 76–103.

42 See Rick Bonus, *Locating Filipino Americans*; Benito Vergara Jr., *Pinoy Capital*; and Dawn Mabalon, *Little Manila Is in the Heart*

43 Allan Isaac, *American Tropics*, 47.

44 See Alexandra Vazquez, *Instrumental Migrations*.

45 As Lum notes, this "particular way of life" is an everyday performance that embodies and enacts "process(es) of human interactions and practices whereby certain values, meanings, or social realities are created, maintained, and transformed as part of culture" (7).

46 Isaac's comment during California Dreaming workshop (June 2010).

47 See Patrick Flores's "Palabas," 8–10.

48 Lori Mersh, "Cuteness and Commodity Aesthetics," 185–203.

49 Jane O'Connor as cited in Jacqueline Warwick's essay on Michael Jackson, "'You Can't Win, Child,'" 241–59.

50 Catherine Ceniza Choy, *Empire of Care*; Rhacel Parreñas, *Servants of Globalization*; Robyn Rodriguez, *Migrants for Export*.

51 Note Allan Isaac's new work on call center workers, as presented at "A Symposium on Call Centers in India and the Philippines," Thursday, May 30, 2013, UCLA Center for Southeast Asian Studies, Los Angeles.

52 See Balance, "Dahil sa Iyo," 119–40.

53 See Balance, "How It Feels to Be Viral Me: Affective Labor and Asian American YouTube Performance."

54 For more on "compassion politics," see Lauren Berlant's introduction, "Compassion (and Withholding)."

55 For a short bibliographic list of Oprah studies books, see Eva Illouz, *Oprah Winfrey and the Glamour of Misery*; Janice Peck, *The Age of Oprah*; Trystan Cotten and Kimberly Springer, eds., *Stories of Oprah*; Cecilia Farr and Jaime Harker, eds., *The Oprah Affect*; and Vicki Abt and Leonard Mustazza, *Coming after Oprah*.

56 As quoted in Jon Caramanica's *New York Times* important performance review, "Emotions with Exclamation Points."

57 As Jane O'Connor describes the "Christ-like child star"—"1. Has a natural, inherent talent that has not been taught; 2. Embodies physical perfection; 3. Has a special, almost supernatural quality; 4. Does not engage in annoying or irritating behaviour which would otherwise be typical of a child of their age; 5. Has a purpose in life to uplift or inspire others; 6. Is often unusually intelligent and/or demonstrates developmental proclivity" ("Beyond Social Constructionism," 219–20).

58 As D. Dasein writes in "Tribute Albums: Looking Back in Honor," "In the best tributes, the covering artist steals a song from the original and makes it their own, while they keep, even exaggerate its original spirit" (as quoted in Plasketes, "Re-flections on the Cover Age").

59 For more on this visual discourse of the Filipino (as) child, see Abe Ignacio, Enrique de la Cruz, Jorge Emmanuel, and Helen Toribio, eds., *The Forbid-*

den Book. In the 2011 concert at the Philippine International Convention Center, Charice made it a point to "pay respects" to her elders (older Filipino pop musicians/singers) and situated herself within these celebrity circles by naming folks Kuya (older brother), Tito (uncle), and so on.

60 Herman Gray, *Watching Race*.

61 As Rachel Devitt writes about the marketing of hip-hop group the Black Eyed Peas, which features one of the most prominent Filipino musicians in the U.S. today, Apl de Ap (Allan Pineda): "The Black Eyed Peas' negotiations and articulations of multiculturalism are sanctioned by, subject to, and, at times, aimed at the powerful dollars and discourses of the multi-national music industry. Thus, while Apl's ethnicity helps sell Peas albums in the Philippines, where the group's sold-out shows are attended by President Gloria Macapagal-Arroyo, their label, A&M, shows no signs of supporting the Tagalog tracks or their videos in the United States" (*Lost in Translation*, 124).

Chapter 3: Jessica Hagedorn's Gangster Routes

1 Notable critical writing that deals with *Dogeaters* includes book chapters in Victor Bascara's *Model Minority Imperialism*; Allan Isaac's *American Tropics*; Lisa Lowe's *Immigrant Acts*; Viet Nguyen's *Race and Resistance*; and Lucy Burns's *Puro Arte*. Essays include M. Mendible, "Dictators, Movie Stars, and Martyrs"; Victor Roman Mendoza, "Queer Nomadology"; Jeffrey Santa Ana, "Feeling Ancestral"; Stephen Sohn, "From Discos to Jungles"; Juliana Chang, "Masquerade, Hysteria"; Susan Evangelista, "Jessica Hagedorn and Manila Magic"; S. Koshy, "The Fiction of Asian American Literature"; and A. E. Quintana, "Borders Be Damned."

2 Many thanks to Mark Pangilinan for our conversations on this point.

3 Martin Joseph Ponce, "Cross-Cultural Musics," in *Beyond the Nation*, 120.

4 Ponce, "Cross-Cultural Musics," 120.

5 Ponce, "Cross-Cultural Musics," 124.

6 Amanda Weidman, *Singing the Classical, Voicing the Modern*, 13.

7 Lesley Wheeler, *Voicing American Poetry*, 3.

8 Ponce, "Cross-Cultural Musics," 120.

9 Ponce, "Cross-Cultural Musics," 121.

10 Ponce, "Cross-Cultural Musics," 121.

11 Nashira Priester, "Jessica Hagedorn and the West Coast Gangster Choir," October 30, 1975, SFSU Poetry Center (DVD).

12 Stephen Vincent, "Poetry Readings/Reading Poetry," 23.

13 Vincent, "Poetry Readings/Reading Poetry," 12 and 25.

14 Thulani Nkabinde Davis, "Known Renegades," 75.

15 Davis, "Known Renegades," 71.

16 Jessica Hagedorn, introduction to *Charlie Chan Is Dead*, xxiii.

17 Hagedorn, introduction to *Charlie Chan Is Dead*, xxiv.

18 For more on the Third World internal colonial approach, see Daryl Maeda's *Chains of Babylon* and William Wei's *The Asian American Movement*.

19 Janice Mirikitani, Janet Hale, Roberto Vargas, Alejandro Murguia, and Luis Syquia Jr., eds., *Time to Greez!*; *Third World Women*; Ishmael Reed and Al Young, eds., *The Yardbird Reader*.

20 Hagedorn, introduction to *Charlie Chan Is Dead*, xxiv.

21 For more on this Third World literary aesthetic, see Brian Christopher Flota's "Flight to San Francisco."

22 Hagedorn, "Smokey's Getting Old," *Danger and Beauty*.

23 Hagedorn, "Smokey's Getting Old."

24 Hagedorn, introduction to *Danger and Beauty*, viii.

25 A cassette taped copy of an interview that Hagedorn, as a KPFA correspondent, conducted with Betty Davis in the early 1970s is a rare gem that can be found in Hagedorn's collection at the Bancroft Library.

26 I use the term *tropicalization* as a nod to Frances Aparicio and Susana Chavez-Silverman's definition (and work): "To tropicalize [. . .] means to trope, to imbue a particular space, geography, group or nation with a set of traits, images, and values." See their introduction to the edited collection *Tropicalizations*. Likewise, it is the title of an earlier poetry collection by Victor Hernandez Cruz; see *Tropicalization* (New York: Reed, Cannon, and Johnson Communications, 1976).

27 Author's interview with Jessica Hagedorn, November 24, 2012.

28 Ponce, "Cross-Cultural Musics," in *Beyond the Nation*, 124–28.

29 Kathy Mackay, "A Diverse and Inspired Group."

30 Author's interview with Jessica Hagedorn, October 10, 2009.

31 Hagedorn, "Make-Believe Music," in *The Poetry Reading*, 140.

32 During its inaugural performance, the group also featured a musician named Sam on the keyboards (whom Linda Tillery refers to near the end of the last song). Despite my efforts, I was unable to track down this musician's last name.

33 As Hagedorn recalls, this shorthand often took the form of simply telling Priester, "Here are the lyrics. I'm hearing something like . . . an ominous groove" (from author's interview with Jessica Hagedorn, October 10, 2009).

34 As Hagedorn realized early on, "'Okay . . . clearly I'm not going to be working in night clubs because we're not a dance band.' You know, this thing was like, such a strange notion at the time . . . so I thought, 'We're not going to get those kinds of gigs, so why not just go straight forward and make a concept album? Shoot, why not?'" (from author's interview with Jessica Hagedorn, October 10, 2009).

35 Jessica Hagedorn and the West Coast Gangster Choir, SFSU Poetry Center, October 30, 1975, DVD. Sam played piano/keyboard that night.

36 Hagedorn recalled one label executive's comment: "'You know, it's going to be a hard sell because you're not quite this and you're not quite that.' And I saw that as . . . a plus. And he was like, 'No'" (from author's interview with Jessica Hagedorn, October 10, 2009).

37 Hagedorn, introduction in *Danger and Beauty*, ix.

38 Author's personal interview with Jessica Hagedorn, November 3, 2009.

39 Author's personal interview with Jessica Hagedorn, November 3, 2009.

40 Marvin Taylor, "'I'll Be Your Mirror, Reflect What You Are,'" 35.

41 Carlo McCormick, "A Crack in Time," in *The Downtown Book*, 85.

42 McCormick, "A Crack in Time," 75.

43 McCormick, "A Crack in Time," 67.

44 For more, see Moten's chapter, "Resistance of the Object: Adrian Piper's Theatricality," in *In the Break*, 233–55.

45 For a salient example of this, see an excerpt from his 1986 interview with filmmaker Tamra Davis, featured in her 2010 film, *Jean-Michel Basquiat: Radiant Child*.

46 See José Esteban Muñoz's chapter, "Famous & Dandy Like B. & Andy: Race, Pop, and Basquiat," in *Disidentifications: Queers of Color and the Performance of Politics* (Minneapolis: University of Minnesota Press, 1999).

47 For more on this, see Ricardo Montez's chapter "Theory Made Flesh?: Grace Jones, Bill T. Jones, and Haring's Neoprimitive Line" from his forthcoming manuscript, "Keith Haring's Line: Race and the Performance of Desire."

48 Author's interview with Jessica Hagedorn, October 10, 2009.

49 Author's interview with Jessica Hagedorn, October 10, 2009.

50 McCormick, "A Crack in Time," 67.

51 Deirdre McKay, "Everyday Places," 2.

52 McCormick, "A Crack in Time," 70.

53 For more on the artistic kinship between these two cities, see Bernard Gendron's *Between Montmartre and the Mudd Club: Popular Music and the Avant-Garde*, and Stew's 2008 musical, *Passing Strange*.

54 McCormick, "A Crack in Time," 70.

55 Author's interview with Vernon Reid, August 31, 2012.

56 Author's personal interview with Hagedorn, November 3, 2009.

57 McCormick, "A Crack in Time," 70.

58 Nicky Paraiso, "Laurie Carlos."

59 Author's interview with Vernon Reid, August 31, 2012.

60 Author's interview with Vernon Reid, August 31, 2012.

61 Fred Moten, *In the Break*, 67.

62 Danielle Goldman, *I Want to Be Ready*, 73.

63 Goldman, *I Want to Be Ready*, 57.

64 Goldman, *I Want to Be Ready*, 83.

65 Author's personal interview with Jessica Hagedorn, November 3, 2009.

66 Goldman, *I Want To Be Ready*, 83.

67 Author's personal interview with Jessica Hagedorn, November 3, 2009.

68 For example, "Dog Eat Dog," as harbinger to the title for Hagedorn's canonical novel, and a nascent version of Carlos's later solo performance piece *White Chocolate*.

69 Laurie Carlos, Jessica Hagedorn, and Robbie McCauley, "Teenytown," 91.

70 Carlos, Hagedorn, and McCauley, "Teenytown," 91.

71 Carlos, Hagedorn, and McCauley, "Teenytown," 103.

72 Carlos, Hagedorn, and McCauley, "Teenytown," 103.

73 Carlos, Hagedorn, and McCauley, "Teenytown," 103.

74 For more on accent puns, see Sarita See's chapter, "Why Filipinos Make Pun(s) of One Another," in *The Decolonized Eye*.

75 Over the span of two decades, Bonetti conducted interviews with contemporary writers for the American Audio Prose Library, all of which were published in *The Missouri Review*. Thus, both audio recordings, as well as print transcriptions, of these interviews remain.

76 Kay Bonetti, "An Interview with Jessica Hagedorn."

77 Hagedorn, *Gangster of Love*, 62.

78 For more on "inside jokes," "aural be/longing," see See's chapter, "Why Filipinos Make Pun(s) of One Another," in *The Decolonized Eye*.

79 Hagedorn, *Gangster of Love*, 17.

80 Hagedorn, *Gangster of Love*, 17.

81 Angela McRobbie and J. Garber, "Girls and Subcultures," 1–15; Tia DeNora, *Music and Everyday Life*; Simon Frith, *Taking Popular Music Seriously*.

82 Hagedorn, *Gangster of Love*, 31.

83 Hagedorn, *Gangster of Love*, 52.

84 Hagedorn, "Souvenirs," in *Dangerous Music*, 4.

85 Susan Stewart, *On Longing*, 135.

Chapter 4: Pinoise Rock

1 Bindlestiff Studio was started in 1989 by puppeteer Chrystene Ellis and a cadre of local theater artists. In 1995, Filipino community-based arts group Teatro ng Tanan (TnT or "Theatre for Everyone") and Filipino American experimental comedy troupe Tongue in a Mood joined the theater's consortium and, until the sale of the building and the theater's demolition in 2002, Bindlestiff fostered emerging Filipino and Filipino American performing/visual/literary artists, scholars, and audiences in realizing new and innovative ways of "performing Filipino." After many years of protests, renovations, and begotiations, it reopened its doors in September 2011.

2 Author's interview with Ogie and Jesse Gonzales, December 15, 2011.

3 For more on the Epicenter Zone, see Mimi Nguyen's *Pop Matters* article,

"A Place Full of Punks," October 18, 2004, http://www.popmatters.com/feature/tttp-5nguyen/, accessed August 26, 2015.

4 Remarkably, the Eraserheads were the first Philippine band to win the award.

5 Author's interview with Ogie and Jesse Gonzales, December 15, 2011.

6 November 20 and 21, 1998. Planning and publicizing that initial festival required a large leap of faith for, as Ogie remembers, "First, we thought, 'Are there any Fil-Am bands?' We didn't know any except for (SF indie rock band) Julie Plug."

7 The list of bands that performed at piNoisepop over those seven years runs long and wide. For a complete listing that includes bands' hometown locations and musical genre, visit the Bindlestiff Studio: piNoisepop archives' Facebook page, https://www.facebook.com/Bindlestiff-Archives-piNoisepop-Music-Festival-1998–2005–144159418936184/, accessed October 15, 2015.

8 Sara Cohen, *Rock Culture in Liverpool*, 240.

9 I mark the beginning of this time period with the 1991 publication of Will Straw's now-canonical essay, "Systems of Articulation, Logics of Change."

10 Will Straw, "Systems of Articulation, Logics of Change." See also Cohen's *Rock Culture in Liverpool*, Holly Kruse's *Site and Sound*, and Barry Shank's *Dissonant Identities*.

11 For more on this topic, see Sarah Thornton's "Strategies for Reconstructing the Popular Past," *Popular Music* 9, no. 1 (January 1990): 87–95.

12 For more on indie rock's genealogies and "indebtedness" to punk/postpunk rock music, see Kaya Oakes's *Slanted and Enchanted: The Evolution of Indie Culture* (New York: Holt, 2009), and Michael Azerrad's *Our Band Could Be Your Life: Scenes from the American Indie Underground, 1981–1991* (Boston: Little, Brown, 2012).

13 Wendy Fonarow, *Empire of Dirt*, 39.

14 Fonarow, *Empire of Dirt*, 29.

15 Fonarow, *Empire of Dirt*, 54.

16 As Fabian Holt writes: "Following Frith and Negus, I adopt the term *genre culture* as a concept for the overall identity of the cultural formations in which a genre is constituted. It makes sense to view popular music genres as small cultures because they are defined in relation to many of the same aspects as general culture." See Holt's *Genre in Popular Music*, 19.

17 Carl Wilson's 2015 *Slate* article, on the aging of indie rock and its necessary death as a viable musical category solely due to its unbearable whiteness, serves as the most recent example of this ongoing trend. See Wilson's "Against Indie," http://www.slate.com/articles/arts/music_box/2015/04/against_indie_new_albums_from_modest_mouse_sufjan_stevens_and_more_show.html, accessed October 15, 2015.

18 To reiterate, the importance of these texts is twofold: first, they do not

presume indie rock musical culture as strictly white and therefore, without that assumption, they move forward in carefully analyzing the relationship between race and musical genre. See Jose Anguiano's "Latino Listening Cultures"; Aileen Dillane, Martin J. Power, and Eoin Devereux, "'I Can Have Both,'" 149–63; Gustavo Arellano's "Their Charming Man"; James Spooner's landmark 2003 documentary *Afro-Punk*; Aaron Thompson's "From Bad Brains to Afro-Punk"; Jayna Brown, Patrick Deer, and Tavia Nyong'o, "Punk and Its Afterlives Introduction," 1–11; Dengue Fever, John Pirozzi, and Josh Otten's film *Sleepwalking through the Mekong*; and Joshua Chambers-Letson's "'No, I Can't Forget,'" 259–87.

19 Sasha Frere-Jones, "A Paler Shade of White."

20 Holt, *Genre in Popular Music*, 5.

21 Holt, *Genre in Popular Music*, 13.

22 Holt, *Genre in Popular Music*, 2.

23 Holt, *Genre in Popular Music*, 19.

24 "If we pay close attention to how individuals choose a station on a radio or respond to a street musician, we quickly learn that such everyday routines are more complex than most people think. Through the acts of identification and negation, our filters define ourselves and others" (Holt, *Genre in Popular Music*, 151).

25 Holt, *Genre in Popular Music*, 19.

26 Within a local music scene, performance venues and events—such as piNoisepop—act as that scene's heart or core. But, within a translocal scene network, they operate as one of many "social hubs"—such as record shops, rehearsal studios, online forums, YouTube channels, Facebook fan pages, television/radio programs, fanzines/newsletters—that gather, produce, and disseminate a certain genre of music.

27 See new work, including Grace Wang's *Soundtracks of Asian America* and Patricia Ahn's "Aftermarkets of Empire."

28 See P. H. Kim and H. Shin, "The Birth of 'Rok,'" 199–230; Joshua Chambers-Letson's " 'No, I Can't Forget,'" 259–87; David Novak's *Japanoise*.

29 Wendy Hsu, "Redefining Asian America."

30 See Sara Cohen's *Rock Culture in Liverpool: Popular Music in the Making* (Oxford: Oxford University Press, 1991) and *Decline, Renewal, and the City in Popular Music Culture: Beyond the Beatles* (Farnham, UK: Ashgate Press, 2007).

31 From KulArts' web page, http://www.kularts.org/contemporary.php, accessed October 15, 2015.

32 Benjamin Jaime, "piNoisepop: OPM Goes West (alternative Fil-Am bands find a home in this Bay Area music festival)," July 11, 2000, Philmusic.com, accessed through copy scanned by Jesse Gonzales, December 10, 2011.

33 Mimi Nguyen and Thuy Linh Tu, introduction to *Alien Encounters*, 12–13.

34 Nguyen and Tu, introduction to *Alien Encounters*, 13.
35 Jean-Luc Nancy, *Listening*, 3.
36 Neferti Tadiar, *Things Fall Away*, 145.
37 Tadiar, *Things Fall Away*, 144.
38 Jocelyn Valle, "The Eraserheads."
39 For more on the Eraserheads and their fan base, see Jing Garcia's edited collection, *Tikman Mo Ang Langit: An Anthology on the Eraserheads* (Manila: Visual Print Enterprises, 2006).
40 Albert Ascona, "Pinoy Punk," 101.
41 Tadiar, "Metropolitan Dreams," *Fantasy Production*, 84.
42 Author's interview with Myrene Academia, June 22, 2009.
43 Henry Jenkins, *Convergence Culture: Where Old and New Media Collide*.
44 Author's interviews with Diego Mapa, September 10, 2011; Diego Castillo, June 13, 2009; and Jason Caballa, September 15, 2011.
45 As Philippine music critic Aldus Santos points out, "These days, Marasigan, despite favoring the declarative over the figurative, is still lyrically exciting, employing, as always his choice tool: the *kanto* (street) vernacular." Santos, "Top Ten Pinoy Lyricists of the Past Decade," in *Repeat While Fading*, 103.
46 Author's interview with Diego Castillo, June 13, 2009.
47 Author's interview with Ogie and Jesse Gonzales, December 15, 2011.
48 Author's interview with Diego Castillo, June 13, 2009.
49 Eric Caruncho, "Last Tango in Olongapo," in *Punks, Poets, and Poseurs*, 50.
50 Ascona, "Pinoy Punk," 103.
51 Ascona, "Pinoy Punk," 104.
52 Author's informal conversation with Raimund Marasigan, June 20, 2010.

Epilogue: Rakenrol Itineraries

1 Roland Tolentino, "Burgis na Juvenilia," August 7, 2012, http://pinoy weekly.org/new/2012/08/burgis-na-juvenilia/, accessed October 15, 2015.
2 Patrick F. Campos, "The Intersection of Philippine and Global Film Cultures in the New Urban Realist Film," *Plaridel: A Journal of Communication, Media, and Society* 8, no. 1 (2011): 4.
3 Campos, "Intersection of Philippine and Global Film Cultures," 4.
4 Lumbera (1984), in Campos, "Intersection of Philippine and Global Film Cultures."
5 Campos, "Intersection of Philippine and Global Film Cultures," 8.
6 Campos, "Intersection of Philippine and Global Film Cultures," 8.
7 Mara Coson, "On Privilege in Independent Cinema: Every Cloud Has a Silver Spoon Lining," *Manila Review* 1, no. 1 (December 2012), http:// themanilareview.com/issues/view/on-privilege-in-independent-cinema -every-cloud-has-a-silver-spoon-lining, accessed October 15, 2015.

8 Alice Sarmiento, "What Isn't in *What Isn't There*," *Manila Review* 1, no.
   4 (February 2014), http://themanilareview.com/issues/view/what-isnt
   -in-what-isnt-there, accessed October 15, 2015.

9 Author's interview with Marie Jamora, December 8, 2013.

10 *Rakenrol* has screened at Visual Communications' (VC) Los Angeles
   Asian Pacific Film Festival (LAAPFF), where it garnered the Audience
   Choice Award (May 2011); a private fundraiser screening cosponsored by
   San Francisco-based organizations Bindlestiff Studio, Center for Asian
   American Media (CAAM), and KulArts (May 2011); Asian Cinevision (ACV)
   New York Asian American International Film Festival (AAIFF) (August
   2011); Manila's Cinemalaya Film Festival (September 2011); and San
   Francisco-based Yerba Buena Center for the Arts' (YBCA) New Filipino Cin-
   ema series (June 2012). *Ang Nawawala* has screened at the Cinemalaya Film
   Festival, where it garnered the Best Original Score and Audience Choice
   Award in the New Breed Category (May 2012); Hawaii International Film
   Festival (HIFF) (April 2013); VC's LAAPFF (May 2013); Honolulu Museum
   of Art's Filipino Film Festival (May 2013); and YBCA's New Filipino Cinema
   series (June 2013), to name a few.

11 For more on film festival studies, see Cindy Wong, *Film Festivals: Culture,
   People, and Power on the Global Screen* (New Brunswick, NJ: Rutgers University Press, 2011).

12 For more on this internationalizing trend within the history of Asian
   Pacific American film festivals, see curator Chi-hui Yang's foreword to the
   special issue, "Documenting Asia Pacific," *Concentric: Literary and Cul-
   tural Studies* 39, no. 1 (March 2013): 3–6; and Sonjia Hyon's "The Right to
   Be Whoever the Hell They Want to Be: *Better Luck Tomorrow* and Asian
   American Cultural Politics of Normal," in "Anxieties of the Fictive: Asian
   American Politics of Visibility," Ph.D. diss., Department of American Stud-
   ies, University of Minnesota, 2011.

13 For more on U.S. imperialism's impact on the Philippine film industry, see
   Nick Deocampo's *Film: American Influences on Philippine Cinema* (Manila:
   Anvil Publishing, 2011); José B. Capino's *Dream Factories of a Former Colony:
   American Fantasies, Philippine Cinema* (Minneapolis: University of Minne-
   sota Press, 2010); Roland B. Tolentino's edited collection *Geopolitics of the
   Visible: Essays on Philippine Film Cultures* (Manila: Ateneo de Manila Univer-
   sity Press, 2010); and Nicanor Tiongson's writings, especially "The Filipino
   Film Industry," *East-West Film Journal* 6, no. 2 (1996).

14 Timothy Dowd, Kathleen Liddle, and Jenna Nelson, "Music Festivals as
   Scenes," 149.

15 Dowd, Liddle, and Nelson, "Music Festivals as Scenes," 158.

16 Monica Sassatelli, "Urban Festivals and the Cultural Public Sphere," 13.

17 Jasper Chalcraft and Paolo Maguadda, "'Space Is the Place,'" 184.

18 Diego Mapa, "Taken by Cars Takes Manila by Storm with Their Debut CD."

19 From SXSW website, www.sxsw.com/about, August 14, 2014.

20 "Taken by Cars and the Road to Austin," http://www.bakitwhy.com/articles
    /taken-cars-and-road-austin, accessed October 15, 2015.

21 Mike Shih interview in "Pinoy Band Taken by Cars Performs at Major U.S.
    Music Fest," http://ph.omg.yahoo.com/news/pinoy-band-taken-by-cars
    -performs-at-major-u-s—music-fest-.html, accessed October 15, 2015.

22 For more on the interconnected state and music industry infrastructure in
    the K-Pop example, see Patty Ahn's dissertation, "Aftermarkets of Empire:
    South Korean Pop Music and the Global Logics of Race and Gender in the
    U.S. Media Industries," Ph.D. diss., Critical Studies Department, USC
    School of Cinematic Arts, 2014.

23 Erwin Romulo, "Ciudad's New Song and How You're Getting Old without a
    Choice," http://radiorepublic.ph/ciudad-sifil/, accessed October 15, 2015.

24 See "Brooklyn Sessions," http://ciudad.bandcamp.com/album/brooklyn
    -sessions, accessed October 15, 2015.

25 Ted Reyes, "For Ciudad, New York Rain Is New York Love," http://www
    .examiner.com/article/for-ciudad-new-york-rain-is-new-york-love,
    accessed October 15, 2015.

26 For more on Asian American cool, see Mimi Nguyen and Thuy Linh Tu's
    introduction to their edited collection, *Alien Encounters: Popular Culture in
    Asian America*; on global cineaste, see Wong's *Film Festivals*.

27 Thanks to Raimund Marasigan for helping me further formulate this
    notion of "nostalgia tours."

28 Over the past few years, I have had the honor of coproducing and organiz-
    ing, with artists and musicians from Manila, New York, and Los Angeles,
    the following Pinoy indie rock shows: Ciudad's New York tour, featuring
    the Jack Lords Orchestra, Black Sonny, and Youngster (November 8, 2009,
    at the Delancey); Red Datsun, Velta, and Sandwich Halloween Party (Octo-
    ber 31, 2011, at Local 269, New York); Taken by Cars' "Abduction Tour LA"
    (March 16, 2012, at Mr. T's Bowl); the Jack Lords Orchestra with Sandwich
    (November 23, 2013, at Fontana's NYC); Rakenrol film screening, featuring
    Spazzkid and Sandwich (December 5, 2013, at Busby's East, Los Angeles).

29 "Apl de Ap Takes You to the Philippines: A Celebration of Global Filipino
    Music," http://www.hollywoodbowl.com/tickets/apldeap-takes-you-to
    -philippines-celebration-of-global-filipino-music/2012–07–08, accessed
    October 15, 2015.

30 Author's interview with Marie Jamora (September 2011). As Jamora
    recalls, "my band mates . . . not just the people from Boldstar but from my
    previous band, as well, they all just ADORE Versus. Even in college . . . like,
    I met this guy, he was Jason . . . you know, Jason Caballa . . . he was intro-
    duced to Versus by his block mate who had them on 7-inch. Like, we all got

to know the band through different avenues but we all got to love them equally."

31 Author's interview with Marie Jamora, September 21, 2011.

32 From Super Astig Blog's short video, "The Excursion Tour Baguio," https://www.youtube.com/watch?v=oWxFvw4auuU, accessed October 15, 2015.

33 Merlin Magallona and Jay Batongbacal, in their collection *Archipelagic Studies: Charting New Waters*, 8.

34 These titles reference albums by the following bands: *Quiet Life* (Japan), *Do You Really Want to Hurt Me?* (Culture Club), *Paranoid* (Black Sabbath), *Are We Not Men?* (Devo), and *Virgins and Philistines* (The Colourfield).

35 My thanks to Marie Jamora for reading an earlier version of this chapter and for her insights regarding the film.

Abt, Vicki, and Leonard Mustazza. *Coming after Oprah: Cultural Fallout in the Age of the TV Talk Show*. Bowling Green, OH: Bowling Green State University Press, 1997.

Ahn, Patricia. "Aftermarkets of Empire: South Korean Pop Music and the Global Logics of Race and Gender in the U.S. Media Industries." PhD diss., Department of Critical Studies, School of Cinematic Arts, University of Southern California, Los Angeles, 2014.

Anguiano, Jose. "Latino Listening Cultures: Identity, Affect, and Resilient Music Practices." PhD diss., University of California, Santa Barbara, 2012.

Aparicio, Frances, and Susana Chavez-Silverman, eds. *Tropicalizations: Transcultural Representations of Latinidad*. Hanover, NH: University Press of New England, 1997.

Arellano, Gustavo. "Their Charming Man." *OC Weekly*, September 12, 2002.

Ascona, Albert. "Pinoy Punk." *Rogue* magazine, June 2, 2008.

Azerrad, Michael. *Our Band Could Be Your Life: Scenes from the American Indie Underground, 1981–1991*. New York: Little, Brown, 2012.

Balance, Christine Bacareza. "Dahil sa Iyo: The Performative Power of Imelda's Song." *Women and Performance: A Journal of Feminist Theory* 20, no. 2: 2010, 119–40.

Balance, Christine Bacareza. "How It Feels to Be Viral Me: Affective Labor and Asian American YouTube Performance." *WSQ: Women's Studies Quarterly* 40, nos. 1–2 (spring/summer 2012): 138–52.

Bascara, Victor. *Model Minority Imperialism*. Minneapolis: University of Minnesota Press, 2006.

Battaglia, Debbora, ed. *E.T. Culture: Anthropology in Outerspaces*. Durham, NC: Duke University Press, 2005.

Berlant, Lauren, ed. "Compassion (and Withholding)." *Compassion: The Culture and Politics of an Emotion*. New York: Routledge, 2004.

Bernstein, Charles, ed. *Close Listening: Poetry and the Performed Word*. New York: Oxford University Press, 1998.

Bonetti, Kay. "An Interview with Jessica Hagedorn." Recorded in April 1994 for the American Audio Prose Library. Accessed October 15, 2015. http://www.missourireview.com/archives/bbarticle/an-interview-with-jessica-hagedorn/.

Bonus, Rick. *Locating Filipino Americans: Ethnicity and the Cultural Politics of Space*. Philadelphia: Temple University Press, 2000.

Bowe, John. "How Did House Bands Become a Filipino Export?" *New York Times Magazine*, May 29, 2005.

Brown, Jayna, Patrick Deer, and Tavia Nyong'o. "Punk and Its Afterlives Introduction." *Social Text* 31, no. 3 (2013): 1–11.

Buenconsejo, José S. "Parodies of Traditional Comedia and Hollywoodish Spectacle in Francisco Buencamino Sr.'s Film Music *Ibong Adarna* (1941)." Paper presented at ICOPHIL 2011 conference.

Burns, Lucy San Pablo. *Puro Arte: Filipinos on the Stages of Empire*. New York: NYU Press, 2012.

Campomanes, Oscar. "Filipinos in the United States and Their Literature of Exile." In *Reading the Literatures of Asian America*, edited by Shirley Geok-lin Lim and Amy Ling. Philadelphia: Temple University Press, 1992.

Campos, Patrick F. "The Intersection of Philippine and Global Film Cultures in the New Urban Realist Film." *Plaridel: A Journal of Communication, Media, and Society* 8, no. 1 (2011): 1–20.

Capino, José B. *Dream Factories of a Former Colony: American Fantasies, Philippine Cinema*. Minneapolis: University of Minnesota Press, 2010.

Caramanica, Jon. "Emotions with Exclamation Points." *New York Times*, September 16, 2008.

Carlos, Laurie, Jessica Hagedorn, and Robbie McCauley. "Teenytown." In *Out from Under: Texts by Women Performance Artists*, edited by Lenora Champagne. New York: Theatre Communications Group, 1990.

Carluccio, John, Ethan Imboden, and Raymond Pirtle. *Turntablist Transcription Methodology* handbook. Accessed October 15, 2015. www.battlesounds.com/transcription/ttm.pdf.

Caruncho, Eric. "Last Tango in Olongapo." *Punks, Poets, Poseurs: Reportage on Pinoy Rock and Roll*. Manila: Anvil Publishing, 1996.

Castro, Christi-Anne. *Musical Renderings of the Philippine Nation*. New York: Oxford University Press, 2011.

Chalcraft, Jasper, and Paolo Maguadda, "'Space Is the Place': The Global Localities of the Sonar and WOMAD Music Festivals." In *Festivals and the Cultural Public Sphere*, edited by Liana Giorgi, Monica Sassatelli, and Gerard Delanty. New York: Routledge, 2011.

Chambers-Letson, Joshua. "'No, I Can't Forget': Performance and Memory in Dengue Fever's Cambodian America." *Journal of Popular Music Studies* 23, no. 3 (2011): 259–87.

Chang, Juliana. "Masquerade, Hysteria, and Neocolonial Femininity in Hagedorn's *Dogeaters*." *Contemporary Literature* 44, no. 4 (winter 2003): 637–63.

Choy, Catherine Ceniza. *Empire of Care: Nursing and Migration in Filipino American History*. Durham, NC: Duke University Press, 2003.

Chuh, Kandice. "It's Not about Anything." In "Being-With: A Special Issue on the Work of José Esteban Muñoz." *Social Text* 32, no. 4 (winter 2014): 125–34.

Chuh, Kandice. *Imagine Otherwise: On Asian Americanist Critique*. Durham, NC: Duke University Press, 2003.

Chun, Kimberly. "'Scratch' and Sniff with DJ QBert." *Asian Week*, March 8–14, 2002.

Cohen, Sara. "Mapping the Sound: Identity, Place, and the Liverpool Sound." In *Ethnicity, Identity, and Music: The Musical Construction of Place*, edited by Martin Stokes. Oxford: Berg, 1994.

Cohen, Sara. *Rock Culture in Liverpool: Popular Music in the Making*. New York: Oxford University Press, 1991.

Cohen, Sara. *Decline, Renewal, and the City in Popular Music Culture: Beyond the Beatles*. Burlington, VT: Ashgate Press, 2007.

Constantino, Renato. "The Miseducation of the Filipino." In *Vestiges of War: The Philippine-American War and the Aftermath of an Imperial Dream, 1899–1999*, edited by Angel Velasco Shaw and Luis Francia. New York: NYU Press, 2002.

Cotten, Trystan, and Kimberly Springer, eds. *Stories of Oprah: The Oprahfication of American Culture*. Jackson: University Press of Mississippi, 2010.

Cristal, Marko. "The Evolution of Dance Crews in Southern California and Its Influence on the Filipino-American Experience." Thesis, Departments of History and Asian American Studies, UC Irvine, June 2012.

Dasein, D. "Tribute Albums: Looking Back in Honor." *Illinois Entertainer*, March 5, 1995, 52.

Davis, Tamra. *Jean-Michel Basquiat: the Radiant Child*. Film. Fortissimo Films/ Arthouse Films, 2010.

Davis, Thulani Nkabinde. "Known Renegades: Recent Black/Brown/Yellow." In *The Poetry Reading: A Contemporary Compendium on Language and Performance*, edited by Stephen Vincent and Ellen Zweig. San Francisco: Momo's Press, 1981.

Dengue Fever, John Pirozzi, and Josh Otten. *Sleepwalking through the Mekong*. Film. M80/Film 101 Productions, 2009.

DeNora, Tia. *Music in Everyday Life*. New York: Cambridge University Press, 2000.

Deocampo, Nick. *Film: American Influences on Philippine Cinema*. Manila: Anvil Publishing, 2011.

Devitt, Rachel. "Lost in Translation: Filipino Diaspora(s), Postcolonial Hip Hop, and the Problems of Keeping It Real for the 'Contentless' Black Eyed Peas." *Asian Music* 39, no. 1: 108–34.

Dillane, Aileen, Martin J. Power, and Eoin Devereux. "'I Can Have Both': A Queer Reading of Morrissey." *Journal of European Popular Culture* 5, no. 2 (2014): 149–63.

DJ Babu (Chris Oroc). "Interview with Christo Macias." May 1996. Accessed January 14, 2004. http://www.bombhiphop.com/newbomb/bombpages /articles/DJ/Turntablism%20Mailing%20List%20FAQ.htm.

Dowd, Timothy, Kathleen Liddle, and Jenna Nelson. "Music Festivals as Scenes: Examples from Serious Music, Womyn's Music, and SkatePunk." In *Music Scenes: Local, Translocal, and Virtual*, edited by Andy Bennett and Richard A. Peterson. Nashville: Vanderbilt University Press, 2004.

Drew, Rob. *Karaoke Nights: An Ethnographic Rhapsody.* Walnut Creek, CA: AltaMira Press, 2001.

Enriquez, Elizabeth L. *Appropriation of Colonial Broadcasting: A History of Early Radio in the Philippines, 1922–1946.* Quezon City: University of the Philippines Press, 2008.

Eshun, Kodwo. In *Modulations: A History of Electronic Music: Throbbing Words on Sound*, edited by Peter Shapiro. New York: Caipirinha, 2000, 102.

Evangelista, Susan. "Jessica Hagedorn and Manila Magic." MELUS 18, no. 4 (1993): 41–52.

Farr, Cecilia, and Jaime Harker, eds. *The Oprah Affect: Critical Essays on Oprah's Book Club.* Albany: State University of New York Press, 2008.

Fernandez, Doreen. *Palabas: Essays on Philippine Theater History.* Manila: Ateneo University Press, 1996.

Flores, Patrick. "Palabas." *Ctrl + P Journal of Contemporary Art*, March 2008, 8–10.

Flota, Brian Christopher. "Flight to San Francisco: Bay Area Literature and Multiculturalism, 1955–1979." PhD diss., George Washington University, 2006.

Fonarow, Wendy. *Empire of Dirt: The Aesthetics and Rituals of British Indie Music.* Middletown, CT: Wesleyan University Press, 2006.

Foucault, Michel. *Discipline and Punish: The Birth of the Prison.* New York: Pantheon, 1977.

Frere-Jones, Sasha. "A Paler Shade of White: How Indie Rock Lost Its Soul." *New Yorker*, October 22, 2007. Accessed October 15, 2015. http://www .newyorker.com/magazine/2007/10/22/a-paler-shade-of-white.

Friar, William. "QBert (aka Richard Quitevis): The Turntable Pioneer Takes a Solo Spin." *Contra Costa Times*, October 4, 1998.

Frith, Simon. *Performing Rites: On the Value of Popular Music.* Cambridge, MA: Harvard University Press, 1998.

Frith, Simon. *Taking Popular Music Seriously.* Burlington, VT: Ashgate, 2007.

Fuentes, Marlon. "Extracts from an Imaginary Interview: Questions and Answers about *Bontoc Eulogy*." In *F Is for Phony: Fake Documentary and Truth's Undoing*, edited by Alexandra Juhasz and Jesse Lerner. Minneapolis: University of Minnesota Press, 2006.

Garcia, Jing, ed. *Tikman Mo Ang Langit: An Anthology on the Eraserheads*. Manila: Visual Print Enterprises, 2006.

Gendron, Bernard. *Between Montmartre and the Mudd Club: Popular Music and the Avant-Garde*. Chicago: University of Chicago Press, 2002.

Gitelman, Lisa. *Always Already New*. Cambridge, MA: MIT Press, 2006.

Glissant, Edouard. *Caribbean Discourse: Selected Essays*. Charlottesville: University of Virginia Press, 1992.

Goldman, Danielle. *I Want to Be Ready: Improvised Dance as a Practice of Freedom*. Ann Arbor: University of Michigan Press, 2010.

Gray, Herman. *Watching Race: Television and the Struggle for Blackness*. Minneapolis: University of Minnesota Press, 1995.

Hagedorn, Jessica, ed. *Charlie Chan Is Dead: An Anthology of Contemporary Asian American Fiction*. New York: Penguin Books, 1993.

Hagedorn, Jessica. *Danger and Beauty*. San Francisco: City Lights Publishers, 2002.

Hagedorn, Jessica. *Dangerous Music*. San Francisco: Momo's Press, 1975.

Hagedorn, Jessica. *Dogeaters*. New York: Penguin, 1991.

Hagedorn, Jessica. "Interview with Betty Davis." Banc phonotape 3840. Jessica Tarahata Hagedorn A/V collection, Bancroft Library, UC Berkeley.

Hagedorn, Jessica. *The Gangster of Love*. New York: Penguin, 1997.

Hagedorn, Jessica. "Makebelieve Music." In *The Poetry Reading*, edited by S. Vincent and E. Zweig. San Francisco: Momo's Press, 1981.

Hall, Stuart. "Notes on Deconstructing the 'Popular.'" In *Cultural Theory and Popular Culture: A Reader*, edited by John Storey. Athens: University of Georgia Press, 2006.

Hartman, Saidiya. *Scenes of Subjection: Terror, Slavery, and Self-Making in Nineteenth-Century America*. Oxford: Oxford University Press, 2007.

Henares, Quark, director. *Rakenrol*. Film. 2011.

Hila, Antonio C. *Musika: An Essay on Philippine Music*. Manila: Sentrong Pangkultura ng Pilipinas, 1989.

Hillenbrand, Margaret. "Of Myths and Men: Better Luck Tomorrow and the Mainstreaming of Asian America Cinema." *Cinema Journal* 47, no. 4 (2008): 50–75.

Hogg, Bennett. "The Cultural Imagination of the Phonographic Voice, 1877–1940." PhD diss., University of Newcastle upon Tyne, 2008.

Holt, Fabian. *Genre in Popular Music*. Chicago: University of Chicago Press, 2007.

Hsu, Wendy. "Redefining Asian America: Cultural Politics, Aesthetics, and

Social Networks of Independent Rock Musicians." PhD diss., Critical and Comparative Studies in Music program, University of Virginia, 2011.

Hyon, Soyoung Sonjia. "Anxieties of the Fictive: Asian American Politics of Visibility." PhD diss., Department of American Studies, University of Minnesota, 2011.

Ignacio, Abe, Enrique de la Cruz, Jorge Emmanuel, and Helen Toribio, eds. *The Forbidden Book: The Philippine-American War in Political Cartoons*. San Francisco: T'Boli, 2004.

Illouz, Eva. *Oprah Winfrey and the Glamour of Misery*. New York: Columbia University Press, 2003.

Irving, D. R. M. *Colonial Counterpoint: Music in Early Modern Manila*. Oxford: Oxford University Press, 2010.

Isaac, Allan. *American Tropics: Articulating Filipino America*. Minneapolis: University of Minnesota Press, 2006.

Iyer, Pico. *Video Night in Kathmandu: And Other Reports from the Not-So-Far-East*. New York: Knopf, 1988.

Jackson, Sarah. "Bay Area 51." Unpublished paper, May 6, 1998.

Jamora, Marie, dir. *Ang Nawawala* [What Isn't There]. Film. 2012.

Jenkins, Henry. *Convergence Culture: Where Old and New Media Collide*. New York: New York University Press, 2008.

Jessica Hagedorn and the West Coast Gangster Choir. SFSU Poetry Center. DVD. October 30, 1975.

Joaquin, Nick. *Manila, My Manila*. Manila: Bookmark, 1999.

Johnson, E. Patrick. *Appropriating Blackness: Performance and the Politics of Authenticity*. Durham, NC: Duke University Press, 2003.

Kang, Laura. *Compositional Subjects: Enfiguring Asian/American Women*. Durham, NC: Duke University Press, 2002.

Katz, Mark. *Capturing Sound: How Technology Has Changed Music*. Berkeley: University of California Press, 2010.

Kelly, Caleb. *Cracked Media: The Sound of Malfunction*. Cambridge, MA: MIT Press, 2009.

Kim, Jodi. *Ends of Empire: Asian American Critique and the Cold War*. Minneapolis: University of Minnesota Press, 2010.

Kim, P. H., and H. Shin. "The Birth of 'Rok': Cultural Imperialism, Nationalism, and the Glocalization of Rock Music in South Korea, 1964–1975." *positions: east asia cultures critique* 18, no. 1 (2010): 199–230.

Kirshenblatt-Gimblett, Barbara. "Objects of Ethnography." In *Exhibiting Cultures: The Poetics of Museum Display*, edited by Ivan Karp and Steven Lavine. Washington, DC: Smithsonian Institute Press, 1990.

Kittler, Friedrich. *Gramophone Film Typewriter*. Stanford, CA: Stanford University Press, 1999.

Koshy, S. "The Fiction of Asian American Literature." *Yale Journal of Criticism* 9 (1996): 35–65.

Kruse, Holly. *Site and Sound: Understanding Independent Music Scenes*. New York: Peter Lang, 2003.

Kun, Josh. *Audiotopia: Music, Race, and America*. Berkeley: University of California Press, 2005.

Kun, Josh. "Unexpected Harmony." *New York Times*, June 20, 2010.

Lovink, Geert. "Everything Was to Be Done—All the Adventures Are Still There: A Speculative Dialogue with Kodwo Eshun." *Telepolis*, February 10, 2000.

Lowe, Lisa. *Immigrant Acts: On Asian American Cultural Politics*. Durham, NC: Duke University Press, 1996.

Lum, Casey M. K. *In Search of a Voice: Karaoke and the Construction of Identity in Chinese America*. Mahwah, NJ: Lawrence Erlbaum, 1996.

Mackay, Kathy. "A Diverse and Inspired Group." *San Francisco Sunday Examiner and Chronicle*, February 8, 1976.

Maeda, Daryl. *Chains of Babylon: The Rise of Asian America*. Minneapolis: University of Minnesota Press, 2009.

Mallat, Jean. *The Philippines: History, Geography, Customs, Agriculture, Industry, and Commerce of the Spanish Colonies in Oceania*. Manila: National Historical Institute, 1983.

Manalansan, Martin. *Global Divas: Filipino Gay Men in the Diaspora*. Durham, NC: Duke University Press, 2003.

Mapa, Diego. "Taken by Cars Takes Manila by Storm with Their Debut CD." *Manila Standard Today*, February 9, 2008.

Massumi, Brian. *Parables for the Virtual: Movement, Affect, Sensation*. Durham, NC: Duke University Press, 2003.

McCormick, Carlo. "A Crack in Time." In *The Downtown Book: The New York Art Scene, 1974–1984*, edited by Marvin J. Taylor. Princeton, NJ: Princeton University Press, 2006.

McKay, Deirdre. "Everyday Places: Philippine Place-Making and the Translocal Quotidian." Paper given at Cultural Studies Association of Australasia Conference, *Everyday Transformations: The Twenty-First Century Quotidian*, Murdoch University, Perth, 2004.

McRobbie, Angela, and J. Garber. "Girls and Subcultures." In *Feminism and Youth Culture: From Jackie to Just Seventeen*, edited by A. McRobbie. London: Macmillan, 1991.

Mendible, M. "Dictators, Movie Stars, and Martyrs: The Politics of Spectacle in Jessica Hagedorn's *Dogeaters*." *Genders* 36 (January 2002): 1–15.

Mendoza, Victor Roman. "A Queer Nomadology of Jessica Hagedorn's *Dogeaters*." *American Literature* 77, no. 4 (December 2005): 815–45.

Mersh, Lori. "Cuteness and Commodity Aesthetics: Tom Thumb and Shirley Temple." In *Freakery: Cultural Spectacles of the Extraordinary Body*, edited by Rosemarie Garland-Thomson, 185–203. New York: NYU Press, 1996.

Millet, Frank. *The Expedition to the Philippines*. New York: Harper and Bros. Publishing, 1899.

Mirikitani, Janice, Janet Hale, Roberto Vargas, Alejandro Murguia, and Luis Syquia Jr., eds. *Time to Greez!: Incantations from the Third World.* San Francisco: Glide Publications, 1975.

Montez, Ricardo. *Keith Haring's Line: Race and the Performance of Desire.* Durham, NC: Duke University Press, forthcoming.

Moten, Fred. *B Jenkins.* Durham, NC: Duke University Press, 2010.

Moten, Fred. *In the Break: The Aesthetics of the Black Radical Tradition.* Minneapolis: University of Minnesota Press, 2003.

Moten, Fred. "The Phonographic *Mise-en-scène.*" Special issue on "Performance Studies and Opera," *Cambridge Opera Journal,* 16, no. 3 (November 2004): 269–81.

Muñoz, José Esteban. *Disidentifications: Queers of Color and the Performance of Politics.* Minneapolis: University of Minnesota Press, 1999.

Nancy, Jean Luc. *Listening.* New York: Fordham University Press, 2007.

Nelson, Alondra. "Introduction: Future Texts." *Social Text* 20, no. 2 (summer 2002): 1–15.

Ng, Stephanie. "Performing the 'Filipino' at the Crossroads: Filipino Bands in Five-Star Hotels throughout Asia." *Modern Drama: World Drama from 1850 to the Present* 48, no. 2 (summer 2005): 272–96.

Nguyen, Mimi, and Thuy Linh Tu, eds. *Alien Encounters: Popular Culture in Asian America.* Durham, NC: Duke University Press, 2007.

Nguyen, Viet. *Race and Resistance: Literature and Politics in Asian America.* New York: Oxford University Press, 2002.

Novak, David. *Japanoise: Music at the End of Circulation.* Durham, NC: Duke University Press, 2013.

Oakes, Kaya. *Slanted and Enchanted: The Evolution of Indie Culture.* New York: Holt, 2009.

O'Connor, Jane. "Beyond Social Constructionism: A Structural Analysis of the Cultural Significance of the Child Star." *Children and Society* 23, no. 3 (2009).

Ong, Walter. *Orality and Literacy: The Technologizing of the Word.* London: Methuen, 1982.

Onishi, Norimitsu. "Sinatra Song Often Strikes Deadly Chord." *New York Times* (Asia Edition), February 7, 2010.

Paraiso, Nicky. "Laurie Carlos." BOMB: *Artists in Conversation* 43 (spring 1993). Accessed October 15, 2015. http://bombmagazine.org/article/1655/laurie -carlos.

Parreñas, Rhacel. *Servants of Globalization: Women, Migration, and Domestic Work.* Stanford, CA: Stanford University Press, 2003.

Peck, Janice. *The Age of Oprah: Cultural Icon for the Neoliberal Era.* Boulder, CO: Paradigm, 2008.

Pisares, Elizabeth. "Do You (Mis)Recognize Me: Filipina Americans in Popular Music and the Problem of Invisibility." In *Positively No Filipinos Allowed: Building Communities and Discourse,* edited by Antonio Tiongson, Edgardo

Gutierrez, and Ricardo Valencia Gutierrez, 172–98. Philadelphia: Temple University Press, 2006.

Plasketes, George. "Re-flections on the Cover Age: A Collage of Continuous Coverage in Popular Music." *Popular Music and Society* 28, no. 2 (2005): 137–61.

Ponce, Martin Joseph. *Beyond the Nation: Diasporic Filipino Literature and Queer Reading*. New York: NYU Press, 2012.

Pray, Douglas. *Scratch: The Movie*. New York: Palm Pictures, 2001. DVD.

Pugh, Jonathan. "Island Movements: Thinking with the Archipelago." *Island Studies Journal* 8, no. 1 (2013): 9–24.

Quintana, A. E. "Borders Be Damned: Creolizing Literary Relations." *Cultural Studies* 13, no. 2 (1999), 358–66.

Rafael, Vicente. *White Love and Other Events in Filipino History*. Durham, NC: Duke University Press, 2000.

Reed, Ishmael, and Al Young, eds. *The Yardbird Reader*. Berkeley, CA: Yardbird Books, 1972–1976.

Reyes, Ted. "For Ciudad, New York Rain Is New York Love." Accessed August 14, 2014. http://www.examiner.com/article/for-ciudad-new-york-rain-is -new-york-love.

Rice, Mark. "His Name Was Don Francisco Muro: Reconstructing an Image of American Imperialism." *American Quarterly* 62, no. 1 (March 2010): 49–76.

Richardson, Clairborne. "The Filipino-American Phenomenon: The Loving Touch." *Black Perspective in Music* (1982): 3–28.

Roach, Joseph. *Cities of the Dead: Circum-Atlantic Performance*. New York: Columbia University Press, 1996.

Romulo, Erwin. "Ciudad's New Song and How You're Getting Old without a Choice." Accessed October 15, 2015. http://radiorepublic.ph/ciudad-sifil/.

Rodewald, Stew and Heidi. *Passing Strange: The Stew Musical*. Performance. Public Theater, New York, 2008.

Rodriguez, Dylan. *Suspended Apocalypse: White Supremacy, Genocide, and the Filipino Condition*. Minneapolis: University of Minnesota Press, 2009.

Rodriguez, Robyn. *Migrants for Export: How the Philippine State Brokers Labor to the World*. Minneapolis: University of Minnesota Press, 2010.

Santa Ana, Jeffrey. "Feeling Ancestral: The Emotions of Mixed Race and Memory in Asian American Cultural Productions." *positions: east asia cultures critique* 16, no. 2 (2008): 457–82.

Santos, Aldus. *Repeat While Fading: Pinoy Rock Biographs*. Quezon City: Poppy and Plume, 2009.

Sarmiento, Alice. "This House Is Open but You'll Have to See It My Way." Accessed August 5, 2014. http://alicesarmiento.wordpress.com/2012/04/13 /this-house-is-open-but-youll-have-to-see-it-my-way.

Sassatelli, Monica. "Urban Festivals and the Cultural Public Sphere: Cosmopolitanism between Ethics and Aesthetics." In *Festivals and the Cultural Public*

Sphere, edited by Liana Giorgi, Monica Sassatelli, and Gerard Delanty. New York: Routledge, 2011.

Schechner, Richard. *Between Theater and Anthropology*. Philadelphia: University of Pennsylvania Press, 1985.

Schneider, Rebecca. *Performing Remains: Art and War in Times of Theatrical Reenactment*. New York: Taylor and Francis, 2011.

See, Sarita. *The Decolonized Eye: Filipino American Art and Performance*. Minneapolis: University of Minnesota Press, 2009.

Shank, Barry. *Dissonant Identities: The Rock 'n' Roll Scene in Austin, Texas*. Middletown, CT: Wesleyan University Press, 1994.

Shaw, Angel Velasco, and Luis Francia, eds. *Vestiges of War: The Philippine-American War and the Aftermath of an Imperial Dream, 1899–1999*. New York: NYU Press, 2002.

Shimakawa, Karen. *National Abjection: The Asian American Body Onstage*. Durham, NC: Duke University Press, 2002.

Snapper, Juliana. "Scratching the Surface: Spinning Time and Identity in Hip-Hop Turntablism." *European Journal of Cultural Studies* 7, no. 1 (2004): 9–25.

Sohn, Stephen. "From Discos to Jungles: Circuitous Queer Patronage and Sex Tourism in Jessica Hagedorn's *Dogeaters*." MFS *Modern Fiction Studies* 56, no. 2 (2010): 317–48.

Sohn, Stephen Hong. "Introduction: Alien/Asian: Imagining the Racialized Future." *MELUS* 33, no. 4 (winter 2008): 5–22.

Spooner, James. *Afro-Punk*. Documentary. Image Entertainment, 2003.

Stadler, Gustavus, ed. Introduction to "The Politics of Recorded Sound," a special issue of *Social Text* 102, no. 87 (spring 2010).

Sterne, Jonathan. *The Audible Past: Cultural Origins of Sound Reproduction*. Durham, NC: Duke University Press, 2003.

Stewart, Susan. *On Longing: Narratives of the Miniature, Gigantic, the Souvenir, the Collection*. Durham, NC: Duke University Press, 1993.

Straw, Will. "Systems of Articulation, Logics of Change: Scenes and Communities in Popular Music." *Cultural Studies* 5, no. 3 (1991): 368–88.

Tadiar, Neferti. *Fantasy Production: Sexual Economies and Other Philippine Consequences for the New World Order*. Hong Kong: Hong Kong University Press, 2004.

Tadiar, Neferti. *Things Fall Away: Philippine Historical Experience and the Makings of Globalization*. Durham, NC: Duke University Press, 2009.

Talusan, Mary. "Music, Race, and Imperialism: The Philippine Constabulary Band at the 1904 St. Louis World's Fair." *Philippine Studies* (2004): 499–526.

Tarocco, Francesca, and Xun Zhou. *Karaoke: The Global Phenomenon*. London: Reaktion Books, 2007.

Taussig, Michael. "The Talking Machine." *Mimesis and Alterity: A Particular History of the Senses*. 193–211. New York: Routledge, 1993.

Taylor, Marvin J. "'I'll Be Your Mirror, Reflect What You Are': Postmodern Doc-

umentation and the Downtown New York Scene from 1975 to the Present."
RBM: A Journal of Rare Books, Manuscripts, and Cultural Heritage 3, no. 1
(March 20, 2002): 32–51.

Third World Women. San Francisco: Third World Communications Group, 1972.

Thompson, Aaron. "From Bad Brains to Afro-Punk: An Analysis of Identity,
Consciousness, and Liberation through Punk Rock from 1977–2010." MA
thesis, Cornell University, 2010.

Thornton, Sarah. "Strategies for Reconstructing the Popular Past." *Popular
Music* 9, no. 1 (January 1990): 87–95.

Tiongson, Antonio. "Filipino Youth Cultural Politics and DJ Culture." PhD
diss., Ethnic Studies, University of California, San Diego, 2006.

Tiongson, Nicanor. "The Filipino Film Industry." *East-West Film Journal* 6, no. 2
(1996): 23–61.

Tolentino, Roland B., ed. *Geopolitics of the Visible: Essays on Philippine Film Cultures.* Manila: Ateneo de Manila University Press, 2010.

Tompkins, Dave, James Tai, and Brian "B+" Cross. "Science Friction." *URB*, February 1998: 45–47.

Toop, David. "Hip Hop: Iron Needles of Death and a Piece of Wax." In *Modulations—A History of Electronic Music: Throbbing Words on Sound*, edited by
Peter Shapiro, 88–101. New York: Caipirinha, 2000.

Valle, Jocelyn. "The Eraserheads Are Better Musicians and Persons." *Philippine
Daily Inquirer,* May 6, 2000.

Vazquez, Alexandra. "Instrumental Migrations: The Transnational Movements
of Cuban Music." PhD diss., Department of Performance Studies, New
York University, 2006.

Vergara, Benito, Jr. "Betrayal, Class Fantasies, and the Filipino Nation in Daly
City." In *Cultural Compass: Ethnographic Explorations of Asian America*,
edited by Martin Manalansan, 139–58. Philadelphia: Temple University
Press, 2000.

Vergara, Benito, Jr. *Displaying Filipinos: Photography and Colonialism in Early
Twentieth-Century Philippines.* Quezon City: University of the Philippines
Press, 1995.

Vergara, Benito, Jr. *Pinoy Capital: The Filipino Nation in Daly City.* Philadelphia:
Temple University Press, 2010.

Vincent, Stephen. "Poetry Readings/Reading Poetry: San Francisco Bay Area,
1958–1980." In *The Poetry Reading: A Contemporary Compendium on Language and Performance*, edited by Stephen Vincent and Ellen Zweig. San
Francisco: Momo's Press, 1981.

Wang, Grace. *Soundtracks of Asian America: Navigating Race through Musical Performance.* Durham, NC: Duke University Press, 2014.

Wang, Oliver. *Legions of Boom: Filipino American Mobile DJ Crews in the San
Francisco Bay Area.* Durham, NC: Duke University Press, 2015.

Wang, Oliver. "Spinning Identities: A Social History of Filipino American DJs in the San Francisco Bay Area (1975–1995)." PhD diss., University of California, Berkeley, 2004.

Warwick, Jacqueline. "'You Can't Win, Child, But You Can't Get Out of the Game': Michael Jackson's Transition from Child Star to Super Star." *Popular Music and Society* 35, no. 2 (2012): 241–59.

Watkins, Lee. "Minstrelsy and Mimesis in the South China Sea: Filipino Migrant Musicians, Chinese Hosts, and the Disciplining of Relations in Hong Kong." *Asian Music* 40, no. 2 (2009): 72–99.

Weaver, Suzanne. *Phil Collins: The World Won't Listen*. Dallas: Dallas Museum of Art, 2008.

Weheliye, Alexander G. *Phonographies: Grooves in Sonic Afro-modernity*. Durham, NC: Duke University Press, 2005.

Wei, William. *The Asian American Movement*. Philadelphia: Temple University Press, 1993.

Weidman, Amanda. *Singing the Classical, Voicing the Modern: The Postcolonial Politics of Music in South India*. Durham, NC: Duke University Press, 2006.

Weinstein, Deena. "The History of Rock's Pasts through Rock Covers." In *Mapping the Beat: Popular Music and Contemporary Theory*, edited by Thomas Swiss, John Sloop, and Andrew Herman, 137–51. Malden, MA: Blackwell, 1998.

Weinstock, Jeffrey A. "Freaks in Space: 'Extraterrestrialism'and 'Deep-Space Multiculturalism.'" In *Freakery: Cultural Spectacles of the Extraordinary Body*, edited by Rosemarie Garland-Thomson, 327–37. New York: NYU Press, 1996.

Wheeler, Lesley. *Voicing American Poetry: Sound and Performance from the 1920s to the Present*. Ithaca, NY: Cornell University Press, 2008.

White, Hayden V. *Tropics of Discourse: Essays in Cultural Criticism*. Baltimore: Johns Hopkins University Press, 1978.

Wilson, Carl. "Against Indie." *Slate*. Accessed October 15, 2015. http://www.slate.com/articles/arts/music_box/2015/04/against_indie_new_albums_from_modest_mouse_sufjan_stevens_and_more_show.html.

Wong, Deborah. *Speak It Louder: Asian Americans Making Music*. New York: Routledge, 2004.

Yang, Chi-Hui. "Foreword: Documenting Asia Pacific." *Concentric: Literary and Cultural Studies,* 39, no. 1 (March 2013): 3–6.

Yano, Christine R. *Tears of Longing: Nostalgia and the Nation in Japanese Popular Song*. Cambridge, MA: Harvard University Press, 2003.

Page numbers followed by *f* indicate photographs.

www.ingramcontent.com/pod-product-compliance
Lightning Source LLC
Chambersburg PA
CBHW050349270326
41926CB00016B/3668